Adolescence in Pacific Island Societies

ASAO Monograph Series

Andrew J. Strathern, General Editor

Pamela J. Stewart, Associate Editor

Adolescence in Pacific Island Societies

~~~~~~~~~~~~~~~~~~~~~~~~~~~~~~~~~

Edited by

GILBERT HERDT

and

STEPHEN C. LEAVITT

UNIVERSITY OF
PITTSBURGH PRESS

ASAO Monograph #16

Published by the University of Pittsburgh Press, Pittsburgh, Pa.

15261, by arrangement with the Association for Social Anthropology in Oceania

Copyright © 1998, Association for Social Anthropology in Oceania

Manufactured in the United States of America

Printed on acid-free paper

10 9 8 7 6 5 4 3 2 1

Library of Congress Cataloging-in-Publication Data

Adolescence in Pacific Island societies : edited by Gilbert Herdt and
Stephen C. Leavitt.
      p. cm. — (ASAO monograph   ;   #16)
   Includes bibliographical references and index.
   ISBN 0-8229-4068-X (cloth   :   acid-free paper)
   ISBN 0-8229-5672-1 (pbk.   :   acid-free paper)
      1. Adolescence—Oceania—Cross-cultural studies.   2.   Teenagers—Oceania—
Cross-cultural studies.   3.   Social change—Oceania—Cross-cultural studies.
4.   Oceania—Social conditions—Cross-cultural studies.   I.   Herdt, Gilbert H., 1949–
II.   Leavitt, Stephen C., 1959–   III.   Series: ASAO monograph   ;   no. 16.
GN663   .A53 1998
305.235'0995—ddc21   98–9053

A CIP catalog record for this book is available from the British Library.

We dedicate this book to the memory of
Margaret Mead, pioneer in the study of Pacific adolescence.

CONTENTS

PART III.
ADOLESCENCE AND SOCIAL CHANGE
IN THE PACIFIC

ACKNOWLEDGMENTS

This project has a long history. It began as a symposium at the 1990 Association for Social Anthropologists in Oceania (ASAO) meetings in Lihue, Hawaii, organized by Gilbert Herdt. The participants there recognized the need for a published comparative assessment of adolescent experience in Pacific Islands societies, so they set out to put together a volume. The plan was to build a tightly coordinated comparative volume. Material on adolescence and social change from a range of societies would be addressed in a context of explicit comparison. Carol Worthman agreed to collect the material from other contributors and write an explicitly comparative chapter. The unusual degree of collaboration for an edited volume requires that we acknowledge with gratitude the contributions of those whose individual studies do not appear here. Participants in the original symposium included Paula Brown, Mark Busse, Leslie Marshall, Fitz J. P. Poole, Donald Rubinstein, and Rebecca Stephenson. Several of these participants submitted to Carol Worthman detailed reports on their field data on adolescence, and she discusses their data in her chapter in this volume.

We would also like to thank Andrew Strathern, editor for ASAO publications, for his continued commitment to publishing quality anthropological work in the Pacific Islands. Editors at the University of Pittsburgh Press took great care with the manuscript and directed the project with skill and patience. Finally, we thank Janet McQuade for all her work on the manuscript, from editing and translating files to building the final index. For her assistance we are grateful.

Adolescence in Pacific Island Societies

I

COMPARATIVE
PERSPECTIVES
ON
PACIFIC
ADOLESCENCE

Introduction

STUDYING ADOLESCENCE IN CONTEMPORARY PACIFIC ISLAND COMMUNITIES

Gilbert Herdt and Stephen C. Leavitt

All of us, at some moment, have had a vision of our existence as something unique, untransferable and very precious. This revelation almost always takes place during adolescence. Self-discovery is above all the realization that we are alone: it is the opening of an impalpable, transparent wall—that of our consciousness—between the world and ourselves. It is true that we sense our aloneness almost as soon as we are born, but children and adults can transcend their solitude and forget themselves in games or work. The adolescent, however, vacillates between infancy and youth, halting for a moment before the infinite richness of the world. He is astonished at the fact of his being, and this astonishment leads to reflection: as he leans over the river of his consciousness, he asks himself if the face that appears there, disfigured by the water, is his own. The singularity of his being, which is pure sensation in children, becomes a problem and a question.
— OCTAVIO PAZ (1985:9)

If culture and individual development are interdependent processes of historical change, then surely no phase of the life course is more ripe with possibilities of renewal, rebellion, and recreation of cultural life than adolescence. As scholars since the time of Dewey, Margaret Mead, and Erikson have suggested, the adolescent embodies culture since he or she reworks social relations and knowledge systems toward an indefinite future. Erikson (1968) argued a generation ago during the turmoil of the student movement of the 1960s that history must respond to the strivings of youth. Developmental studies have since then contributed enormously to our understanding of adolescence in Western countries. But the cross-cultural record is less complete. Modernizing societies around the globe face dizzying change, with youth culture in the forefront, yet we still have few systematic comparative studies of adolescence to draw upon in understanding culture change. Indeed, this book constitutes the first detailed study of adolescence in any culture area; it presents a unique set of cultural case studies of youth in the rapidly developing societies of the Pacific Islands. We look at how adolescence—as refracted through local contexts—helps to define what these societies are becoming.

Anthropology's place in the intellectual world owes much to its early studies of adolescent development in Pacific cultures. Beginning with Malinowski's (1922, 1927a, 1927b, 1929) significant works on the Trobriand Islands, a critical line of inquiry in cultural psychology and psychological anthropology can be identified from more than sixty years ago. Malinowski's portrait of the "amorous adolescent" in *The Sexual Life of Savages* is remarkable both for its challenge to Freudian views of sexual repression and Oedipal development in nonwestern societies and for its vision of egalitarian sexual relations that seemed to mirror the notion of "free love" in the age of the flappers of the 1920s (see D'Emilio and Freedman 1988). At about the same time, Margaret Mead's *Coming of Age in Samoa* (1928) inaugurated an immense change in our view of how social environment shapes development. Her argument in that book challenged the received view that adolescence was an inherently conflictual process of internal distress and external rebellion. Mead (1930, 1935) worked on the Admiralty Islands off the coast of New Guinea in the late twenties and early thirties and again returned to work in the Sepik River societies in the 1930s along with Gregory Bateson (1936). By the later 1930s, John Whiting (1941) initiated fieldwork among the Kwoma of the Sepik area too, resulting in the first effort to apply social learning theory principles to the study of another culture. His discussion of adolescence is a detailed ethnographic study of the moral and social development of Kwoma youth, situated in ecological settings and observations that have endured as a standard of cross-cultural developmental study (see J. W. M. Whiting and E. H. Chasdi 1994; B. B. Whiting and C. P. Edwards 1987). These studies used the very different characteristics of adolescent life in Pacific societies to help redefine our most basic sense of culture's role in adolescent development.

From the 1950s through the 1980s, though, anthropological study of adolescence had been dormant, even nonexistent, except for occasional ethnographic pieces scattered in monographs. The reasons for this hiatus have to do primarily, we think, with the decline of developmental perspectives in anthropology following the demise of culture and personality studies, especially those anchored in the Freudian tradition (see LeVine 1982; cf. Shweder 1991). Within anthropology, the ensuing scholarship seemed less concerned with the individual, with phases of the life course, with biosocial influences upon development, and with the measurement of "person" or "culture" concepts in the usual empirical sense (Spiro 1986). Meanwhile, adolescent psychology as a field of study continued to expand, resulting in the creation of several scholarly journals dedicated to adolescence as well as a professional society. Perhaps in response to the gap, the

Whitings (1987) initiated a significant training project across cultures that has led to the publication of the most significant monographs since the time of Malinowski, Mead, and Whiting. Condon's (1987) study of Eskimo youth and Burbank's (1988) examination of Australian aboriginal girls initiated a series of monographs. Schlegel and Barry's (1991) significant cross-cultural survey of adolescence and their findings regarding gender differences will be addressed below. Amit-Talai and Wulff (1995) and Schlegel (1995b) use cross-cultural comparisons to reveal the ways adolescents contribute to their societies in the context of change. The time is optimal, then, for an even more focused set of comparative contributions to examine the meaning and context of adolescent development in a particular culture area.

This book attempts for the first time to document and compare a range of adolescent development issues among traditional societies of the Pacific Islands. Some of the societies we discuss remain rooted in relatively traditional concerns, but all, in one way or another, have had to respond to the relatively dramatic social changes in the postcolonial era. We have chosen, therefore, to direct our attention to those issues we believe are central to a cross-cultural understanding of adolescence in contexts of social change. The volume's division into sections on cultural constructions and social change in the Pacific reflects only the *relative* attention devoted to these issues in those chapters. All our contributors, to one degree or another, consider issues pertinent to changes occurring throughout the Pacific.

Early studies of adolescence in the Pacific took the relative influence of biology and culture as a central theme in understanding adolescence. Margaret Mead and Bronislaw Malinowski had to argue against views that deemed biology decisive in defining adolescent experience. Margaret Mead's (1928) Samoan research was instigated by a contentious perspective on the biological nature of adolescence in Western conceptions of human nature: Are teenagers innately unruly and rebellious? Must they act out their sexual and aggressive impulses? Here, cultural relativism theory was battling the powerful form of evolutionary and biological reductionism, as well as the insidious eugenics movement (Freeman 1983). Yet Mead's book must be seen as a response to Freudian theory, too, which in its strongest form placed the adolescent in "defiant rebellion against any and every authority" (A. Freud 1966:138). Derek Freeman's (1983) work has strongly criticized Mead's ethnographic data, interpretations, and scientific paradigm. No doubt many of these criticisms are cogent and indicate flaws in her study; however, her work was also undertaken long ago, in a different period of scientific canons. And, in the meantime, Samoan culture has changed. Nevertheless, the work of Mead, like that of Malinowski (1927a, 1929), set the terms for a broad challenge of received wisdom on human nature, personality, and culture.

Despite the cogency of relativist arguments, we find ourselves now insisting that biology play at least *some* role. All humans experience the physical changes of puberty—the biological transformation of passing from childhood to adulthood—and in many societies these physical changes are central to defining social roles. In the Pacific, recent decades have brought changes in diet that have affected rates of physical maturation, so that boys and girls are reaching puberty at earlier chronological ages. These changes, in turn, affect the way these youths are understood as well as the roles deemed appropriate for them. For this reason, among others, we consider it essential to adopt a cultural *life-course perspective* (LeVine 1982) in considering adolescence and social change.

Such a perspective begins by emphasizing what is generally agreed in Western science: that adolescence is a unique phase of the life span because of simultaneous changes in physical maturation, psychological adjustment, and social relations (Steinberg 1987; Petersen 1988; Offer et al. 1988). Adolescence is also generally regarded as a critical period for the emergence of adult forms of social competence and adaptation (Peterson 1988; Steinberg 1987). Historical studies demonstrate that change in youth must be seen as both a developmental stage and as a social age (Elder 1980; Tanner 1981). The social-psychological literature has long associated social change with problems of adolescent development and behavior (cf. Erikson 1968; Davis and Dollard 1940), and the high school, in particular, has been a focus of social conflict and maturation (Lynd and Lynd 1929; Simmons and Blythe 1985; Elder 1980:11–14). We need to distinguish between earlier and later age phases of adolescence, along with the historical/sociocultural context of these phases of development, including important social groups in which youth spend time and are socialized (Boxer et al. 1984; Offer et al. 1988).

A synthetic approach has to hold local cultural constructions of development as central to understanding the place of adolescence in social change. Several of our chapters (see especially chapters 4, 5, and 6) stress that Pacific Island societies build basic understandings of body, person, and gender from vital distinctive ideas about the maturation process. In considering the impact of social change, it is essential to see how those understandings affect how adolescents actually experience events in their social world. It is not enough to know, for example, that Bumbita Arapesh men (described in chapter 8) define their growth as a literal sapping of their parents' vital spiritual essence—what we need to look at are the *implications* of that idea for the way a young man sees himself growing up to face challenges his parents never encountered. How does his view of himself as an embodiment of his parents' essence affect his capacity to confront a new world? A focus on adolescent experience means coupling detailed articulations of cultural constructs with careful observation of individual cases and analysis of actual personal narratives. Rubinstein (1995, 1983) has used this approach to build a sensitive study of alarming trends in adolescent suicide rates in Micronesia.

Another aim of the life course approach is to do away with constructions of adolescents as somehow "marginal" or even "deviant" figures in society, and here we agree with points made by Wulff (1995) regarding the significance of "youth culture." Adolescents in all societies occupy structural positions that contribute to the overall makeup of the social world. Indeed, the populations of the Pacific Islands are demographically young—and may continue to get younger in the future. Young people have the most direct exposure to agents of social change, such as schools, technological innovations, and popular culture. It could be argued that they therefore play a disproportionately large role in defining how social changes will be construed locally.

Finally, a life course perspective demands that one consider adolescence in light of a broader historical process. Because of the recent dramatic changes that come with development, the societies of the Pacific Islands offer an opportunity to look both at how adolescents contribute to the character of changes through time and at how these changes have in turn affected the lives of adolescents themselves. It often has been said that adolescence represents developmentally that part of the cultural life course that is "betwixt and between" normative social and biological roles and states of being (Boxer et al., 1984; Mead 1928; Offer et al. 1988; Petersen 1988; Worthman, chap. 2, this volume). This liminal nature is complicated in the Pacific, perhaps more than elsewhere, by several interlocking dimensions of adolescent study: the demographic processes of youth as influenced by age (roughly ages eleven to nineteen in the United States), gender, and socioeconomic status within and across cultural populations; the historical processes of dependence (colonialization), independence (postcolonialization), and nation status of these groups; maturational processes and rates of pubertal development in these populations; and cultural processes—categories and representations of "youth" and "adolescence"—in relation to social structure and culture change at large.

DEMOGRAPHICS AND BIOLOGY: THE "TIMING" OF PUBERTY

The place of adolescent experience in the life course has been affected dramatically in the Pacific by shifts both in the demographic distributions of whole populations and in the pace of biological development in the individual. These shifts mean that social systems that had established well-defined roles for adolescents must respond to situations which may no longer reflect their underlying assumptions about development. In chapter 2, Carol Worthman explores the implications of these changes for a range of Pacific societies. The principal brief for Worthman's chapter was originally to integrate the ethnographic material presented in other chapters into a biosocial analysis of adolescence in the Pacific.

To assemble a more comparable ethnographic database pertaining to the biosocial dynamics that are the focus of this book, Worthman sent a survey in February 1990 to each contributor who also participated in the session on adolescence in the Pacific organized by Gilbert Herdt for the Association for Social Anthropology in Oceania annual meetings in Lihui, Kauai, in March, 1990. Of the sixteen societies represented in Worthman's analysis, six are the explicit focus of other chapters in this volume. Worthman's chapter underscores the importance of considering biological factors in any analysis of the relationship between adolescence and social change.

Changes in Pacific Island demographics have wide-ranging effects, especially on the character of gender relations and relationships between generations. Pacific Island societies are demographically youthful as well as being historically young nation-states. Like many developing countries, those of the Pacific have populations whose average age may be in the teens or twenties. Thus, the links among recent history, adolescence, and emerging national identity are strong (cf. Keesing and Tonkinson 1982); for example, Papua New Guinea is, as a political entity, both young in population and politically young in its neocolonial statehood (founded in 1975). In 1980, 43 percent of the population (about 1.3 million) was under the age of fifteen. By 1990, 50 percent or more of the population will be fifteen or younger (Townsend 1985:3), and the population will have risen to almost three million.

This demographic transformation is significant because of the traditional emphases in Melanesian cultures upon age and gender as categories of social structure and organization, a topic discussed explicitly by Aletta Biersack in chapter 4. Pacific Island societies are at a critical moment historically in the transforming effects of social change upon gender and sexuality. Increasing discontinuity between generations related to modernization and history is stratifying relations between generations (Mead 1956; Schwartz 1976). Gender differentiation in the life span has taken on a new meaning. Whereas at one time same-sex identifications took precedence in virtually all social action (see especially Cantrell's Gebusi study in chapter 5), today opposite-sex relations have a new political and social importance (Herdt 1987). The old split between gender and age is being reconfigured so that same-aged peers of either sex sometimes and in some contexts have more in common than different-aged persons of the same sex of alternate generations. Biersack's study of Paiela youth gives an idea of this changing thematic. The horizontal stratification of age is replacing gender as the vertical stratifier in culture and developmental experience (reviewed in Herdt 1989a; see Lepowsky 1990a; Rossi 1980).

The focus on demography reveals powerful correlations among physical maturation, development, and social change in the Pacific. No area of research on adolescence has interested Westerners more than the psychophysiological parameters of puberty and menarche. An immense amount of literature now shows the critical nature of biological and social timing at the confluence of pubertal events (Boxer et al. 1984; Brooks-Gunn et al. 1985; Hill et al. 1985; Freud 1958; Lerner 1985; Meyer-Bahlberg 1985; Petersen and Crockett 1985; Steinberg and Hill 1978; Simmons and Blythe 1985).

Demographic variations are instructive. Worthman's pioneering research has shown important pubertal differences between Western and Kikuyu adolescents. Kikuyu males, for instance, enter puberty before their female peers, unlike a comparison British sample. However, age of menarche in Kikuyu girls (median 15.9 years) is later and more variable than that of British girls (mean 13.5 years) (Worthman 1987:33). In her chapter for this book, Worthman shows how New Guinea societies go to great extremes in accentuating pubertal changes for symbolic purposes, and this stands out as a distinctive human pattern. Because cultural categories construct not only the social but also the physical life history of the individual, demographic differences in maturation will have a bearing on the character of local beliefs.

The general effects of cultural change upon physical development, specifically the timing of puberty (see Dennett and Connell 1988), are also important in understanding how people have had to adjust their basic categories for development and for defining differences between male and female. A growing body of research in the United States has examined biological and social "timing" events in normative adolescence (Offer et al. 1988; Petersen 1988). However, these developmental studies are usually decontextualized and insensitive to influences of the cultural setting on self-concept, peer interactions, pubertal and menstrual changes, and what is now called the growth of "social competence" in adolescents (Burbank 1988; Whiting and Edwards 1988).

Beliefs about adolescence in Pacific Island societies show effectively the value of considering biological and social maturational timing in a cross-cultural context. Many Highland New Guinea peoples, for example, have detailed and explicit beliefs about the differential growth and maturation of the sexes. To illustrate, consider the dual roles of biology and social age-grading among the Sambia of the Eastern Highlands. Sambia place extraordinary emphasis upon ritual initiation practices to categorize, celebrate, and institutionalize status advancements in males (Herdt 1981). From age seven to the early twenties, boys undergo six successive initiation ceremonies. Adolescence, in Sambian thought, is an event related to third-stage initiation, which highlights biological-pubertal changes, especially those related to the maturity of the glans penis. As Van Gennep (1960) might have said of such rites of passage, Sambia make the biological changes secondary to the social status events; and indeed, because of age cohorts, Sambia boys vary from ages fourteen to sixteen and are at different maturational states when they jointly undergo the ritual. Yet this social structural view is also incomplete. In the case of intersexed hermaphrodites assigned to the male sex (Herdt 1987; 1990b), Sambia initiate them, but not completely. They take the hermaphrodites through first- and second-stage rites, but no further: such persons do not undergo the puberty ceremony. Sambia men say that this is because the hermaphrodites achieve incomplete masculinization and will probably not be married or reproduce like biologically normal males. Sambia do not go a step further to argue that the initiations could complete the biology of these persons. Hence, the social transitions are critical timing events, but these also depend upon individual biological maturity achievements to activate them. Thus, biology and culture figure into the Sambia conception of adolescence.

How much recent dietary patterns have changed growth, and thus the temporal and spatial bases of beliefs such as these, is still open to question (Malcolm 1976). Clearly, though, social change has affected the rate of maturation. Traditional Highland New Guinea populations have provided some of the most extreme examples of delayed maturation (Eveleth and Tanner 1976). Malcolm (1970a) surveyed maturation and nutrition among the Bundi, a Gende-speaking people of the northern highlands, in 1966–67. Despite a near absence of clinical signs of malnutrition, he found a median age at menarche of eighteen years, with delay to the early twenties by both sexes in final attainment of adult stature. Gainj women studied in 1978 also reported very late menstrual onset (Wood et al. 1985). Diverse evidence indicates nutritional factors as significant contributors to maturational delay in these populations (Dennett and Connell 1988). The Mountain Ok speakers, another short-stature group with late maturation, show signs of chronic undernutrition at all ages. Mountain Ok speakers with access to markets in mining towns, however, were taller and heavier. Cultural patterns of diet and resource allocation, then, may contribute to patterns of chronic undernutrition in childhood (Crittenden and Baines 1985; B. Shaw 1986). As development changes the dietary patterns of these societies, it is likely that the age of menarche will drop significantly.

What Carol Worthman's comparative chapter shows in rich detail is that because of the relationship between beliefs and established patterns of maturation, any changes in the biology of maturation (such as age of menarche) will have an effect on the concepts, practices, and interpretations surrounding development. As a result, social processes depend on the biological domain in ways that are often hidden. On this basis, Worthman makes a compelling case for the value of a "biosocial view" of adolescence in the context of cultural change.

ADOLESCENCE AS A CULTURAL CATEGORY

Pacific Island societies exhibit a strikingly wide range of ideas about physiological development and its relation to social roles. In many cases, these ideas justified ritual practices considered fundamental to the proper maturation of young people. New ideas have meant that the cultural conception of "adolescence" in these societies is changing, so that concepts of the person and recipes for social action have had to respond to the particular meanings of adolescent development at this moment in world history. Some societies traditionally had no explicit category for "adolescence." Others marked identity categories of "child" and "youth" roughly akin to those of the West. In either case, the introduction of Western norms and institutions, especially the chronologically age-graded school system, is creating a more uniform category of the adolescent in the social and ethnic processes of emerging national identity, itself a product of the ideology of "modernization" across the Pacific.

Given the range of traditional ideas about life stages, it is worth considering whether the study of something called "adolescence" is even viable when looking across cultures. What is "adolescence?" How did it come into being? And what has it done to aid in understanding human nature and culture?

"Adolescence" as a domain worthy of study is, of course, a Western cultural category, and probably a recent one at that. Historical research suggests a close link between industrialization and the emergence of adolescence as an expanded stage in human development in the West (Bullough 1981; Tanner 1981). Some evidence suggests that the ancient Egyptians and Romans recognized adolescence as a phase of life (Ariès 1962). Prior to the Industrial Revolution, though, the transition from childhood to adulthood generally appears to have been much more abrupt than it is now. It is instructive to reflect upon the etymologies of both *adolescence* and the associated term, *puberty*. *Adolescence* comes from the Latin *adolescere* (to grow up), while puberty comes from the Latin *pubescere* (to grow hairy). Thus, both adolescence and puberty are derived from words that emphasize maturational processes rather than stages of development. The processual nature of adolescence, together with the cultural events that mark off youth in local places, indicates the difficulty of defining adolescence solely by chronological age.

Difficulties with the definition have contributed to relativist arguments that *adolescence* be considered only in terms defined by local traditions. This relativist position is critiqued and a universal adolescent model is offered in a major recent study (Offer et al. 1988:110–11). On the basis of a survey conducted in ten countries, these investigators believe that they found sufficient "similarities" to "constitute a portrait of the 'universal adolescent'" (110). They list six traits: (1) universal adolescents are happy, enjoy life, and feel in control of their lives; (2) they are caring, enjoy interaction, and dislike being alone; (3) they value work and school, and do well in both, because these domains are important for now and the future; (4) they regard their parents positively; (5) they feel confident about their "sexual selves" and are unafraid of discussing or thinking about sex;

and (6) universal adolescents cope well with life's problems; they feel they can make decisions and put things in order: "They are confident in that they feel certain that they will be able to assume responsibility for themselves in the future" (111).

These generalizations are useful as predictive hypotheses for future research, but their cross-cultural validity is questionable. For example, what does it mean to suggest that adolescents are "happy," "enjoy life," and "feel in control" across all these countries? (see the critique in Triandis 1988). Such subjective states are open to widely differing cultural interpretations. The "happiness" of the Gebusi girl (Cantrell, chapter 5) and Australian girl (Burbank and Chisholm, chapter 3) differ widely, though each is socially adjusted. Perhaps what we see is the result of a standardized stimulus modality back-translated to produce consistent results; we cannot know for sure, nor does this concern rob the study of its importance. It does, however, remind us of the perennial problem of anthropology: how to work in another language and culture; how to translate another people's experience into something that is accurate but also recognizable to our own culture (Herdt and Stoller 1990). These concerns are especially acute in relation to ethnopsychology and emotional development (see Stigler et al. 1990; Lutz 1985; White and Kirkpatrick 1985).

Consider Victoria Burbank and James Chisholm's arguments in chapter 3 about adolescent mothering: conventional views of the "problem" of teenage pregnancy rely on visions of limited social choices for pregnant girls and on assumptions about their immature mothering skills. Such ideas are, in fact, cultural constructions based on a particular view of adolescence. Burbank and Chisholm's research among Australian Aboriginals shows that, in that cultural context, premarital sex and subsequent pregnancies are part of an adolescent strategy for autonomy located in a particular sociocultural context (see also Burbank 1995). It is not appropriate in this context to define the pregnancies as a "problem." Burbank and Chisholm go on to argue that the Aboriginal case of a different cultural construction of adolescence should lead us to reconsider assumptions about the "teen pregnancy problem" in the West. Varying understandings about what adolescence means can have significant effects on how events such as teenage pregnancy actually play out in a given situation. In chapter 8, Stephen Leavitt makes a similar argument about local constructions of behavior commonly labeled "delinquent" in Western contexts.

In chapter 4, Aletta Biersack outlines how subtleties in local constructions of adolescence can significantly affect the way we see these societies in relation to others, especially when such ideas are viewed in life cycle perspective. The traditions of the Paiela and Porgera Valleys in Enga Province, Papua New Guinea, dictate that sexual development occur in a context of magicoritual maintenance of body growth. These traditions use horticultural metaphors to frame physical maturation and explain a hierarchical relationship between men and women. The emphasis is on cultivating the potential for fertility in both males and females, but at the expense of the body itself. As Biersack puts it, "Through coitus, childbearing, and nursing, couples are fertile but only on the condition that they diminish, even extinguish, their own lives in the process." Such an ideology of fertility in adolescent growth cuts across conventional typologies of Papua New Guinea societies, such as Lindenbaum's contrast between "homosexual" and "heterosexual" societies (1987). The rationale behind fertility practices in heterosexual Paiela and Porgera resembles explicitly, for example, the Sambia justification for homosexual relations with adolescents (see Herdt 1981). Biersack's attention to the intricacies of local constructions of adolescent development enables her to make that point.

At the same time, in spite of the widely varying ways to construct this step in the life course, it does not make sense to assert that something called "adolescence" as a life stage and its concomitant "youth culture" are simply the products of particular sociopolitical contexts. In chapter 6, Maria Lepowsky argues against the often implicit assumption in sociological work that distinctive "youth cultures" are a relatively recent phenomenon. She describes a well-developed youth culture as part of the traditional Vanatanai understanding of adolescence. The effects of recent changes have to be considered in light of a very high level of autonomy for both males and females and a view that the transition to adulthood is a gradual process marked by specific activities. One way males used to acquire prestige as a way of emerging into adulthood was through the warrior role, and with pacification older youths have had fewer opportunities to gain a reputation. Lepowsky shows as well that the transition to adulthood for older youths depends on negotiating a wide array of specific cultural expectations based on a traditionally defined category of adolescence.

SOCIAL CHANGE AND PACIFIC ISLAND SOCIALIZATION

A critical issue in the social-psychological study of adolescence deals with how culture change and the march of time can change the basis for local socialization practices, introducing conflict within and between generations. Glen Elder's influential work has suggestive implications for ethnographic studies in rapidly developing societies (Elder 1975; 1980; Rosow 1978). We note in particular Elder's suggestions that change may enhance competition and conflict between historical generations, historical age cohorts, and chronological age groups. A developmental perspective locates these historical/generational differences in the context of major social institutions and role conflicts (LeVine 1982:85–98; Petersen 1988).

Take, for instance, an example from close to home: the relationship between adolescence and the institution of the high school in American culture is historically recent, but profound. In their classic study *Middletown*, Robert and Helen Lynd (1929) discovered how much small-town Indiana life was shaped for youth by the high school. By the 1920s, a new social era had arrived: "Adolescents moved in a youth-centered world, based in the high schools that most now attended" (D'Emilio and Freedman 1988:240). Schooling had been infrequent for males and rare for females, but "by the 1920s, high school had become a mass experience, with almost three-quarters of the young enrolled" (257). Automobiles allowed free movement, dating, and a revolt against certain kinds of parental standards. Among these generational changes was the "petting party," which signaled new sexual norms and middle-class lifestyles. Frederick Lewis Allen, who wrote the best-selling novel of the decade, referred to this as a "revolution in manners and morals" (240).

A generation later, as Elder (1980:15) suggests, the meaning of adolescence was changing. Hollingshead's (1949) famous study, *Elmtown's Youth*, revealed the extent to which the changes of the 1920s had made things problematic. He singled out four changing "social properties" of adolescence: (1) its social status contradictions ("adolescence is an ill-defined no man's land"); (2) the conflicts and competition between different youth-training agencies; (3) the age segregation typical of middle-class students, youth isolated from their parents (see also Mead 1961); and (4) the significant class variations in the social transition to adulthood.

Such changes in the American landscape were striking. What was responsible for them? One potential cause lay in the effects of the Great Depression (Elder 1975), which created a unique historical cohort by virtue of the difficulties of economic survival. Elder (1980:16) suggests that for the adolescent, the Great Depression encouraged schooling and graduation, delayed adult tasks such as marriage, and, for the youth who experienced deprivation, forced adult realities upon them at an earlier age. Structural patterns of this kind, relating historical time to demographics and social events, offer a promising way to look at the dramatic changes in Pacific Island societies in recent years.

However, applying these approaches to the Pacific context requires some revision of conventional approaches. The influential view of Erik Erikson (1968) underlies much of the work on conflicts between generations. The transition to adulthood, he suggests, finds "society" replacing the "family" as the context of identity development. Family-based initiations and roles remain enormously critical to identity in Pacific Island societies, and Erikson's emphasis upon the youths' "overconcern" with a newfound social image is useful (1968:128). But Erikson goes on to argue that adolescent intolerance toward others, idealism and a felt conflict of loyalties, and the suffusion of Self in the Other—"falling in love"—were all key indicators of an emotional intensity and identity transformation intrinsic to adolescence. When considered in a cross-cultural perspective, such assertions are problematic, as we will recall from Mead's Samoan case, and for the reasons of historical contingency suggested by Elder (1980). Erikson's concern more with universals than particulars reminds us of the greatest source of conceptual conflict between psychological developmentalists and anthropologists (see Burbank 1987; Herdt, 1990b; Lutz 1985; reviewed in Stigler et al. 1989). From an anthropological perspective, it is important to consider those cases that transformed the received wisdom of the influence of culture on development. Mead's 1928 study on Samoa was the first of these, but her second study on Manus Island was no less instrumental in cautioning us against general assumptions about relations between generations.

Mead (1930) emphasized, of course, the discontinuity between childhood and adulthood—the extent to which the children of Manus were to become different persons as adults. To what extent are intracultural differences between age cohorts (see Schwartz 1976) influential for development? Mead was concerned to "test" the Levy-Bruhl and Piagetian reductionisms on the thought processes of "primitives." Manus people are no less logical than we are, Mead felt. By showing that Manus adults were preoccupied with sex, wealth, and work, compared to children who were uninvolved and disinterested in these domains of cultural life, Mead opened the possibility of an alternative moral/cognitive developmental pathway, a kind of "children's culture." While that idea has not generally been explored, it remains of great interest to culture theory (see Herdt 1989c).

Mead's research highlights the extent to which Manus children live completely different lives from the adults. This work sets a precedent for understanding the particularly problematic relationships between generations that have been observed throughout the Pacific. Adolescent Manus boys continued to live a life without responsibilities. There was no single puberty ceremony for boys, but between ages twelve and sixteen, their ears were pierced. The timing of this event depended more on the group's finances—the event requires various ceremonial exchanges—than on a boy's physical development (see, by comparison, Gewertz 1982). At sixteen or seventeen, these youth became warriors; in the men's house they could initiate sex, possibly with women taken as spoils in war.

Today, social change has made the situation quite different. On Manus, youth of this age leave the village to work on plantations, where they have coastal jobs or go to school (Carrier and Carrier 1989). Traditionally, the period from age sixteen until marriage (traditionally around the ages of twenty to twenty-four), did little to prepare youth for their domestic lives as married men. The role of a young warrior in many ways prolonged the freedom of childhood, and modern life away from the village working on plantations has little in common with village sociality. Marriage changes this. A young man becomes obligated at marriage to the maternal uncles who have gathered the bride-wealth that finances the marriage. The youth, we are told, also feels ashamed in front of his wife's male relatives because his uncles have not completed the marriage payment. Disjunction in development is thus more abrupt for males but also present among females—whose experience of menstruation and adult sexuality is a matter of difficult developmental transition.

What Mead's research suggests is that the issue of identity transformation, so important to Erikson's views, must be considered on quite different terms in the Pacific, both because of the heightened discontinuities between a child's and an adult's life and the significance of the local community on the adolescents' perceptions of themselves.

Traditionally, there were two kinds of sociopolitical orders across the Pacific: ranked, hierarchical societies, found primarily in Polynesia and its outliers (Mead 1928; Ortner and Whitehead 1981; Sahlins 1963), and egalitarian, achieved-status societies, common to Micronesia, Melanesia, and Aboriginal Australia. These are of course ideal types, and the contrast may be "less real than apparent" (Feil 1987:93; Douglas 1979). However, adolescence in its traditional and modern forms is constructed differently, as different types of personhood, in each system. For example, the egalitarian mode of Highlands New Guinea departs significantly from the ranked systems of Trobriand culture.

Pacific societies generally emphasize kinship relationships rather than political authority in social relations. In the absence of overarching political authority, rules concerning the rights and obligations of individuals toward others are based upon cultural ideas of status, kinship, and descent. Because traditional social relations are primarily kinship-based, education was also traditionally kinship-based. An important implication of this is that a distinction is drawn in New Guinea societies between those individuals who are within the kinship sphere—individuals with whom most face-to-face interactions take place and who are involved in a complex and morally binding network of rights and obligations—and those individuals who are outside the kin-based security circle (Lawrence 1964). The latter are often considered enemies toward whom one has ill-defined or nonexistent obligations. One usually did not learn or receive instruction from non-kin, except perhaps in ritual domains (Keesing 1982) and in relation to trade. Furthermore, moral conceptions of persons and things are situationally specific (Read 1955). This cultural pattern has many implications for the success of culture change in general. One significant consequence is Western-style schools and their inroads in rural areas; here students interact with teachers outside the sphere of traditional kinship relations, introducing new social influences.

Marriage is another important aspect of kinship vital for understanding the effect of social change on adolescence in the Pacific (Ward 1994). Traditionally, marriages in New Guinea societies were arranged by senior members of exogamous clans or lineages who were primarily concerned with forging links between adjacent territorial or descent groups. As Cantrell shows in chapter 5, gender and kinship were often structurally aligned here. Today, however, with increasing opportunities to meet individuals from other groups through schools and towns, and with increasing exposure to Western ideas of romantic love, young people in New Guinea have begun to make their own decisions concerning sexuality, marriage, and reproduction. For instance, how are children to be valued in the person's life career? Sometimes these decisions are in opposition to those of their parents and other kin of their group. Increasingly, gender, marriage, and sexuality are domains that involve rapid social change rather than the maintenance of tradition (Jolly and Macintyre 1989). Thus, a widening circle of social contacts is influencing romantic, sexual, and gender norms and roles in villages, further transforming meanings of traditional personhood development and education.

These changes have to be viewed against the backdrop of traditional domains of socialization. For example, there are in traditional Sambia culture two global contexts for gender-stratified socialization: early childhood and subsequent ritual initiation. These contexts are associated with the changing focus of cultural competence in development: women are the children's first influence; men are the later exclusive socializers. To fully recognize these differences, we must distinguish early from late training—"primary" and "secondary" socialization regimes (LeVine 1982; see also Mead 1963). It is likely that such a sociocultural thematic applies to many Pacific societies (Whiting 1941; Chowning 1973).

The primary socialization group includes the mother or her substitutes and others socially responsible for the child's protection, care, and training. The secondary group, though, is particularly important in the context of social change in the Pacific. It includes all trainers responsible for teaching, evaluating, monitoring, and enforcing the social rules of the child's eventual incorporation into adult institutions and roles. The transition from primary to secondary socialization group is necessary to attain social status positions in the wider society. Secondary social groups such as age sets, school playmates, castes, religious organizations, and so forth become expanded reference groups for the developing child. In Western society the school is crucial, gradually supplanting the family in importance. In these transitions, as among the Sambia, the child moves from being defined as a nonresponsible dependent of his or her primary group to being an independent social, economic, and moral agent in the society as a whole. Adolescence consolidates this process (Erikson 1968; Whiting et al. 1986). In many places, the initiated adolescent, as among the Mountain Arapesh, is a moral agent whose actions newly affect and may even magically harm parents

(Mead 1970:415). In adolescence, then, a significant transformation in social purpose begins.

By contrasting early and later socialization we begin to see that, in learning how to be a socializer—by teaching norms and rules—the adolescent undergoes a final stage of socialization. Some teaching, such as the elders' ritual instruction to youth, reveals how society requires an expertise in sacred knowledge before one is allowed to socialize as an adult (Poole 1982). Elders must actively supervise sophisticated tasks such as arranging ceremonial exchanges or performing sacred myths (Keesing 1982). The rule that only certain elders are allowed to train for these traditions suggests that age, canonical knowledge, and little innovation are expected of the trainees (see also Schwartz 1976). To put it differently, such elders are closer to being the big men or heroes of myths who embody the desired characteristics and actions of culture heroes (Herdt 1981; Leenhardt 1979; Poole 1981). As long as the mythic figures are honored, they provide a means not only of linking the present with the past, but of interpreting lived experience through the lens of myth (Herdt and Stephen 1989; Hutchins 1987).

How such factors may play a role in adolescent experience in the context of social change is explored in detail by Stephen Leavitt in chapter 8. Leavitt argues that among the Bumbita Arapesh of the East Sepik Province of Papua New Guinea, much of the behavior associated with "delinquency" in Western contexts has more to do with adolescents' efforts to emulate elders in a situation where many of the traditional methods for conveying knowledge between generations—such as male initiation—have been lost. The elders retain their status as culture heroes but no longer have a formalized context in which to transfer their wisdom across generations. Young Bumbita adolescent males face this sense of loss with considerable anxiety, and their efforts to build on a tradition of belligerence and independence in respected leaders leads to behavior that is often considered "delinquent." Leavitt shows how important it is to consider the distinctive cultural frames for transferring knowledge between generations when discussing adolescent behaviors.

Donald Rubinstein (1995) also conveys with poignancy the social structural factors contributing to the dramatically high rate of adolescent suicide in contemporary Micronesia. Rubinstein argues that traditional Micronesian societies, like many elsewhere in the Pacific, require the individual to negotiate a series of wider social relations in the process of growing up, from the intimacy of the individual's nuclear family and security circle to a broadly defined and structured series of formal relationships in adulthood. He links many adolescent suicides to conflicts with figures of authority and suggests that recent increases are related to the loss of the lineage men's house and clubhouse institutions so that today, "young men at puberty are metaphorically flung into a social abyss, rather than into the supporting arms of the lineage and men's house. The compensatory social mechanisms no longer operate as before" (40). In chapter 7 here, Alan Howard documents some similar trends away from formal social mechanisms to greater personal freedom in Rotuma, but without the dramatic social consequences.

Christine Jourdan (1995) describes how the freedom associated with unemployment among youths in Honiara, Solomon Islands, encourage them to make active contributions to contemporary culture in the town. She argues that their dislocation puts them in a position to help carry out a "creolization" of introduced cultural traits, where they put "new meanings into old shells," allowing them to "find an identity niche in town" (205). The youths' disaffection and independence from the influence of older generations set up conditions that influence the tone of culture change in the town.

These studies underscore the need to consider changes in local social organization, especially as they affect relations between generations, as a central factor in any analysis of Pacific adolescence in the context of social change. The adolescent has become a major agent of social change and continuity in Pacific Island cultures. Prior to colonization, several critical domains were instrumental to the construction of adolescence as a stage of life in the Pacific. Among these, kinship, gender, marriage, politics, and warfare were the most salient themes. In the precolonial order, societies differed much more than today, we suspect, on the structure and meaning of "adolescent" experience. While social change brings with it a certain homogenization of contexts, it remains important to consider the distinctive social environments that have influenced contemporary situations.

GENDER AND SEXUALITY

Adolescence, being a time of transition through biological puberty, brings the youth into the social definitions of adult gender and sexuality. In many traditional Pacific societies, the adolescents' new sexual desires are constrained by highly restrictive social mores, documented, for example, in Whiting's classical account of the Kwoma (1941). The Kwoma youth tentatively yearns for social and sexual contact with the opposite sex, but must socially avoid it. Several significant ethnographic accounts of adolescence across cultures now fortify our understanding of gender relations. These studies in general demonstrate that adolescent girls are more socially controlled and less able to articulate sexual desires than males (see Whiting et al. 1986). This perspective is strongly inferred from the study of inner-city American adolescent girls as well (Fine 1988). However, across types of social structures, there is enormous variation in the restrictiveness of premarital sexuality and attitudes regarding virginity (see, for example, Burbank and Chisholm in chapter 3). Many detailed studies of adolescents in specific societies demonstrate that girls are often more restricted than boys. This is true, for instance, among the Holman Island Innuit Eskimos (Condon 1987:148), Australian Aborigines (Burbank 1988), and Thai Muslims (Anderson and Anderson 1986:375), and within the Pacific it holds true of the Mountain Arapesh (Mead 1935), Manus (Mead 1930), Kwoma (Whiting 1941), and Sambia (Herdt 1987), among other groups. Social change introduces variation and new innovations, and Lepowsky's chapter 6 is a significant example of contrary trends.

Pacific Island societies are well known for the extent to which ritual plays a role in defining gender. But the role of ritual in adolescent development across the Pacific is quite variable. Initiation does not simply introduce a sex contrast, as one might imagine, with boys initiated and girls not (reviewed in J. Brown 1981; Keesing 1982; M. Strathern 1988). Female initiation occurs as well, albeit less frequently or elaborately (P. Brown 1978). In Melanesia, the relationship between male cults and initiation, and the social distance between the sexes, is of course renown (Allen 1967; Mead 1935). Hogbin's (1970) significant account of Wogeo Island initiation perhaps sums up the relationship best: "The underlying theme of the male cult is again the gulf, physical and social between men and women" (101). The Wogeo themselves have a favorite expression, with regard to men's cult activities and sacred flutes, that echoes from other areas of Melanesia: "Men play flutes, women bear infants." On Wogeo, the social development of men and women is punctuated from babyhood into middle age by genderizing ritual practices, which find their zenith in scarification of the tongue and entry into the men's secret society.

It is important to caution, with Hogbin, that a strong physical basis of ritual activity exists in the ideology of many areas of Melanesia, where "the purpose of the rites . . . is to make certain that the boy will grow into a man" (1970:103). In chapter 4 here, Biersack argues that such ideas need to be held in mind. Her study suggests that ideas about body development and the ritual/nonritual contrast are more salient than male/female in certain societies, a suggestion that helps to explain many puzzling features of the symbolic role of women (see also M. Strathern 1988).

To illustrate the extraordinary influence of socially constructed reality upon adolescent sexual development—and the powerful impact of changing times, consider the issue of ritualized homosexuality in Melanesia. The institutional pattern of same-sex transmission of semen to create masculinity in these cultures was most powerful and widespread (Herdt 1984). We know now that this represented a special cultural ontology of psyche and development that came together especially in adolescence. The interplay of the erotic and key social/ritual roles is stupendously important to male adolescent growth. So much was this the case among the Sambia that the achievements of biological maturity and then fatherhood were believed to be solely the products of ritually constituted insemination (Herdt 1981). In such instances, the social construction of sexuality is part of both the biology and psycho-culture of adolescence.

Social change and modernization in the postcolonial social order have brought to an end these ritual practices, however. Today, as Van Baal (1984) has remarked of Marind-anim cultural practice in general, ritualized homosexuality belongs to the past. Other sexual practices of a radically different ontology have likewise given way to change, resulting in very different adolescent sexual development pathways compared to the past. The suppression of traditional sexuality in general is a major theme of the Pacific. In Tonga, for instance, ceremonial dancing was stopped by missionaries who associated this feature of the religion with sex (Latukefu 1980:76). Of course, missionary suppression of traditional religion (see, for examples, Gewertz 1983; Read 1952; Schieffelin and Crittendon 1991; Tuzin 1989) was prominent in many areas. Alongside this transformation, a change in gender roles has often occurred and instigated a generation gulf.

Gender is another key dimension. An important study by Carrier and Carrier (1989) illustrates the effect of social change on gender stratification. On Manus Island, boys and girls do similarly well in grade school, and they have "roughly comparable chances" of achieving grade 10. However, they differ in other opportunity structures: "Girls were almost completely dependent on regular secondary education if they were to migrate to work" (18). On the other hand, boys depend far less on school; they could leave school and get work easier. Nevertheless, it is difficult to tell how much this differs from traditional culture, which already was changing in Mead's (1930) day.

Likewise, a new order of increasing autonomy by women is indicated by innovative women's social movements (reviewed in M. Strathern 1988), which have replaced the "sexual antagonism" of traditional social relations in some places (Herdt and Poole 1982). In Papua New Guinea, examples of such movements include the *wok meri* of the Goroka area (Sexton 1982) and the Kafaina movement in Chauve area (Warry 1986).

Adolescent development is also often thought of as a kind of emancipation, and this notion emerges in some areas of the Pacific, both for boys and girls. We have already seen how, in the case of Manus, adolescent girls achieve greater autonomy, and the same is true of Sambia girls (Herdt 1987). Parents do not lose all authority, nor do secondary social agents gain all control; rather, autonomy is more valued by individual and group. A new kind of adult sociality enters into adolescent social transactions (see P. Brown 1978:147, on Highlands New Guinea; Schieffelin 1982, on Kaluli youth); the adolescent is now a morally consequential agent. In female developmental experiences, these new social bonds are delimited (as in the Gebusi case in Cantrell, chapter 5) and sometimes highly open (as on Vanatanai in Lepowsky, chapter 6). The male experience is emancipation plus new social obligations.

The study of adolescent freedoms in the context of gender polarities needs to be complemented, though, with accounts of how individual adolescents actually experience these ideas in their own lives. Herdt and Poole's discussion of Melanesian "sexual antagonism" argues that the famed oppositions between men and women need to be qualified by more actual studies of how people experience the opposition. In his study of Bumbita Arapesh sexuality, Leavitt (1991) introduced a methodological distinction between "sexual ideology" and "sexual experience," noting that when young men and women actually talked about how they regarded the other sex, the "antagonism" issues paled considerably when compared to anxieties about sexual competence and maturation into sexual roles.

Eileen Cantrell's chapter 5 on Gebusi men and women draws on the importance of the concept of "experience" to introduce a significant new way of qualifying Melanesian gendered oppositions. She argues that, when looked at from the perspective of women's actual experience, the "antagonism" against men is really an opposition to "those excessive and transgressive areas of men's behavior that threaten gender harmony." Rather than relying on a view of gender as part of an ideology of difference, Cantrell describes a negotiated process whereby men and women stake out positions that strive to make sense of the dominant and culturally defined definitions of gender. When discussed in the abstract, these understandings are not questioned, but in the context of actual practice, men and women argue for very different interpretations.

As views of gender difference change and the social options of young men and women adjust to postcolonial conditions, there are likely to be many similar negotiations over definitions of gender difference in relation to what young men and women actually experience. Herdt and Poole's call for more research on individual experience is now fifteen years old; there is much that remains to be done.

MODERNIZATION, EDUCATION, AND YOUTH

Western education and school has transformed adolescence in much of the Pacific. The issue raises again the general problem of the transformation of persons and genders across social time (reviewed in Mead 1956; Schwartz 1976). As social influences upon adolescent development change, child-rearing styles of socializers, with qualities such as restrictiveness/permissiveness or warmth/hostility, must change as well (Maccoby 1980:380–410). In such contexts, educational systems are, to quote Spindler, "charged with responsibility for bringing about change in the culture" (1974:303). Schools become agents of intended acculturation and, simultaneously, may become unwitting agents of cultural discontinuity (Wilcox 1982). But there is a terrific gap in our knowledge on this issue. If it is true, as Hartup has written, that "the school as a social system has not been well described in relation to the growth of social competence in the individual child" (1979:946) in Western cultures, than how much more significant is this for the Pacific? With the exception of Howard's discussion of Rotuman schooling in chapter 7, this volume does little specifically to close that gap. However, we do offer some observations here as a potential basis for future research.

Culture change suggests a problem in traditional education that arises out of developmental discontinuities across genders (horizontal) and across generations (vertical). Traditionally, affiliation and learning were developmentally timed, with most contact in early childhood years being with the mother and the domestic world. Later socialization, especially for males, was more associated with father and a larger public (Herdt 1989b). Generally, same-sex relationships were egalitarian, whereas opposite-sex relations tended to be hierarchical (M. Strathern 1988).

Two concepts are helpful here: social time and developmental life course time (Elder 1980; Neugarten and Datan 1973). The person ages and matures, just as society is changing. Particular phases of development—such as adolescence— may be experienced during a social time of great unrest, as in the 1960s, or with relative complacence and social conformity, as in the 1980s. Such distinctive developmental experiences must affect all subsequent phases of maturation (Boxer et al. 1984). In the Pacific, to take again the example of Manus Island, someone who came into adolescence during World War II must have had a very different life course than one who, a few years later, came of age during the Paliau "cargo cult" movement (Mead 1956). Indeed, Schwartz (1976) suggests that virtually all social change in stratification was a result of this history in Manus. The island was colonized and educated in the 1880s. Many islanders gained significant positions in the educated work force of New Guinea. Hence, extraordinary migration and change eventuated on Manus Island, and these changes left an indelible imprint of Manus culture on New Guinea society as a whole (Carrier and Carrier 1989).

In Pacific Island societies, the introduction of schools is another vanguard of cultural change. The school is such a key socializing institution that what is needed is a multidimensional model that recognizes the cultural conflicts brought on by schools and explores how new values are actually transmitted through schools. Let us conceptualize the school as a "total institution" (Goffman 1961) in which alternative cultural values and rules (Geertz 1973) prevail. Schools provide centrifugal social values that mediate between local village culture and national state ideology and institutions. Symbolic mediation of this sort entails both social conflict as well as cooperation between persons and groups (see, for instance, Carrier and Carrier 1989).

The concepts of modernity and acculturation have always been problematic and remain so in this regard. The notions of progress (Inkeles 1966), rationalization (Weber 1946), and rationality in means-to-ends schemes and interpretations of cultural practices (Gelner 1992) suggest the difficulties of applying simple folk Western formulations to the concepts and socioeconomic structures of the nonwestern world (Sahlins 1976). A model of social change is needed that takes account of the "insider" understanding of indigenous history and narratives necessary to critically augment acculturation accounts. Thus, new ways of approaching modernization may come from studying adolescents who are bridging changing sociocultural systems.

We might think of the comparison of schooled and unschooled adolescents across the Pacific as an example of the process. Here we are impressed by performance and competence standards that effectively amount to two distinct cultural systems. As an ideal type, traditional village life represents one cultural system; the school as institution and symbolic setting represents another. Studies of culture and literacy are obviously related to this issue. How much does literacy alter traditional thought and change cognition? Greenfield's studies of Wolof children (Greenfield and Bruner 1966) are suggestive because of the many differences she finds in performance on tasks of school and nonschool children, matched for age and residence. How much does the technology implicit in a school curriculum matter in claims of literacy effects? The problem, as reviewed by Cole et al. (1971), is one in which we need to understand the total system's relationship between school and nonschool, and a key problem of analysis concerns how we conceptualize schooled versus unschooled adolescent populations. Do we contrast them purely in terms of intellectual tasks, social dynamics (Hartup 1979), or cultural knowledge (Geertz 1973; Mead 1963)? Obviously, anthropologists opt for the latter. As Tharp (1989:350) has pointed out in the context of contemporary Hawaii, for instance, the problems of culture and education in the implementation of Western classroom tasks supersede the more limited issue of literacy. A dual cultural system model is concerned more broadly with what Tharp has called the "cultural compatibility hypothesis," whereby adjustment and success in two worlds are required of youth.

The high schools of Papua New Guinea are a particularly powerful context in which to understand and compare the effects of acculturation upon youth across a range of societies. Here, too, issues of traditional cultural competence and contemporary education success come to the fore. Precisely how children and young people come to develop new systems of cognitive and cultural schemas, and come to share these in their own and other sociocultural groups as national identity, is of direct interest (Carrier and Carrier 1989; Schwartz 1976). The emergence of the high school as a bureaucratic institution with special exams—a new cultural ethos in the Pacific—is a powerful challenge to the norms and roles of traditional culture (Townsend 1985:92–95; cf. Heath 1989:371; Good and Weinstein 1986:1095; Linney and Seidman 1989; Rogoff and Morelli 1989). The adolescent's social "competence" becomes increasingly problematic; it is not reducible simply to educational success (particularly in village settings).

YOUTH AND NEW NATIONAL IDENTITIES

Acculturation problems are accelerating for the Pacific region in general and for Papua New Guinea in particular. Extraordinary economic and industrial development related to mining, petroleum, timber, and agricultural interests have increased dramatically the importance of Papua New Guinea in relation to the major powers, particularly Japan. The geopolitical significance of these changes is suggestive of the need for understanding the country's emergent social forces, leaders, and goals (see Howard, chapter 7). Of more importance for the study of cross-cultural adolescence, however, is the Pacific's recent booming economy and its extremely heterogeneous, young, culturally pluralistic population. Indeed, these trends suggest the need to model rapid sociohistorical effects upon development through ritual and secular, school and nonschool pathways, into the future.

What part is played by urban elites in modernization? In postcolonial Papua New Guinea, such elites have become the agents of acculturation, with the emerging elite culture in cities idealized as the target to which nonelite groups gradually aspire. The youth of today will of course reproduce these strata. The high school as an "elite" institution can be viewed as a part of this emerging culture. What is the fit between educational policy and the democratizing sociocultural system? Education policies implemented without regard to the needs of the society as a whole create substantial political problems which, if left untended, can lead to widespread political and social discontent.

Papua New Guinea faces the difficulties of many postcolonial countries in its task to forge a national culture and identity from the cultural and linguistic diversity of its peoples. Ideology and nationhood are here very much linked (Geertz 1963). The Melanesian jurist and social philosopher Bernard Narokobi (1980), for instance, has emphasized land, communalism, and the traditional polities of village and clan in his discussion of the distinctive features of Melanesian culture that contribute to Papua New Guinea's national identity. He has appealed to a pluralism based on village sociality (54) and the idea that the education system is "foreign in its design and implementation . . . dominated by expatriate ideologies" (52). Narokobi similarly derides "Christianity" as a national theme of unification (153) in traditional pagan New Guinea societies, even though in the recent New Year's messages the governor-general of Papua New Guinea (himself a New Guinean) referred to the "Christian heritage" of the country. Michael Somare, the first prime minister of Papua New Guinea, has written about the problem of educational elites there. Referring to the situation at the time of independence, Somare states, "There were very few educated Papua New Guineans then. Only a few of us could see and understand what was ... happening" (1975:44; see also Kiki 1968:144–48). Henry Olela (1980:198) has appealed to the high schools and universities of Papua New Guinea as "custodians of the intellectual soul of the nation," which are in search of a "conceptual cultural framework." Here we see powerful signs of tension between change and tradition, between what is authentic or artificial (Latukefu 1980) in Pacific lifeways—tensions that are necessary in the emergence of new national identities but which are particularly burdensome to the adolescents of today.

With societies in such transition, how are youth coping with these burdens? The challenges—and burdens—of identity formation in the changing Pacific scene are reflections of social communities' efforts to remake themselves. For, if we look to the example of Rotuma in Alan Howard's chapter 7, we find that "the vitality of social life" is also the acceptance of adolescent humor and "youthful antics." Rotuma youth have more choices, more identity decisions and burdens to make as well, but somehow these have been integrated successfully so far into an ongoing social fabric. "New lives for old" was Mead's (1956) metaphor for this process of cultural reproduction, and while its functionalism may have been flawed, the moral and psychological sentiments were not. As Howard says, even now, Rotuma involvement is interpreted by their elders as signs of "love and compassion."

Change is never a one-way street, nor a simple process of building up or tearing down, and neither is national identity. Social change affects all of us. The construction of adolescence in Pacific Island contexts is a promotion of an overarching national culture: Youth are seeking their own new and unique historical pathway of development, from the past to the present. Such a search for identity has usually been the most blessed thing in traditional village life in the Pacific. As Malinowski (1929) once remarked of the Trobriand attitude toward youth: adolescents are the very "flower of the village" (64). Not all cultures would provide us with such a rosy metaphor, but surely we must believe that the Trobriand sentiment is by no means unusual. We are reminded of the musing of Oscar Wilde as he made a Dorian Gray comment over a century ago: "Youth! There is nothing like it." The Trobriand sentiment is not so different from this Victorian notion, and we may conclude with Wilde's reason: Adolescents "seem in front of one. Life has revealed to them her latest wonder."

Adolescence in the Pacific

A BIOSOCIAL VIEW

Carol M. Worthman

This essay attempts to frame the largely ethnographic chapters of this volume with a wider developmental perspective by bringing together two anthropological literatures on human development, one that deals with physical variation and another that documents cultural diversity. As in other regions of the world, both kinds of diversity are marked among Pacific peoples. The timing and course of human development—puberty in particular—vary widely within and between populations. Even more disparate are the ways in which societies have constructed the period between childhood and adulthood, known in Western societies as adolescence. Interactions between these two levels of variation will be examined, and two conclusions drawn: first, that human development is inherently biosocial, and, second, that systems of child rearing and socialization rely on the dialectic of body and context that shapes ontogeny. This dialectic is seldom apparent to social actors, who instead see development as a social process sustained by cultural interpretations. This widely held conviction has even convinced many ethnographers that social arrangements largely determine what a child will become.

One strong thread of evidence gives immediate pause to the "Xerox model" of socialization, in which the blank page of the child is put through the copy machine of socialization and turns out like others exposed to the same cultural template: people turn out quite different from one another. Substantial individual variation among adults—in behavior, appearance, and life history—both reflects inherent individual differences and reveals the stochastic nature of development, arising as it does from continuous encounters over time between inherent features, organized social intervention, historical accident, and contextual vicissitudes. Development and socialization to normative outcomes are at best probabilistic. As the developmental psychologist Richard Lerner has observed: "In probabilistic, as opposed to predetermined, epigenetic models of development, biological and contextual factors are seen to be reciprocally (dynamically) inter- active, making developmental changes dependent upon the timing of interact- ing biological, psychological, and social factors" (Lerner 1989:11). Epigenesis is the interaction of context with genotype that is responsible for shaping the phe- notype, or characteristics of the individual. Through this term, developmental biologists tacitly concede the importance of context—that, indeed, organisms (particularly humans) are biologically designed to develop in interaction with their environment. In other words, biology depends on social context in its de- velopment while society depends on biology in shaping persons. The two are mutually defining domains of ontogeny.

At present, anthropologists separate biological from cultural domains and consider human development from two quite disconnected vantage points. The first is contemporary cultural anthropology's concern with the social construc- tion and local constitution of selves. The second is physical anthropology's work on growth and maturation as a window onto human adaptation. Such a divi- sion of labor fosters concepts of development that implicitly divide persons into two constitutive domains: social constitution and physical constitution. How these domains relate in the construction or (if one prefers a less deterministic term) ontogeny of persons remains poorly articulated (LeVine 1990). Recogniz- ing this lacuna, psychologists have lately emphasized that development is a re- ciprocal process that occurs through time between the individual and the envi- ronment (Lerner and Foch 1987; Stattin and Magnusson 1990). The temporal dimension is important because development is a process of differentiation: maturation is directional and cumulative in the sense that a young person, once at point B, cannot return to point A, although state B remains a product of prior events and states.

Both historical/social conceptions and anthropological analyses of adoles- cence express tensions between viewing adolescents as in a state of being or of becoming. On the one side, the content and experience of this life stage can be taken phenomenologically as lived personal history; on the other, it can be con- strued in terms of the adult outcomes toward which it leads. Adolescents are fre- quently seen as not quite being "themselves"; rather, they are seen as being ei- ther in a special state or in transit to some ultimate maturational destination. Pacific societies represent divergent views on what adolescence is "about," from those that foreground being adolescent to those that emphasize becoming adult. Focus in the present volume on adolescents and their socially constructed lived experiences around the Pacific reveals a rich social diversity that can aid our thinking about how socialization works.

Many folk developmental theories treat maturation either as something that happens "naturally"—an unfolding with little intervention—or as a process that culture must influence with strong, conscious, sustained effort. Both views have merit, but where a culture falls on this spectrum shapes the ecology of child development. I will demonstrate that the cultural milieu constructs not just the social but also the physical life history of the individual. I will also show how, reciprocally, the biology of maturation influences cultural concepts, practices, and interpretations of development. As necessary background to this analysis, the biology of puberty will first be reviewed. Then, drawing on examples of peoples around the Pacific, I will examine how social process depends on and acts through the biological domain in ways that are clearly articulated at times or, more often, hidden. This latter observation will lead to a consideration of effects of social change on ontogeny that may also be mediated by alteration of biosocial interactions in development.

PUBERTY AND ADOLESCENCE

The dual constitution of adolescence in scientific discourse is expressed in the terms *puberty* and *adolescence;* confusion over their difference reflects the divided scientific approaches for studying human development. Adolescence is a social construct that varies enormously, but puberty is a universal physiological process.

Puberty is the sequence of physical changes that transforms the child into an adult, most visible by attainment of reproductive maturity, adult size and shape. Thus, puberty is universally experienced as a process of growth while adolescence is not. Onset of puberty is defined by the first rise in gonadotropins (hormones secreted by the brain which initiate the process) or by the first bodily changes of puberty, which are breast buds in girls and genital growth in boys. Puberty ends when this biological sequence of maturational change is complete.

Adolescence, on the other hand, is defined by the culturally constituted meanings of this process, especially the childhood-to-adulthood transition. The beginning, ending, and duration—not to mention content—of adolescence differ greatly across societies. Moreover, the chronological relationship between puberty and adolescence varies widely. The Pacific peoples discussed in this book illustrate the breadth of such diversity: some do not recognize an adolescent period at all while others elaborate and prolong it. Australian Aboriginal peoples, for instance, traditionally married girls at the onset of puberty (Burbank 1988:55–6, and chapter 3, this volume). Bimin-Kuskusmin boys, on the other hand, undergo a ten-year ritual cycle to attain manhood (Poole 1982). Gender differences in social construction of adolescence are often quite pronounced: among the Tiwi, girls were married before puberty, but boys endured a ten-year initiation cycle before they could do so (Hart, Pilling, and Goodale 1988:102–04).

Even within groups, then, adolescence can be constituted differently, with distinctive grades, steps, and meanings.

Does such marked cultural variation correspond to differences in the kinds of persons that members of these societies are expected to become? The interface between puberty and adolescence—biological and social processes—provides an opportunity to examine interaction between the shared biological processes of ontogeny and the particular meanings of the construction of persons and groups. We may, for instance, expect societal differences in sex roles to be reflected by concomitant variation in socialization practices (Whiting and Edwards 1988).

Patterns of physical maturation have been closely studied in Western populations, so that extensive data on endocrine and morphologic changes of puberty in both sexes are available and give a fairly complete picture of the biology of this stage. Unfortunately, equivalent data for any Pacific Island group are lacking. However, comparative studies have shown that the process of puberty is roughly equivalent across populations, so that we can use data from Western groups to form a representative picture of pubertal events and their general sequence. Figure 1 outlines the progression of key physical changes of puberty in well-described Western populations, emphasizing visible alterations in growth, shape, and function, along with the nonvisible endocrine patterns that cause them. The timing of events varies widely across societies, though, complicating attempts to represent the course of puberty. Therefore, figure 1 has been constructed to show the schedule of pubertal change in a particular population at a particular time, namely, a Western postindustrial setting with low child morbidity and mortality along with good nutrition. The figure is a composite, constructed from data on European and American populations to represent a group having a median age at menarche of 13.5 years, the age reported for a large British cohort born in the 1950s and a major source of data on pubertal progression (Marshall and Tanner 1969). Where data are from an American population with a slightly different timing of menarche, ages of reported events have been adjusted slightly to maintain the chronological relationship to median age at menarche.

Puberty is marked by physical growth, morphological change, and the endocrine changes that drive both of these. Alterations in pattern and amount of hormone stimulation of the gonads by the brain (via release of the gonadotropins, LH and FSH) induce increases in gonadal activity that stimulate rises in estradiol and testosterone production (Grumbach et al. 1990). Genital growth in boys and breast development in girls ensue. The combination of gonadal and central nervous system activity drives reproductive maturation and the appearance of primary and secondary sex characters. These features include penile and testicular growth, muscle expansion, voice change, and facial and axillary hair

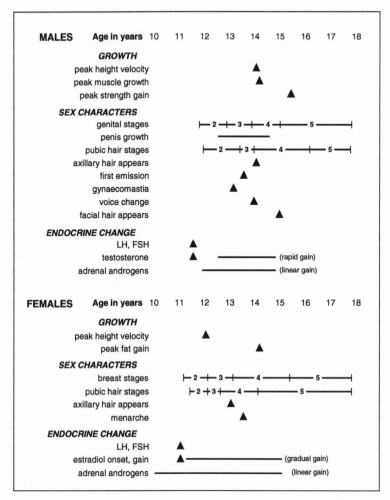

Fig. 1. The course of puberty in Vanatinai, including endocrine changes and the morphological-functional features associated with them. *Sources:* Apter 1980; Ducharme et al. 1976; G. B. Forbes 1986; Kulin et al. 1989; Laron et al. 1980; Lee and Migeon 1975; Lee et al. 1976; Lee 1980; Malina 1986; Marshall and Tanner 1969, 1970, 1986; Nottelman et al. 1987.

in boys, and breast development and altered amount and distribution of fat in girls. Growth markers depicted in figure 1 comprise median time of peak height velocity (PHV), or maximal height gain per unit time; peak rates of growth in muscle bulk and strength in boys; and age at peak rate of fat gain in girls. Figure 1 also depicts median ages of developmental events such as first appearance of axillary (armpit) hair, first emission, onset of gynaecomastia (transient breast enlargement in males), and so on. Horizontal lines in figure 1 refer to gradual or cumulative changes over time, with numbers marking conventional stages of adolescent development. Divisions between numbers mark median age of entry into each stage. Morphological onset of puberty is defined as the appearance of stage 2, or the age at which change first occurs in either of the defining morphological features of puberty (genital development or pubic hair growth in boys, breast development or pubic hair growth in girls). For boys, the period of growth in length of the penis is also indicated by a solid line. For both sexes, median age at first significant daytime rise in gonadotropins (FSH, LH) and gonadal steroids (testosterone, estradiol) is noted as well. Characteristic developmental shifts in adrenal androgen output commence in mid-childhood with a slight increase in slope with age (adrenarche) and increase linearly across puberty after another pronounced flex in slope in early puberty. This pubertal period of increased rates is indicated by the straight line. Such changes in output of adrenal androgens play a significant, but poorly understood, role in puberty. They stimulate pubic hair development and act synergistically with gonadal steroids to produce accelerated growth and skeletal maturation, and, in girls, to induce the appearance of axillary hair. In the case of boys, axillary hair growth is governed largely by levels of testosterone, a very potent androgen that increases with testicular development.

When asked to compare development in both sexes, people from most societies, including our own, will say that boys enter puberty and mature much later than girls. Based on endocrine change and pubertal staging, however, boys in Western postindustrial settings enter puberty just six to eight months later than do girls (see fig. 1). Girls, however, progress more quickly through puberty and display outward signs of maturity earlier on in the process than do their male peers. Peak height velocity in girls occurs about a year after they become pubescent and almost 1.5 years before menarche, while in boys it transpires nearly 2.5 years after entering puberty, about one-half year after sperm production commences. Thus, girls grow fastest shortly after onset of puberty and well before reproductive function is achieved, but boys have their most rapid height gain much later in puberty, after they attain reproductive capacity.

Sexual dimorphism in puberty is due in part to differences in gonadal hormone production that have differential effects on steroid target tissues (Schreiber and Baron 1984). Girls' breasts and growth rate are highly responsive to estradiol production; consequently, stimulation occurs early in the course of slow pubertal increases in ovarian activity. Boys, on the other hand, show very large and rapid rises in testosterone over two years, with maximal increases occurring in individuals over a period of only ten to twelve months. Boys apparently require substantial testosterone stimulation to achieve the most visible pubertal changes—accelerated growth, muscle bulking, voice change, and facial hair. In contradistinction to sex differences in visible attainments, capacity to produce gametes (indicated by menarche and first ejaculation) is achieved almost simultaneously by both sexes. Despite near equivalence in timing of basic reproductive competence, boys and girls appear to mature at quite distinctive rates because of gender differences in the timing of other signs of maturity. Each sex exhibits some dissociation of reproductive maturity from overall physical development, with girls appearing more precocious and boys more juvenile than their actual state of reproductive maturity.

The pubertal transformations, which are charted in figure 1, occur in a social context; they alter adolescents' views of themselves and perceptions of them by others. Reviewing the visible changes of puberty with this point in mind reveals sources for cultural models of development. We have just seen how, in the face of relative gender synchrony in reproductive development, boys and girls are believed to mature at different times. Busse (1990) reports a Boazi saying that deftly captures that perception: "women take a short cut, men go around." While girls show early signs of maturity in growth and breast development, the signs of androgenization in males are more numerous, being expressed in several new traits—new physique (muscle gain, relative fat loss), manly voice, adult genitalia, and whiskers. Girls' genitalia, by contrast, are not transformed in puberty, although their body habitus is altered through breast development and, later, fat gain. The plethora of changes over a prolonged period in boys supports the cultural view of maturation as a more incremental, achieved status in males than in females. One physical change which has not been discussed in the anthropological literature on adolescence is gynaecomastia. In Western populations, as much as 70 percent of boys show breast enlargement in early to mid puberty (Brunstein 1996; Styne 1991). This condition frequently causes consternation for the boy and his parents, though the condition subsequently regresses within a short time. One wonders whether gynaecomastia is also prevalent in nonwestern groups, and how it is seen by them.[1] The fact that an early sign of puberty in some boys is breast expansion, something usually identified only with females, should excite attention in societies with strong gender polarization, including several of the New Guinean groups discussed in this book.[2]

Gaps between different developmental milestones during puberty also create windows for perceived efficacy of social action. Many groups observe menarcheal seclusion and some even deliberately fatten postmenarcheal girls: in Western societies, where such practices are absent, girls show most rapid gain in fat two years after peak height velocity, or in the year after menarche. Rituals at menarche and practices aimed at identifying girls with adult female roles after menarche are reinforced by the propensity of postmenarcheal girls to gain weight and achieve an adult feminine body habitus: girls appear to become more like women as the result of social interventions.[3] In boys, there is a curious lag of about 1.5 years between the time that they acquire muscle mass most rapidly, at peak height velocity, and the time when most accelerated gains in strength are realized. The physiologic reasons for the temporal gap are unclear, but such a gap can reinforce the culturally constituted perception that it is one thing to have male physical *attributes,* and quite another to have a man's *abilities* (Mead 1935, 1949). Practices aimed at "making men" out of boys receive validation from the observation that boys gain muscle but do not become strong as men until after culture has intervened. Thus, belief in nurture can be reinforced by nature.

The wet-dry, soft-hard metaphors for gender frequently encountered in New Guinea provide a further instance of biological concomitants in metaphors of ontogeny.[4] Viewed through this metaphor, men are "dry," but boys are borne and nurtured by women and are "wet" by association. The purpose of ritual cycles commencing in middle to late childhood is in part to purge boys of their "wetness" through diet, bloodletting, masculine work, and trials of physical endurance (stress, sweating, denial of water). The biology of puberty supports this cultural model. Adults exhibit marked gender differences in proportion of body fat and muscle, so that the more muscular men appear hard, or "dry," compared to women. A slight sex difference in percentage of body fat exists in Western children, girls having more than boys, but the difference increases sharply from early puberty (when both sexes gain fat) onward. As boys' growth rate increases, proportionate body fat is reduced, and they appear leaner; at peak height velocity, with increments in muscle mass, they become leaner still. Body density therefore increases relative to water (fat having less and muscle greater density than does water) during puberty in boys: they do dry out, so to speak (G. B. Forbes 1986; Malina 1986; Marshall and Tanner 1986).

Many maturational sex differences can be readily discerned by an observer; others are relatively invisible, being purely physiologic. The gender-differentiated manner in which physiologic changes of puberty are manifested by the body or in behavior can also be seen as reflecting adaptive strategies, for these maturational changes can act as signals to other members of society who "read" them and adjust their expectations and treatment of the adolescent according to the cultural schema for development and scripts for socialization (Worthman 1987). Breast development is frequently interpreted as a significant maturational sign. Of the groups represented in this volume, Australian Aboriginal, Gebusi, Paiela, and Vanatinai societies are known to use breast bud formation as a basis for assigning adolescent status to girls. The evidence clearly indicates that girls' appearance at puberty allows the attribution of maturity before reproductive competence is achieved, while that of boys forestalls attribution of maturity and assumption of adult roles until well after reproductive competence is reached.

The developmental profile shown in figure 1 may be representative on the population level, but it conceals a phenomenologically important fact: individuals in any population vary widely in timing of maturational changes. Because

Western societies place children in age-graded school classes, they are acutely aware of this situation: scanning any junior high school class reinforces the impression of developmental diversity by age. Both in Western (Marshall and Tanner 1969, 1970) and nonwestern (Worthman 1986) groups, there are ages at which one can find same-sex peers who have not entered puberty and those who have already completed it, along with the entire spectrum of attainments in between. Socialization practices that are organized by chronological age, such as schooling, are therefore targeting developmentally diverse groups, whereas those organized by maturational status will obviously target more homogenous ones. The schooling system handles the issue of individual developmental differences by ignoring them, while aspects (not necessarily all) of traditional systems such as that of the Paiela (Biersack, chapter 4, this volume), Gebusi (Cantrell, chapter 5, this volume), or Bimin-Kuskusmin (Poole 1990) implicitly attend to them.

Change in socialization practices can therefore also alter the choreography between social experience and biological maturation. For instance, if the Paiela were to shift to schooling as the primary socializing agent (Biersack 1982 and chapter 4, this volume), it would entail a change from socialization employing the body as a principal metaphor for personal development to one in which external evaluation of performance—behavioral and cognitive—is the yardstick of maturity. Acculturation transition is frequently paralleled by a loss of opportunities for narcissistic display of adolescent beauty, sexuality, or newly acquired status in the formal structure of socialization processes. The opportunities generally occur in the context of ritual processions, courtship and dance, and agonistic male display. But schooling effaces such display, requiring a conforming appearance (often in school uniforms; paint and other adornments are banished) and demeanor that downplay individual differences, diminish opportunities for physical exhibition, and juvenilize adolescents.

In addition to the individual differences observed within populations, maturation schedules establish pronounced variation among them. Age at menarche, which is often used as an index for pubertal timing, may vary widely. Median menarcheal ages reported for Pacific populations represent the full range over which the event occurs worldwide, from 12.7 years of age for New Zealand Maori, to 18.0 for Bundi and 18.4 for Lumi of Papua New Guinea (Eveleth and Tanner 1976:215). Historically, socioeconomic transformations have generally been succeeded by accelerated maturation. Since the nineteenth century, European groups have undergone a pronounced historical trend to reduced age at menarche, so that, for instance, working-class girls in Oslo, Norway, experienced menarche at age 13.3 years in 1940, over two years earlier than they did just eighty years previously (Brudevoll, Liestøl, and Walløe 1979). Because of the accelerated maturation rate, height for age in children has also steadily increased through time (Brundtland, Liestøl, and Walløe 1980). These temporal changes in developmental schedule have been termed *secular trends* (or, more precisely, *positive secular trends*) (Tobias 1985). Secular trends have also been reported in the Pacific (Zemel and Jenkins 1989), but the relevant studies are few. Measures of children in Western and American Samoa, and among Samoan migrants to California, have indicated that Samoan children develop most rapidly in California, less rapidly in American Samoa, and least rapidly in Western Samoa (Bindon and Zansky 1986). These differences were apparently due to effects of modernization.

While myriad causes for secular trends to earlier maturation observed in both Western and developing countries have been proposed, no unified causal model exists; amelioration of nutrition and health and other environmental improvements have been consistently implicated (Bielicki 1986; Liestøl 1982). Similar factors are also thought to mediate the widely observed relationship of socioeconomic status to rate of child development and menarcheal age (Bogin 1988:105–59). Thus, the sensitivity of maturational schedules to environmental quality finds expression in the variation within groups and among populations, as well as in the considerable change within populations over time.

MATURATION AS A BIOSOCIAL PROCESS

In several respects, then, human development can be understood as the result of both social and biological processes (Worthman 1993).[5] Even the timing of maturational events, which is generally considered to be "hard wired," represents an outcome of the interplay between the body and its environment. From this perspective, maturational schedules and developmental outcomes are to a degree socially constructed. Except, perhaps, in the study of cognition, the role of socialization in the actual physical organization and functioning of individuals is rarely studied. Various lines of evidence suggest, however, that this role is an active one.

Indirect support for the importance of social arrangements that shape child development comes from literature on the above-mentioned secular trend, which documents parallel changes in rates of child maturation with temporal change in patterns of nutrition and health. These influences commence in utero. Fluctuations in health conditions of mothers (measured in age-specific mortality rates) in Sweden during the nineteenth and twentieth centuries were followed by parallel fluctuations in menarcheal age of their daughters (Liestøl 1982). Poorly nourished or stressed mothers are also more likely to have low birth weight infants, who, in turn, have poorer prognosis for survival and development (Metcoff 1986; Tanner 1978:46). These data further showed that lower menarcheal age correlates with higher gross domestic product at year of birth (Liestøl 1982). After birth, the influence of behavioral variables intensifies. Culturally determined early patterns of infant feeding (nursing schedules, weaning practices) can interact with other environmental variables such as disease or nutrient availability to influence rates of infant development (Dettwyler and Fishman 1992). Analysis of historical records of annual measures of Oslo school-children reveals that attained height by age closely reflects worsening, then improving, concurrent nutritional conditions during World War II (Brundtland, Liestøl, and Walløe 1980). Children exhibit not only slowdown but also catch-up in growth in response to short-term changes in environmental quality (Tanner 1978:154–60; Ruel et al. 1995). Known mediators for these effects include nutrition and illness; the contributions of other factors (stress, climate, photoperiodicity, activity patterns) are less well understood (Bogin 1988).

Such findings illustrate how behaviorally mediated environmental conditions influence child development on several levels. First, milieu may exert an acute (short-term) effect by acting through immediate, reversible suppression or enhancement of growth rates. Second, environmental circumstances may have an organizational (long-term) effect on the developmental trajectory of the child. For instance, physically stressful treatment of infants in the first two years of life (scarification, circumcision, cradleboarding) appears to lead on average to earlier maturation and increased adult height (Whiting 1965; Landauer and Whiting 1981). Third, conditions may operate on development through selection: one explanation for the secular trend contends that rapid maturers may be more likely to succumb early to poor environmental conditions (Ellison 1981). Improved environmental conditions would presumably lead to differential improvement in the survival of early maturers.

Antecedent experiences and concurrent influences moreover alter the timing and course of puberty. The same early conditions that enhance child growth are also associated with earlier maturation (Khan et al. 1995). In addition, maturation of adolescents is sensitive to concurrent nutritional and activity patterns (Warren 1980; Brooks-Gunn and Warren 1988). Pubertal development is therefore in part an autonomous developmental stage and in part an outcome of prior ontogeny.

This generalized overview of behavioral-environmental influences on physical maturation of children has overlooked an important systemic source of individual variation: gender. Interactions of gender with environment influence development in two ways. There are, for one, sex differences in environmental sensitivities and developmental requirements. Then, social custom frequently dictates differential treatment of boys and girls according to cultural models of child need and value (Worthman 1996). These dual factors generally act in concert and vary so widely across populations that it is difficult to dissociate their effects through comparative studies. There is sound theoretical and some empirical support for the expectation that girls will be more highly buffered from environmental influences on maturation than will boys, who should therefore show greater sensitivity to environmental quality (Stinson 1985). It is known, for instance, that males have higher caloric needs for weight at all activity states than do females (Lowrey 1978:347, 351), and that male mortality exceeds that of females at all ages when conditions are equal by sex. But the picture may be more complex than this (Galler et al. 1985, 1987). As yet unexplored systematically is the extent to which, and in what respects, males and females show differential sensitivity to specific environmental circumstances such as stress, workload, thermal load, photoperiod, or micronutrient availability (see, for example, Angold and Worthman 1993). Furthermore, the degree of environmental vulnerability may vary by gender at different developmental stages. Sex-differentiated sensitivity may explain the consistent disagreement over which sex benefits more developmentally from improved environmental conditions.

Societies regularly differentiate treatment of children by gender; many allocate resources preferentially to boys. These practices may either actually accommodate greater male caloric requirements and vulnerability to disease in nutritionally stressed populations, or they may differentially meet the material needs and demands of boys. In the process, one could conjecture that such practices may also set males and females on developmentally different tracks in the ontogeny of resource use. That is, constitutional energy sparing in girls is reinforced by early deprivation, thus enhancing the apparent gender difference in energetic needs in that population. Socially sanctioned sex differences in health care provision, living conditions, or workload are also abundantly documented in the ethnographic and biomedical literature (Hrdy 1990). Differential treatment of children is often legitimated by perceived differences in need or value by sex and becomes integral to the process of gendered social construction of the life course.

Socialization for gender roles typically dictates sex differences in activity, and material and social living conditions. The removal of boys in mid to late childhood from the maternal household to the masculine world and work in several New Guinea societies (Bimin-Kuskusmin: Poole 1982; Bumbita: Leavitt, survey; Gebusi: Knauft 1987, survey; Marind-anim: Busse 1990; Sambia: Herdt 1981; surveyed in Herdt 1989c) illustrates this phenomenon. While the practices arise from specific ethnopediatric models of masculine development, the de facto effect is to alter the living and sleeping conditions, daily companions, and nutritional status of boys. Ritually determined food taboos or prescriptions, encouragement or requirement of hunting (with attendant meat eating), and strong reductions in domestic workload all reshape the nutritional and energetic status of boys entering the men's world. Girls in these populations have been less carefully studied (but see Cantrell, chapter 5, this volume; Leavitt, survey), but the net effect of their remaining with the maternal unit is that their diet, companions, and living conditions can be expected to show little systematic change over the early life span. If anything, the one systematic change with age is increased domestic and gardening labor, often with the motivation of demonstrating marriageability by displaying compliance, productivity, and diligence (for example, with the Marind-anim; see Busse 1990).

Gender as well as group differences in physical development and body habitus are therefore in part social products, inasmuch as the developmental profile of a gender or a population largely reflects environmental circumstances—including culturally mediated arrangements—under which children develop. In this sense, then, the physical development of children may also be seen as socially constructed. It seems more broadly accurate to say, however, that child development occurs as a result of interacting biosocial processes.

ETHNOPEDIATRICS AND SOCIALIZATION

Culture-specific models of child development are a key basis for understanding systematic ways in which culture interacts with physical development of children in the ontogeny of persons. Ethnopediatric models of child development provide guidelines that inform socialization in others' perceptions, intentions, and evaluations of the developing individual (Harkness and Super 1996). Emic views of child development vary considerably among societies, lending at first glance some support to the notion of culture as detached from biology. Closer inspection reveals that all such models do reflect an awareness of maturation as arising from biosocial process; what varies is the degree of emphasis on the role of nature or of cultural contrivance (Worthman 1995).

The concept that growth and physical maturation occurs, on the whole, "naturally" is common in the Pacific; that is, no cultural interventions are deemed necessary to attain reproductive maturity. Island groups discussed in this volume (Rotuma, Vanatinai) and in the classic ethnographic literature (Manus: Mead 1930; Samoa: Mead 1928; Trobriand: Malinowski 1929, section III.3) view development in this way and do not prescribe social interventions to ensure that proper physical maturation does occur. Such societies do, however, differ in the degree of emphasis on age-grade terms (Lepowsky, chapter 6, this volume), reflecting variation in social marking of developmental or life cycle status: maturation, though viewed as natural, may also be closely monitored by the culture. Further, the cultural perception of development as natural does not preclude applying rites of passage and other ritual markers of maturation. Status markers and rituals are legitimated in this context by their social effects, locating and incorporating the physical maturational process in the social-developmental one.

Alternatively, societies may view physical maturation as socially achieved and contrived, as a process that does not occur without conscious, concerted social intervention. Societies subscribing to this model that are described in this book are in Papua New Guinea (Bumbita, Paiela), but similar beliefs may be found across insular Melanesia (Herdt 1989c). The view of child development as requiring social effort takes alternate forms, one concerning what parents should do *for* their children, the other concerning what elders must do *to* them. In both such schemes, child development is understood in a moral dimension because it includes a notion of social agency. Paiela and Bumbita each ascribe proper child growth to the agency of parents. Bumbita (Leavitt, survey) believe that the spiritual energy of parents (channeled through parental yam cultivation) is expended to make their children grow. Parental aging occurs as a direct function of investment in children; therefore, growth of children occurs at the physical expense of parents. Paiela, on the other hand, believe that stringent maternal observation of menstrual pollution taboos and magic is prerequisite, though not sufficient, for optimal development (Biersack, survey). Both of these societies emphasize what parents do *for* children, while those such as Bimin-Kuskusmin or Marind-anim emphasize what is done *to* them.

Gender ideology appears to drive the complex spiritual-material concepts of social agency in development that prevail among some groups of Papua New Guinea (Keesing 1982). Proper adult gender differentiation is thought to occur only through ritual interventions in masculine development. In this view, the gender of default is female, and masculine identity is contingent; perpetuation of the spiritual-material sphere represented by the masculine requires careful, sustained (often lifelong), coordinated effort by men in the making of boys into men, and the maintenance by men of their masculine integrity. This process involves sometimes elaborate symbolic schemata relating food, body fluids, and gender-differentiated body form and function, through ritual and personal practices, to spiritual concepts of gendered oppositions. For instance, Poole (1982, 1990) details a progression of dietary rules that male Bimin-Kuskusmin initiates must observe. Gebusi (Knauft 1987, survey), Marind-anim (Busse 1990) and Sambia (Herdt 1981, 1989c) each exemplify the cultural belief in some areas of Melanesia that semen transfer is required for proper masculine sexual development (Herdt 1982). This practice is supported by beliefs that semen as a life force is a fixed resource that must be carefully guarded and passed from man to boy: boys are thus thought of as literally *en*seminated by men. Socialization practices concerning male adolescents in such societies apply a concrete biological notion of making boys into men that intercalates directly with gender metaphors and concepts of proper masculine social-behavioral development. Poole (1982, 1990) notes that Bimin-Kuskusmin initiates come to link the process of self-definition with body transformation in that cognitive, emotional, motivational, or behavioral change is associated with bodily reconstitution in an irreversible ontoge-

netic process. The outcome, psychobiological fusion in adult identity maintenance, is reflected in the nosebleeding practices of Sambia men (Herdt 1990a).
In contrast to societies believing in "natural" growth, status markers and rituals
are legitimated in this context through their physical effects, identifying the social-developmental process with the physical maturational metaphor.

"Achieved" growth models can also include notions of personal agency or
responsibility in development. Here, the individual is viewed as being to some
degree responsible for his or her own physical maturation through ritual observations and other appropriate behaviors. Again, Paiela and Bumbita provide an
instructive comparison because each incorporates a concept of personal efficacy,
while their assumptions about agency differ widely. Paiela appear to interpret
individual agency with particular concreteness, expecting that both girls and
boys will "grow themselves" by adhering closely to ritual and personal hygienic
formulas for achieving maximum physical perfection (Biersack 1990; chapter 4,
this volume). That beautiful skin and hair are particularly emphasized as achiev-
able in this way is notable, for both closely reflect physical well-being. Such cultural attitudes lead again to a view of growth and maturation as a manifestation
of behavioral or ritual correctness that places development in a moral framework. Bumbita represent a further approach, by extending responsibility to the
individual for internalizing ritually taught practices (kind and amount of food
or sex; purification and avoidance behavior) and appropriating the process of
personal development. Leavitt (survey) has observed of Bumbita youth: "After
the onset of adolescence, the male's sense of his physical maturation pairs with a
sense of spiritual maturation that he himself controls. He knows that to develop
into a man, he must 'take matters into his own hands.'" In this case, taking matters into one's own hands means that young men must increasingly internalize
responsibility for maintaining their own physical integrity by continually cultivating a balance of spiritual energies through correct behavior. They must, for
instance, avoid sexual intercourse to avoid loss of spiritual force and consequent
stunting of growth. Similarly, self-performed penis bleeding among Bumbita or
nosebleeding among Sambia (Herdt 1990) must be pursued purposefully but in
moderation to maintain spiritual-physical balance. Observation of food taboos
likewise depends largely on self-imposition. With transfers of responsibility
from others to self for continued maturation, socialization and enculturation
become increasingly identified with self-defining acts (Tuzin 1980).

Finally, a society may view physical development as socially facilitated, neither driven by nor requiring social intervention, but influenced by it. Sambia,
for example, believe that physical punishment of children stunts their growth
(Herdt 1987:88). Since female maturation is more frequently viewed as natural,
practices to accelerate or augment female development are more common than
those to direct it. Puberty in girls is at times thought to be induced or hastened

by cohabitation or intercourse with a man: Burbank (1987) reports an Australian Aboriginal notion that cohabitation promotes breast development. Such beliefs legitimate early marriage. A common goal of seclusion at menarche and ritual reintroduction to the community is the protection of a girl from pollution and other dangers to her physical well-being, as well as consolidation of her maturational gains and promotion of her beauty and marriageability (see, for example, Cantrell, chapter 5, this volume, on the Gebusi). For Bumbita or Ilahita Arapesh, a prolonged rite at the time of menarche is meant in part to help enhance the girl's physical attainments (Leavitt, survey; Tuzin 1976:19–21), as it was also thought to do by the Chimbu (Brown, survey; Ross 1965; Whiteman 1965).

Different culturally embedded concepts of physical maturation commonly coexist within a single cultural framework. That is, much of child growth may be assumed to proceed naturally, while elements that are thought to require social or personal agency are foregrounded. Generally, development is viewed as more "natural" for girls than for boys: the previous review of pubertal development demonstrated how gender differences in timing and kind of maturational changes support this view. Hence, societies commonly employ dual, gender-differentiated models of development, with females being more "naturally" and males more "socially" constructed. Gebusi (Cantrell, chapter 5, this volume; Knauft 1987) employ such a dual model, as indeed may all other Strickland-Bosavi groups. In this context, gender-dichotomized tracks for physical as well as social maturation play a powerful role in foregrounding the masculine in social life. Thus, Eileen Cantrell (chapter 5) stresses the need for concerted intervention by Gebusi women to create "developmental space" for "naturally" maturing girls to offset the pervasive masculine social ethos that is reinforced by activities undertaken to make boys into men. Further, one suspects a connection between the unusual features of child development reported in New Guinea and the prevalence of elaborate social constructions of physical-spiritual development. Compared to other Pacific populations, children of Papua New Guinea are quite small, and their growth is markedly slowed. Reported ages at menarche for some highland groups—at 18.0 for Bundi and 20.3 for Gainj—are very late (Malcolm 1970; Wood et al. 1985).[6] The question of cause—whether calorie and protein deficiency, trace element and micronutrient deficiency, disease patterns, or other environmental stressors—has not been resolved, although each of these has been implicated (Dennett and Connell 1988). Introduction of dietary change and urbanized settings has been shown to lead to accelerated growth and earlier age at maturation: rural Bundi have, for instance, experienced a drop of about 1.2 years in age at menarche within an eighteen-year period, and endocrine as well as growth measures indicate that maturation is especially accelerated in urban adolescents (Zemel and Jenkins 1989; Zemel, Worthman, and Jenkins 1993).

What effect do such changes in maturational rates and physical attainments have on the social construction of development? This question has not been explored systematically but may be important because secular trends are occurring worldwide. Under social change and acculturative pressure, one would expect emic schemata of social agency in development to be more vulnerable to challenge than the "natural" or "facilitated" views because the literal notion of social agency can be falsified by empirical observation of other peoples. Tuzin has documented this effect among the Ilahita Arapesh:

> Today's young adults grew up with an easy awareness of the outside world, and it is impossible for them to share the bewilderment and suspicion of their elders in the face of radically alien cultural forms. Increasingly, their concerns and activities lie where the Voice of the Tambaran [a central cultural motif] cannot reach them. (Tuzin 1980:325)

Issues of control appear to be particularly central in societies that view maturation as socially contrived or facilitated. Among other things, such a view gives a semblance of command over biologic process by making it appear accessible to social-behavioral interventions. The relinquishing of that control can be a distressing prospect. As evidenced by Rotuman use of finishing school to demarcate the onset of "youth" (Howard, chapter 7, this volume), school often becomes the pacemaker of development. But the challenges posed by social and biological change to socialization systems arise perhaps from a deeper level of function, one that is often hidden from the conscious domain. Socialization practices, of whatever kind, relate physical with social-behavioral ontogeny in ways that may significantly influence outcome. For instance, Poole (1985) has suggested that high suicide rates among Bimin-Kuskusmin men reflect internal contradictions in the long, elaborate initiation cycle that they undergo. One could conjecture that changes in socialization incur unintended changes in developmental outcomes by altering the relationships of biological with social states or experiences. High suicide rates reported among adolescents (Rubinstein 1992) or adults (Gainj women: Johnson 1981; Bimin-Kuskusmin men) in widely different societies around the Pacific indicate the problem is not associated simply with social change or with a specific age or gender; rather, the causes are to be found in locally specific life history conditions.

This section has examined development as a biosocial process, comprising reciprocal effects of cultural and biological factors. Culturally conditioned behavior and environment (for example, subsistence patterns, housing, dietary practices) exert marked effects on development from infancy through puberty, affecting both timing of maturational events and phenotypic outcomes. Biosocial dynamics in ontogeny are most vividly evidenced in sex differences: constitutional dimorphisms are modulated by both cultural effects, including sex-differentiated care, and phenotypic consequences of differential socialization practices. A further level of biosocial interaction occurs in ethnopediatric models of development that guide social actors. Pacific Island societies show a range of approaches, viewing development alternatively as natural, socially facilitated, or socially achieved: each encodes distinct views of relations between individual and society. Societies commonly subscribe to multiple models; a number view female ontogeny as more "natural" and that of males as more "contrived." Social change affects socialization and physical maturation and thus alters biosocial relations in development throughout the Pacific.

RELATIONS OF INDIVIDUAL AND SOCIETY IN ONTOGENY

Anthropologists have tended historically to study socialization practices on the generalized, shared formal, or group level. More recently, some Pacific ethnographers have attended to the individual level of subjective experience and construction of life history (R. I. Levy 1973; Herdt 1982; Leavitt 1991, 1995a). Socialization systems must operate in both these dimensions; that is, they act at the interface between individual and other. Analysis of how socialization practices work on the individual, everyday level may allow construction of a pragmatic view of how the two dimensions—individual and formal/shared—are linked in ontogeny. An analytic framework for addressing this issue should not presuppose whether, how, or to what degree individuals or societies elaborate a distinction of self and other, for the latter is itself culturally shaped. On the one hand there is the field of social action composed of both individual and others. In this arena, only the visible or enacted aspects of the individual participate. On the other hand is the nonvisible arena, composed of physiological states and processes, as well as cognition and affect. Internal states and experiences are not directly observable by or shareable with others, and are therefore necessarily at some remove from the external, transindividual field of action. In this scheme, then, transduction between intraindividual domains that lie outside the realm of social communication, or even of cognition, and the social domain is effected by individual behavior and appearance, and the biosocial construction of the field of transduction becomes an object for analysis of socialization.

A socialization system can only work within some phenomenological framework that mediates between social process and the young, the new members of society. However elaborate the superstructure of metaphor and conceptual complexity that informs the content of socialization, the model must be one of directional change. How a society channels developmental change does, again, vary widely, but must include prescriptions for the treatment of young persons. While, on the phenomenological level, such prescriptions involve the visible, corporeal person, the nonvisible, internal dimension is also necessarily involved.[7]

This internal domain is where physiological processes occur and effect physical maturation, and where knowing, understanding, and motivation are organized to allow the individual to perform in a socially competent, appropriately productive manner. While the existence of an internal domain is constant, the degree to which internal states are attended to, cognized, and elaborated varies across cultures and is itself a target of socialization of self and the relationship to nonself.

Consequently, socialization faces an inherent problem: it can only work indirectly, for internal states cannot be accessed directly. For one thing, socialization practices can only attempt to organize intrasubjectivity through manipulation of experience and environment, with reliance on processes of "internalization." For another, the sole means by which internal states can be known to others is through discernable, corporeal manifestations that allow monitoring of the process of individual development. These cues include behaviors (speech, demeanor, activity and work patterns, and other social performances) and physical appearances or functions (growth, physical well-being, and other maturational changes) from which the developmental status of the person is inferred. Inferences are drawn through the filter of cultural norms and expectations about the goal and content of the developmental process—local ethnopediatric schemas about development, caregiving, and socialization (Worthman 1995). The resultant evaluation (that the person is, for instance, "old enough," "just a silly kid," "too lazy," "ready to marry") guides further treatment of the youngster. Discernable cues, then, entrain socialization; because the nonvisible domain is not directly accessible, the visible person often stands proxy for it and is the benchmark of individual ontogeny. Implicitly, the duality in loci (visible and not visible) engaged by socialization recognizes that culture is as much a product of the organizational bases of behavior as of the behaviors themselves.

On the level of social action and everyday experience, then, the nonvisible, internal domain is a "black box" to others, although cultural identification of the external with the internal self may be so strong as to render them experientially seamless. The phenomenologically hidden dimension of internal states comprises physiological, cognitive, and affective facets that are tightly interwoven (Shore 1988, 1996; Worthman 1992). While socialization practices expose individuals to experiences that may indeed restructure aspects of cognition and affect, these experiences often have recondite effects on physiology. A simple instance can be drawn from previous discussion concerning growth rate and diet: a dietary regimen to which boys are subjected may be intended to establish masculinity (conceived in terms of spiritual forces), but may also influence growth rate and enhance pubertal development by altering protein and calorie intake. More subtly, forging of links between cognitive-affective and physiologic states through ritual experiences that tightly entrain them both may establish biological as well as cognitive dimensions to the organization of behavior. Indirect evidence of this phenomenon is provided by the differences in organization of male aggression across the Pacific: aggression (comprised of physical and cognized elements) is quite differently expressed by Tahitian or Marquesan *taure'are'a* (Levy 1973:280–288, 467–9; Kirkpatrick 1987) and Bumbita *bikhet* (Leavitt, chapter 8, this volume). *Bikhet* and *taure'are'a* channel assertiveness and frustration quite differently, so that the "wild" behavior by each differs in context, content (the former is defined by aggressive-instrumental display,[8] the latter in opportunistic-hedonistic exploration), social interpretation, and proximate organizational basis.

So far, this discussion has identified two general ways in which indirect effects are exerted by the social conditions under which young people grow up, first through influences on the physical maturational process itself, and then by shaping internal organization of behavior and experience (cognition, affect, physiology, and the interactions among these). This notion can illuminate effects of social change: alterations in social arrangements and formal socialization systems may have multiple and unintended, unanticipated consequences in the kinds of persons the young become. Social change rends the seams of developmental process to reveal a "hidden" dynamic between culture and biology. This dynamic core, while generally intangible and transparent to the actors and the formal system (Berger and Luckmann 1966), plays a role in driving the process of differentiation and thus aids in literally constructing the individual. The importance of social arrangements to rates and attainments in physical development has been stressed above. Therefore, altered patterns of physical maturation can be expected to follow from changes in social arrangements so that even the physical person targeted in socialization would no longer be the same.

Biosocial dynamics are set in train by a system of socialization that can be disturbed when social conditions change, and disruption of this dynamic can provoke or reinforce crises of socialization in unexpected ways. This point finds clearest expression in societies with elaborate traditional socialization. Bimin-Kuskusmin or Ilahita Arapesh men are the product of a complex dynamic between individuals and their socially constructed experiences (ritual, diet, activity, housing, relationships): if the dynamic is altered, then men will indeed be different. Recognition of the depth of acculturative transformation is reflected in the continuation of the passage from Tuzin on Ilahita Arapesh, quoted above: "The older people view this trend with sad resignation; for they know that the Tambaran will not sing if it is not heard, and that when its song stops, the world—*their* world—will end forever" (1980:325; see also 1997). The tone of change in socialization is not always one of wistful regret: often, parents become convinced that a new order offers the best opportunity for their children, and that that order requires new sorts of persons, persons that they do not know how to create. Such parents, whether eager or ambivalent about social transformation, then pack their children off for novel experiences—in mission or government schools, in migratory and other new forms of labor—in the hope of establishing a toehold in the emerging modern regional or national sector. Some chapters in this book provide a look at the effects of social change. Burbank and Chisholm, and also Howard, deal with transformations of adolescence and young adulthood in schooled youngsters, where the horizons of what children are socialized for have widened dramatically but have lost some, but by no means all, of their local specificity and legitimacy. For Australian Aboriginals, issues appear to revolve around social control of reproduction, while for Rotumans, youth as labor source appears key. Rubinstein (1992) traces these threads to the high rates of adolescent suicide that punctuate the social map of Melanesia.

Levy (1973:466–68) has proposed that mastery of the most critical and central behavioral repertoires for a society are overdetermined by multiple redundant socialization influences, and "that such redundancies of control are a necessary feature of the most culturally-determined behavior." Redundancies should render the socialization system more resistant to erosion through social change, and indeed we see that the descriptions of more acculturated Micronesians or Aboriginals given by Howard (chapter 7, this volume) and Kirkpatrick (1987) or Burbank and Chisholm (chapter 3, this volume), respectively, do not show young people thoroughly identifying with national or world perspectives. Rather, there is a complex reweaving of life history that draws threads from traditional and modern forms. Still, these are, in a biosocial sense, different persons from their historical counterparts.

SAME SOCIETY, DIFFERENT PEOPLE

While the literature may impress us with the tremendous cultural diversity of adolescence, there is a large residue of variation within cultures that anthropologists have explored less carefully. However lax or rigorous the system of socialization, children, adolescents, and the adult men and women they become are not homogeneous persons, even when the social intent appears to be to make them so. Instead, there is considerable personal diversity. Social as well as biological factors account for this. First, all socialization systems have stochastic properties, so that the timing, quality, and quantity of formative experiences can vary widely among individuals. Through historical accident or even formal social design, strong deviations in life history are nearly a norm: for instance, children may find themselves in large or in small households with missing or older parents, boys may be initiated at seven or twenty-two, and young people experience varying degrees of environmental or social support. Mead's (1928, chapters 5, 10) observations of how variation in household composition and social status affected the behavior development of young Samoan women illustrate this point.

Constitutional variation—in appearance, temperament, physical functions, and developmental programs—supplies another source of individual differences. Not only do these constitutional features shape developmental outcome directly, they also affect the pattern of biosocial interactions between child and context. That is, how children look, function, and behave influence how they are treated and set up dynamics that significantly alter their experience (Lerner and Busch-Rossnagel 1981; Scarr and McCartney 1983).[9] In addition, the degree of congruence between demands and opportunities offered by a social setting and the abilities and characteristics of the child clearly differs widely among individuals and settings. For instance, the contrasts between traditional village settings described by Biersack or Cantrell (chapter 4 and 5, this volume) and the settled Aboriginal community described by Burbank and Chisholm (chapter 3, this volume) or modern, educated, wage-oriented, entrepreneurial Papua New Guinea described by Paula Brown (1988) lead to the prediction that a timid, compliant girl would perform quite differently in each. Social management of adolescent sexuality also demonstrates the point: papers in this volume reinforce our awareness of the degrees of documented cross-cultural variation (Whiting, Burbank, and Ratner 1986), from the self-structured permissiveness of the Trobrianders (Malinowski 1929), Vanatinaians (Lepowsky, chapter 6, this volume), or Tahitians (R. I. Levy 1973), to the closely regulated and circumscribed sexual activity prescribed for adolescent Bimin-Kuskusmin (Poole 1982), Kwoma (Whiting 1941), Gebusi (Cantrell, chapter 5, this volume), and Bumbita (Leavitt, chapter 8, this volume). Domains of highly prescriptive socialization can be expected to be far more demanding and less tolerant of personal vagaries. For instance, the importance of properly arranged "straight" marriages in traditional Aboriginal life fuels current intergenerational struggles over reproductive control or autonomy (Burbank and Chisholm, chapter 3, this volume).

Individual variation also poses a challenge to socialization systems, which must somehow accommodate not just the modal normative child, but all (or most) children. This must be done in the face of developmental vicissitudes created by systematic and stochastic variations in social landscape, environmental quality, and individual constitution and ability. The social setting may indulge individual variation by bending socialization rules, shifting expectations of conformity in performance, and tacitly or formally recognizing alternate developmental pathways. Or it may recognize but refuse to tolerate certain deviations and seek to suppress them through socialization. But alternate development pathways must be allowed and often are fostered in socialization. The most usual divergence in a developmental course is organized around gender: males and females are placed on their own tracks through life. In Papua New Guinea, boys being initiated are often called shiftless, weak, and feminine: initiation is designed to eradicate these traits, while girls are left to occupy their "natural" and "not-male" qualities (Herdt 1982). But even something so fluid as "personality" defines separate niches in the microecology of social space, for the partitioning of social roles often occurs in response to individual differences (see, for example, Schieffelin 1985). Accommodation may be made for a series of expected variants that range across conceptual spectra defined in emic terms: good-bad, small-large, fast-slow, difficult-easy, strong-weak, attractive-unattractive. Both biology and behavior play a role in recognized individual variation. Personal differences may be ascribed to inherent/biological or acquired/learned causes, and people may even debate the hereditary or behavioral components of a person's being short, stocky, or aggressive (Chowning 1990; Schieffelin 1985). Such classification and discussion alone imply that individual variation is socially engaged.

Societies may also winnow for talent, to channel people into social roles. Even in small egalitarian societies, there are developmental pathways that lead to special niches (performer, artist, healer-diviner, leader) (see Samuel 1990, for an attempt to model such processes). In more stratified groups, there is a greater diversity of niches but greater social regulation in their attainment. Societies, then, incorporate a finite multiplicity of recognized life course alternatives.

A key means, of course, by which social change influences the social organization of the life course lies in rewriting the menu of life history alternatives. "Goodness of fit" between individuals and the developmental courses open to them is thereby altered: characteristics that were favored or enforced may be deleterious (as when tribal warfare is eliminated), while others that had scarcely found expression may be advantageous (as with the introduction of schooling and jobs for girls). In settings of social change, there is an apparent proliferation of alternatives, but the accessibility or viability of any one of them may appear attenuated. Introduction of schooling, wage economy, entrepreneurship, Christianity, and nationhood ushers in another array of factors shaping life history, factors over which it is much more difficult to take control because the scale is so altered and their modus operandi is relatively unknown. As P. Brown (1988) describes, Chimbu girls may today "hit the road" in search of boyfriends and new experiences, or they may stay home with the precarious security of an eroding way of life. Their male counterparts may try diligence in school, peer solidarity in opportunistic endeavors (gangs or stealing), or individual seeking of the main chance. For both sexes, the characteristics defining mate selection and the process by which it occurs also change dramatically. As the situation described in this volume by Burbank and Chisholm for Australian Aboriginals portrays, rifts between generations open when youth and elders disagree in their perceptions of viable choices for directing the life course.

Instances of erosion of the formal traditional system of constructing life his-

tory found in this volume reflect of course a long-standing theme in the literature (Mead 1949, 1966). Institutionalized "time out" for narcissistic expression
and sexual freedom in adolescence/young adulthood has often been reported for
Pacific peoples (Tahiti: Levy 1973; Samoa: Mead 1928; Marquesas: Kirkpatrick
1987; Vanatinai: Lepowsky, chapter 6, this volume). The *taure'are'a* of Tahiti and
ka'ioi of the Marquesas were distinctly adolescent statuses that Levy suggests may
have had the quality of "antistructure" (1973:469). These have become more
vague categories (*mapu* and *taure'are'a*, respectively) that are defined in terms
of behavior content because they now compete with other conflicting identities
(student, Christian), among which clear pathways to adulthood are not easily
discernable (Kirkpatrick 1987). *Taure'are'a* roles, then, simultaneously express
and conceal real problems and uncertainties in the transition to adulthood: the
resolution of their apparent enviable freedom, self-expression, and exploration
to a well-grounded everyday adult life is left largely to the individual. The roles
reflect gaps in the system of socialization that are created by general social uncertainties about how life histories are to be constructed and meaningful situations secured in the modernizing world.

Such ethnographic cases indicate that social change in the Pacific radically
restructures the relationship between the physical and the social self in life
course development. Chronological age is substituted for reading the body and
behavior as signs of maturity that entrain socialization efforts; schooling proceeds regardless of developmental status of the individual pupil. Inscription of
culture on the body (incision, supercision, culturally mediated regulators of
maturation and physical well-being) and the biosocial processes of internalized
self-definition assume novel forms and individual developmental trajectories
appear to happen in spite of, or against, some prevailing social arrangement. An
outstanding feature is the often radical modification of the relationship between
the reproductive self and the social self. Biological maturation schedules shift
downward in age so that young people are faced with reproductive decisions earlier. Spouse selection and timing of marriage slip the bounds of traditional forms
and become more self-determined. Timing of marriage is set by new priorities
such as schooling and wage labor. The meaning, as well as the realities, of reproduction assume new forms. All these transformations reflect, in yet another way,
the interdependency of biologic and social process in human development and
life history.

CONCLUSION

While contemporary anthropologists have problematized the relationship
between individual and society, the present analysis has sought to cast the problem rather differently, in a way that includes both biological and social processes.

Historic divisions of labor between cultural and biological anthropology in the study of human development have led to a disarticulated understanding of social and physical ontogeny: adolescence has been separated from puberty. Thus, the biological domain has not been adequately addressed in contemporary ethnography and social theory. This chapter suggests a different developmental perspective that may better account for variations across time and space by taking an explicitly biosocial stance. The necessity for a reformulation is demonstrated here through analysis of interactions between social and biological factors in adolescence: biology relies on social context in physical development, while society relies on biology in shaping persons.

Rapid social change has emerged as an important issue in this chapter and in this volume. It accentuates the need for a biosocial perspective on human development, for the present analysis suggests that the lack of such a perspective has impaired our ability to understand and predict the effects of social change on people's lives and experiences. The ethnographic accounts in this volume document societies from the "pristine" traditional to the strongly acculturated; yet nearly all contemporary peoples in the Pacific are experiencing accelerated social change. As has been reviewed here, such social change has been associated repeatedly with changes in socialization as well as with alterations in physical maturational schedules, yet the relationship between these two parameters of change in human development has scarcely been explored by anthropologists. Pacific societies document biological and cultural diversity in puberty and adolescence, but the existing literature on these peoples demonstrates the paucity of analyses that include biological and social measures in studies of socialization. The rich ethnographic record in this region is not matched with a wealth of data on child growth and development.

The present analysis has therefore been more suggestive than definitive in its exploration of the value of a biosocial approach to human development. It has indicated that the production of individual differences may be as important a product of socialization as the production of similarities. Certainly, in the case of gender, biological differences as well as systematic social processes lead to sex differences in development that vary markedly across societies. Thus, in the face of wide biological and cultural diversity, the key element for understanding individual ontogeny would appear to be not so much formal content of socialization per se, but the local (historical-contextual) process through which the individual develops. Therefore, this discussion has focused largely on dynamics of socialization and how the process is constituted in relation to individuals under specific social conditions. Within a given social context, development can run along numerous socially recognized alternate pathways. While availability of divergent developmental trajectories is fairly ubiquitous, these (with the major exception of gender) have received scant attention from ethnographers, whose goals have usually been to characterize the general, normative workings of cultural systems. How those systems create and accommodate, rather than simply eliminate, differences has been less a matter of concern.[10] Understanding of social change may thus be furthered by studying its effects on the channels regulating production and accommodation of individual differences.

Contemporary anthropology has attended to the individual and the social construction of persons and their life histories. Yet modern anthropological devotion to particularism has sown a meager harvest in understanding social process in a more generalized, prospective way. Work in human development that draws on our past (see, for example, Malinowski, Mead, and Whiting) and the present store of ethnographic documentation (such as that presented in this volume), and incorporates it with a biological perspective, should focus our attention on the systematic, but local and contingent, sources of commonality and difference within and between societies and across time.

II

CULTURAL CONSTRUCTIONS OF ADOLESCENCE

THREE

Adolescent Pregnancy and Parenthood in an Australian Aboriginal Community

Victoria K. Burbank and James S. Chisholm

INTRODUCTION

Single pregnancy and parenthood in America (particularly that of teenagers) is associated with myriad developmental problems for children born to unwed mothers, ranging from low birth weight to problems of intellectual performance at school (Lancaster and Hamburg 1986; Scott et al. 1981). Teen pregnancy in America is also associated with diminished prospects for single mothers, even beyond the racism, poverty, and lack of education that some of them may have suffered before their pregnancies (Cramer 1989; Crockenberg and Soby 1989; Furstenberg 1976; Hayes 1987). There is a growing sense, however, that negative outcomes are more a creation of the sociocultural context into which an unwed mother bears a child than an inevitable outcome of single parenthood. It has been argued, for example, that young mothers are not necessarily bad mothers, either physiologically or behaviorally. As Charles Super puts it, "The developmental consequences of school-age pregnancy and motherhood are socially constructed" (1986:379). A study of African American and Cuban teenage mothers demonstrates that the effects of teenage parenthood may vary, depending upon such factors as child-rearing attitudes and types of family support systems (Field et al. 1986). And as the massive Collaborative Perinatal Study showed some years ago, teenage girls in the United States who are not subject to the "special stress" of being young mothers (for example, lack of support from the baby's father) have even more uneventful pregnancies and lower rates of infant morbidity and mortality than do older women (Niswander and Gordon 1972). There is also a growing sense that young women who become single mothers perceive their pregnancies not as "uncontrolled fertility" but as "alternative life-course strategies" (see, e.g., Burton 1990; Geronimus 1987, 1996; Hamburg 1986; Luker 1991; Phoenix 1988, 1993). Linda Burton, for example, argues that teenage childbearing in the African American community that she calls Gospel Hill is a "life-course strategy of choice" linked to "accelerated family timetables, the separation of marriage and childbearing, patterns of intergenerational caregiving in age-condensed families, and grandparental child-rearing systems" (1990:136). Early childbearing is not a "problem" for these women; it is a solution.

In this chapter, we present an analysis of the cultural construction of single pregnancy and parenthood in the Australian Aboriginal community that we call Mangrove. We discuss premarital sex as an adolescent strategy in the struggle for autonomy, describe the consequences of this behavior for adolescent girls, and detail how developing responses and adjustments are being made to ensure the care of young mothers and their offspring. These issues illustrate the ways in which outcomes of single pregnancy and parenthood may be socially constructed and help us to see the implications that different adolescent experiences with pregnancy and parenthood have for adolescent development and the successful adoption of adult roles.

This analysis is an example of "thinking through the other," using the self-consciousness of others to help us discover that which is less conscious in our own thinking (Shweder 1991:108). In order that readers may better understand our interpretations and conclusions, we try to recreate something of our experience at Mangrove, primarily through records of our questions and discussion with Aboriginal men and women and their replies. In the final part of this chapter, we bring the Aboriginal construction of single pregnancy and parenthood to bear on Western constructions of "teenage pregnancy" in order to better appreciate how our understanding of this social issue impinges not only on adolescents who become pregnant, but on adolescents in Western societies generally.

THE SETTING

Mangrove is an isolated Aboriginal settlement located about three hundred miles from Darwin in the wilderness of the Arnhem Land Reserve. In 1988 Mangrove's population numbered about 575 Aborigines and 25 whites. Begun as a mission in the early 1950s, today this settlement is governed by elected Aboriginal officials in consultation with various government agencies and their representatives. Funding for the settlement's school, clinic, housing, and work programs is provided almost exclusively by the Australian government. The legacy of Mangrove's Western founders and the culture of greater Australia that has been both imposed upon and embraced by its residents for nearly three decades can be seen in almost all aspects of settlement life. In the approximate half square mile of coastal land that forms Mangrove, people live in Western-style houses, drive vehicles, eat food purchased from the local store, send their children to the local English-speaking school and their sick to the local health clinic. They use washing machines, stoves, and refrigerators, go to church, and amuse themselves with tape recorders, TV, movies, and videos. Nevertheless, Aboriginal models of etiquette, religion, kinship, and marriage, however modified by the contact experience, continue to inform the lives of Mangrove's people. Elements of Western culture are incorporated into distinctively Aboriginal schemes. Vehicles, for example, are used for hunting and gathering trips, and chartered airplanes take men to circumcision ceremonies. Clans and moieties are important social categories, kin terms are significant social labels, certain affines continue to avoid one another, sisters continue to "be careful" of their brothers, and the concept of "straight"—referring to marriages between partners in structurally correct genealogical positions—continues to have salience in discussions about marriage. Adolescent sexuality, pregnancy, and parenthood must be understood within the context of the settlement, where elements of Western and Aboriginal culture meet, blend, contradict, and dominate.

THE STUDY

Burbank has been visiting this community since 1977. In 1981, as a part of the Harvard Adolescence Project, she spent nine months at Mangrove learning about female adolescence on the settlement (see Burbank 1987; 1988). In 1988 she was joined by Chisholm during a seven-month study of the cultural construction of parenting and how it relates to the treatment and health of children. An important component of this study was a follow-up on developments in adolescent pregnancy and parenting.

ADOLESCENCE, PREGNANCY, AND MARRIAGE AT MANGROVE

Adolescence begins for the "young girls" and "young boys" of Mangrove when a girl's breasts begin to bud and a boy's body grows, voice deepens, and facial hair appears. Both become adults—"men" and "women"—when they marry and have children. Thus the definition of adolescence at Mangrove parallels our understanding of adolescence as "the transitional period between the end of childhood and the attainment of adult social status" (Whiting and Whiting in Burbank 1988:xii).

In the past girls were married during adolescence—ideally before menarche.[1] Today, adolescence signals the beginning of reproductive heterosexual activity, the search for marital partners, and, for some, premarital pregnancy. As

Burbank (1988) details in previous work on female adolescence at Mangrove, major changes in marriage arrangements have attended the recent shift from a nomadic to settled life—in a word, partners who were once chosen for each other now choose each other. These changes, however, are not accepted by many of the adults in the community, particularly those once held responsible for betrothing girls. The resulting conflict between generations appears to have led to a growing number of premarital pregnancies and an increase in the number of single mothers.

Premarital pregnancy has come to be seen, at least by some in the adolescent population, as a means of marrying a partner of choice (Burbank 1988). In brief, expectations are that otherwise obstructive adults may permit a marriage should a couple bear a child. There are also indications that it has come to be seen as a means of being a mother without being a wife.

Premarital pregnancy is clearly on the rise at Mangrove. Marriage histories were obtained for fifty-nine women, those with at least one child between the ages of zero and five at the beginning of our fieldwork in 1988. Fifteen of these women were married before 1981, forty-four were married, or had borne a child out of wedlock between 1981 and 1988. Of the fifteen married before 1981, 53 percent were reportedly married before becoming pregnant and 20 percent were reportedly pregnant before marriage. In 27 percent of the fifteen cases it was unclear if women had first married or become pregnant. Of the forty-four women marrying or bearing a child outside marriage from 1981 onwards, 7 percent were reportedly married before becoming pregnant, 43 percent were pregnant before marriage but subsequently did marry, and 34 percent continued to be single mothers. In 16 percent of the forty-four cases it was not clear if women had married before becoming pregnant or vice versa. It should be noted that even if all these cases are in fact cases of marriage before pregnancy, this category would account for only 22 percent of the total.

The fact that over 50 percent of the marriages of women marrying after pregnancy were said by at least one person to be "not right" or "not straight," and the fact that none of these marriages involved bestowal, suggest that adolescent girls have continued in increasing numbers to seek pregnancy, or at least not to avoid it, as a means of marrying a partner of choice.

Single parenthood is also on the rise as premarital pregnancy does not always lead to marriage. Several reasons were offered for the single status of some mothers. In some cases it was said that the families of either the boy or the girl would not give permission for them to marry. Some of the families of single mothers had withheld permission to marry because they did not approve of the boy. For example, they might see him as a philanderer or as an incorrect partner. In other cases it was said that a couple had not married because either the boy or the girl had not chosen to marry. In several of these cases, it was said that the boy had found another girlfriend and/or had married her. In at least one case it was said that the pregnant girl had found another boyfriend and had not wanted to marry the father of her child. In a few cases it was said that the father of the child was unknown and in one instance because the adolescent mother had several partners.

SINGLE MOTHERS AND THEIR BABIES AT MANGROVE

From medical records, Chisholm obtained prenatal, neonatal, and child health, growth, and development data on a total of ninety-five children born to forty-six women whose marital status at birth was clear (see above). Of the women, nineteen were known to be unmarried when their children were born, and twenty-seven were known to be married. Chisholm was also able to weigh and measure forty-five of these children once during 1988.

The single mothers tended to be younger than the married mothers, but not significantly so. The married mothers, however, had been pregnant significantly more often and correspondingly had significantly more living children.

A series of t-tests showed that the children of single and married women did not differ significantly on birth weight, length at birth, head circumference, or ponderal index (a measure of body mass). Each of these neonatal measures is an indicator of one or more intrauterine growth processes, and the absence of significant differences suggests that the single and married women do not differ in the sort of prenatal environment they provide for their children. Additional support for this interpretation comes from the finding of no significant group differences in one- and five-minute APGAR scores, which reflect both physiological and neurological functioning of the newborn.

A comparison of the children's weight-for-height, height-for-age, and weight-for-age with National Center for Health Statistics (NCHS) standards (World Health Organization 1983) suggests that the nutritional status of the entire sample of children is generally mediocre. Most appear to receive adequate nourishment currently, while also showing evidence of past undernourishment, or "stunting." Here it must be observed that disease—for example, the bacterial, fungal, and parasitic infections that are rife at Mangrove—rather than the quantity or quality of children's food may account for this undernourishment (see also Beck 1985).

Analyses of the height and weight data reveal considerable single-married group differences, with the children of single women appearing generally better nourished than those of married women, especially in height-for-age, which indicates a better nutritional history (WHO 1983). These differences, however, were due entirely to the fact that the children of the single women in the sample were significantly younger than those of the married women. Many were still breast-feeding and thus receiving near ideal nutrition. Being younger, they had had a shorter time to experience disease and undernutrition and consequently were relatively less "stunted" than the older children. Analysis of variance showed there were no significant single-married group differences in any of these measures of child health and development after controlling for child's age, number of mother's pregnancies, number of surviving children born to mother, interval preceding birth of each sample child, and length of gestation. We conclude that at Mangrove a mother's marital status has no effect on child health or physical growth and development, at least through age five.

We note, however, that single pregnancy and parenthood is a relatively new development at Mangrove and these data do not necessarily predict future developments in this area. For example, the fact that single mothers have borne fewer children, and have fewer children to care for, may currently give them an advantage that will be lost should they have larger families out of wedlock.

THE SOCIAL CONSTRUCTION OF TEENAGE PREGNANCY

Assuming, as we do here, that the developmental outcomes of single pregnancy and motherhood are socially constructed, we ask how the people of Mangrove conceptualize "single" pregnancy and parenthood. As one means of addressing this question we asked men and women to tell us a story about a single mother or a single father.

Many of the thirteen women who responded to Burbank's request for a story about a single mother had more or less direct experience with single pregnancy and parenthood. Three of these women were single mothers themselves. Two others were divorced women living with dependent children. Three were mothers of women who had gotten pregnant out of wedlock and three were sisters (one of these a half-sister) of single mothers. Because of the relatively high overall number of single mothers, the others were likely neighbors, kin, or friends of single mothers.

We have identified three issues or themes from an analysis of these stories: marriage, the social identity of "single babies," and childcare. We discuss each of these below, providing illustrations from the stories and other statements from Aboriginal men and women.

MARRIAGE: PRO AND CON

As we have indicated above, pregnancy is sometimes seen as a means of marrying a partner of choice. The perceived connection between pregnancy and marriage is made very clear in the following story:

> There was once a single mother. She was wishing to have a kid and then one
> day she had a boyfriend and she had a baby. Then when the baby was born,
> the boy's family thought it wasn't that boy's baby. Then when it grew and
> started crawling they recognized that little kid. Then the boy's family went and
> got that kid. Then the young girl got married [to the baby's father] and lived
> happily ever after.[2]

But not all the stories indicate that marriage is seen as a desirable goal: "She
doesn't want to marry. She wants to be single. She thinks single life is the better
life, better than being a married woman."

It seems clear that in these Aboriginal women's scheme of things the difference between being a single and married woman pivots on the absence or presence of a husband. The stories and other statements indicate reasons why some
mothers are unmarried mothers. Among these, negative evaluations of men are
noticeable. Here, for example, is a response to Burbank's question about why
the mother and father of a little baby girl were not married:

> The mother and father of Tim and of Shelly won't let them marry because
> they are proper real close family. . . . But Tim is a cheeky [aggressive] one. If he
> gets that baby girl he won't give it back to Shelly. That's why they won't let him
> marry her. When Tim used to get that little girl, nighttime he used to call out
> to Shelly but Shelly didn't like to go with him. Then he would smack that baby
> and the baby would cry and cry until Shelly went out to get her.

Since being "close family" (part of one's kindred) has been presented as sufficient
reason unto itself for forbidding a marriage (Burbank 1988), we think that this
woman's elaboration of the negative character of a potential husband signals the
growing importance of this facet of gender relations in decisions about marriage.

In a discussion of marriage goals and negative evaluations of men, it is important to point out that such evaluations are not confined to single men. The
stories solicited by Burbank about married mothers are of interest. Of the thirteen women who answered this request, five mentioned the possibility of male
infidelity, three linking it to separation from the husband: "Sometimes marriage
is very hard. When you get married, years pass and then he finds another
woman. It's a good life to stay single with kids."

That such perceptions of married men are shared by men is suggested by a
story about a married father told to Chisholm: "He's thinking he might marry
another woman. 'I like being married to two. Or if my wife dumps me, I'll get
another one.' . . . His wife might think, 'Don't ever come back to me. You went
out at night and were playing around on me.'"

In contrast, only three women mentioned any kind of male contribution to wife or children, and one of these stories included a discussion of noncontributing males:

> It's all right because she's gonna have her husband and he's gonna find money and food. Maybe he works and he gets pay and that money goes to his wife and she does the shopping. . . . If the husband is a lazy one, he won't find money. Maybe that wife is gonna go searching for money or go play cards. Maybe if she wins she can go do shopping. She can get Rinso and do washing for the kids and feed the kids.

This speaker is not the only woman to attribute women's gambling to male neglect. For example, a group of three women made the following statement: "Men don't give any money to women, men take money to beer. Some men are good and some are bad. Women play cards to make money for food. Women need money to feed and clothe their children." At least one man seems to agree with the validity of this perception: "Maybe the husband is away and didn't leave any money, so [the wife] wants to win some money to buy some food. My wife [plays cards], you know, when I go to town."

The perception that men may not assist a woman and their children is not confined to economic contributions:

> Some fathers don't [carry the children when the mother is tired]. . . . 'Cause they are a bit shamed to carry the baby and they tell the mother to mind her own kid.
>
> Q: Why are they shamed to carry their kid?
>
> A: 'Cause some of the fathers have girlfriends too and they shame to carry their kids. And they also get wild with their kids because they have a girlfriend.

We note here that the portrait of young men painted by these texts is not confined to this Arnhem Land community; it is a widespread picture of young men associated around the world with poverty, displacement, and inequality.[3]

The extent to which women with children relied upon husbands to sustain and support them in hunting and gathering days is an open question (see Burbank 1988; 1994, for discussions of this issue). Today the absence of significant differences between the birth weights and early development of children of single and married mothers suggests that husbands are not essential for the well-being of women and their children. Various social arrangements associated with settlement dwelling that appear to make it possible for a woman to live in some degree of comfort without a husband are easy to identify and include: an ethos of cooperation and sharing within the extended family or kindred, welfare, jobs for women, and little or no emphasis on wealth differentials or status through possessions. Although the presence of such institutional factors does not guarantee that the women of Mangrove see things this way, the recent increase in single motherhood itself and statements like, "single life is a good life," suggests that they might.

Burbank asked fifteen women if they would prefer to marry a young man, old man, or middle-aged man. The majority said that they preferred to marry young men. Burbank then asked which man they thought would make the best father of their children. Seven women stated that young men make poor fathers. The following are the words of just one of the women, but more or less identical to the reasons that three others gave:

> Young boy, he's good enough to give a baby to a woman and then leave her behind nursing that kid. He just goes, makes her pregnant and then when she delivers, is nursing it in her arms, he doesn't pay any attention to her now. He starts fooling around with another girl.

Yet six of these seven women said they would prefer to marry a young man. This preference, in spite of the perception that young men are not especially reliable partners, suggests that some women at Mangrove might not look to their husbands for economic support or childcare assistance. On the other hand, two women said old men were less desirable fathers because they were less potent and thus less likely to father a child in the first place. It may be that some women at Mangrove think of men as little more than a means of providing them with a baby to raise with the aid of their kin.

From our perspective, on the other hand, the mediocre nutritional status of the entire sample of children suggests that married and single mothers could benefit from more assistance from those around them. In these circumstances a man who contributes to the household should be a welcome partner. But given expectations that at least some men will contribute little, being single may be perceived as an advantage; a woman without a husband may be seen as a woman without yet another drain on resources she could otherwise use for herself and her children. The potential for husbands and wives to compete for resources received a kind of official recognition when a Mangrove Aboriginal community worker arranged for several married women to receive their welfare allowances separately from those distributed to their unemployed husbands: "Some fathers and mothers get welfare separate; father gets [something] and mother gets [more] because its for her and the kids. If father gets it [all] he just goes."

THE SOCIAL IDENTITY OF "SINGLE BABIES"

There is one manner, however, in which men are recognized as very important:

If women have a lot [of sexual partners], they can't know the father. Some will get pregnant. They'll end up not knowing.

Q: Is it important to know who the father is?
A: Very important.
Q: Why?
A: To follow the traditional society, clan group, skin, like that.

At Mangrove, clans and moieties are social categories that are critical to the organization of social life and which are, normally, acquired from one's father. That is, a child is said to be of a certain clan and moiety because his father is. Single mothers are asked to name the father of their child. Once identified by the mother, it is important that the genitor or his family acknowledge a baby as his offspring. This is not, however, something that single mothers can count on:

Katy was single when she had her [first baby]. She told them the father was [her husband] and the family said, "Let us see the baby." And straight off they said, "Yes, the baby is for [Katy's husband]." Katy was a bit worried about this when she was pregnant, but it turned out all right.

Indeed, one single mother suggested that a family might not acknowledge a baby precisely because it was born out of wedlock: "Families here don't like single babies, so when their sons get girls and they get babies, they say the babies are not for their sons." Once this acknowledgment is made, however, even if the parents never marry, the child's clan and moiety are established.

Without this acknowledgment aid is likely to be withheld by the genitor's family (cf. Hamilton 1982): "We didn't recognize that baby at first because Shelly said Wyatt was the father. But when they saw Wyatt's mother carrying that baby, they said, 'Why is she carrying that baby? That's not for Wyatt, that's for Tim.'" Acknowledgment, on the other hand, may be accompanied by welcomed assistance: "When [my baby] was born her father's family didn't recognize her. They said she wasn't for him. But [a woman of the genitor's clan] said that [the baby's] foot was like her father's and she said, 'This is my little grandchild.'[4] Now they recognize her and give her money." This recognition is also important if the parents wish to marry: "Some of the young girls and young boys, they go around with each other. Then after the baby is born, they get married if they see the baby's face or foot [is like the father's]; they get married 'cause they know the baby is for the father."

If, however, a girl refuses to name the father of her child, or if he or his family refuses to acknowledge the child as his, then the child's structural position must be fixed in some other way. All indications are that this is a relatively new problem for the people of Mangrove, and their actions in this regard must be seen as attempts to find a solution where tradition gives them few guidelines.

One solution has been to give the child the clan of his mother. This, however, places him in the wrong moiety as moieties are exogamous and acquired, as we have said, from the father. Another solution is to place the child in the clan of his maternal grandmother. In this case the child is in the correct moiety vis-à-vis his mother.

The extent to which attempts are made to incorporate children into necessary social categories is illustrated by a recent case of adoption. When it became clear that a young single mother was intending to turn her newborn over for adoption outside the community, a woman of the mother's clan was permitted to adopt the child. The adopting woman, however, was herself unmarried. Two men were nominated as the father of the baby; consensus determined one of them to be the father. But it was decided to assign the child to the clan of the husbands of the adopting woman's sisters.

CHILDCARE

Childcare is also an important theme in the stories of single mothers. Six women raised the topic. While three of them indicated that they thought some single mothers can be good mothers, all of them said single motherhood presents problems for childcare. Four of them contrasted caring for children with a search for romance or sexual pleasure. For example: "A single mother, she just leaves her kids at home, depending on her family [to look after them] and she goes looking for boyfriends. And if she gets one, she goes crazy about him and forgets about the kids and keeps on depending on her relatives to look after them." Two others said that a single mother might neglect her child in order to walk around, gamble, or sniff petrol.

The care of babies and small children must be a concern of any social group, but at Mangrove there are several reasons why this issue might receive special emphasis. These include a physical environment filled with hazards for the growing child, a tradition of childcare characterized by a high degree of nurturance and indulgence, and changing family demographics—such as increasing numbers of children born at shorter intervals—that make such childcare increasingly difficult (see Burbank and Chisholm 1990; 1992).

The stories also indicate what appears to be the current solution to the poor care or neglect attributed to single mothers: others are recruited to take care of the child. Mentioned in the stories are a single mother's mother, father, or sister and the genitor's mother and sister. Here the observation that single mothers of Mangrove may be postponing motherhood for themselves by prolonging motherhood for other women—for example, their mothers (Smith 1989)—is of interest. But, we ask, is it only single mothers who depend on others? A story about a married mother suggests this is not the case: "She's not OK with the first kid.

Some, like single mothers, are depending on others. But when she has two or three children, she is sensible like the other married mothers." Single mothers at Mangrove are largely young mothers and are also usually just beginning their reproductive careers. They are, in short, usually inexperienced mothers. Note the equation of single mothers with young mothers in this story: "Single mothers, when they are young they like to go out with men, but after, when they have a kid . . . and it grows a little bit bigger, it's gonna be hard for that young mother." Observation as well as the comments of Aboriginal people suggest that inexperienced mothers, whether they are married or single, often depend on the assistance of their close kin when it comes to childcare. In this context we believe it is significant that the single woman who was given the above-mentioned child in adoption is an older woman who has, perhaps not incidentally, helped a brother and a sister raise their children to near-maturity.

It may be, however, that the perceived need of single mothers to have some romance or sex in their lives (if not a boyfriend or husband), makes them less able to care for their children, in fact. Here a mother compares the behavior of two of her daughters, one a married woman, the other a single mother:

> [The question] makes me think of my two girls. Lela has three kids and Lucy has one. Lela can look after her sister's baby, but Lucy can't look after Lela's children or her own.
>
> Q: Why doesn't Lucy look after Lela's kids?
> A: Because Lucy wants to go running around, looking for a boyfriend, a boyfriend or someone to marry. It's young people's life.

The perceived incompatibility of adolescence with motherhood is continued in the following discussion of abortion:

> Q: Why would a single girl want to get rid of a baby?
> A: She wants to be young and go on doing what she's been doing and she doesn't want to end up with a baby in her arms. (See also Goodale 1971)

THE VALUE OF CHILDREN AND MOTHERHOOD

We believe that when people at Mangrove think about single mothers they usually think of young mothers. This, according to their definition of adolescence, is a contradiction, for female adolescence normally is the period preceding motherhood. Young mothers are seen as young people, more interested in seeking pleasure, and perhaps seeking future marital partners, than in caring for their children. Their kin, however, ensure this care. The attempts to incorporate children without social fathers into a system that requires fathers, and which their mothers have often attempted to defy by their very pregnancies, signals the high value placed on children. The fact of a single pregnancy is probably greeted at best with equivocation. It is said that family members have "shame" when an unmarried girl gets pregnant. One woman reportedly wanted to "kill" the single baby of her ward (Burbank 1988). But regardless of their origins, such children are ultimately accepted (cf. Hamilton 1982). They are not set against the propriety of traditional structural patterns. Though he is not talking about "single babies" per se, the words of a senior man of considerable political and ritual status make this clear:

> Some communities are really strict about their marriage line. But here, the way we look at it, the child belongs to the father—he has to look after the child—doesn't matter if it's straight or not. He's still got to call that child his. Forget about the mother. Just focus on the baby and put that child in the father's clan. . . . Whenever that child is in a ceremony, that child will follow the father's line, moiety, culture. If a white man finds a child for an Aboriginal lady, then her family finds a place for her child. Like if I had a sister, or, one of my clan sisters, she has two children from a white bloke . . . but we don't say, "Ahhh . . ." We still accept the two kids in our clan.[5]

One manifestation of this value is reflected in the health and development records of single babies. Another is the continuing nurturance and protection of the single mothers, who are, perhaps, still regarded as children themselves (Burbank 1988).

But what about the future of single mothers? In particular, what effect does the experience of single pregnancy and parenthood have on their later development? This question must be addressed with reference to cultural constructions of the adult woman. At Mangrove, there is basically one adult female model— that of wife and mother. Currently, the relevance of husbands for women and children is being questioned and the role of wife reevaluated. In contrast, or so we would argue, the role of mother is expected, accepted, and valued in this Aboriginal community.

The extent to which Aboriginal women's maternal role is celebrated is questioned by Jane Collier and Michele Rosaldo (1981) who observe that women's ceremonies focus on women's sexuality but not on women's fertility and nurturance. We would point out that fertility and nurturance, the human capacities required for the perpetuation of the social group, are so important in Aboriginal Australia that they have been taken on as major themes in socially valued male rituals across Australia (see, for example, Bern 1979; Warner 1937; Maddock 1974; Myers 1986). While we cannot speak about the particulars of ritual at Mangrove, we would expect to find a similar focus in local practice. But are nurturance and fertility only valued in association with male practice? We think not.

That children are highly valued by the people of Mangrove is indicated by efforts to incorporate them without prejudice into the social fabric. For example, when answering questions about happiness or unhappiness, people often talk about children; having children makes people happy, whereas harm to children makes them unhappy. According to women's conceptualizations, both men and women can be expected to fight over harm to a child, and indeed we are aware of fights occurring for this reason. In addition, a desire for children is a major reason given for polygyny by men and women alike (Burbank 1988; 1994). During our most recent study, Burbank asked fourteen women what they liked best about being a mother. The answers to this question make it clear that women at Mangrove have very positive feelings about their children. Six women, for example, replied that they liked, loved, cared for, or wanted their children. Four women replied that their children made them happy or kept them from being lonely.

A high valuation of children, however, does not necessarily coincide with a high valuation of motherhood. On the basis of her own fieldwork in Northern Australia and an extensive review of the literature, Gillian Cowlishaw has argued that Aboriginal women accept their role as mothers with great ambivalence. Women, she says, "are either neutral or favourably disposed towards the idea of bearing children, but observations of the burdens which they impose on the mother makes them think twice" (1979:89). While we do not wish to dispute the validity of this observation across Aboriginal Australia, our data suggest that motherhood at Mangrove is not only an expected role, but is also a valued role. For example, six of the women responding to the above-mentioned question made positive statements about being a mother. For some, mothers are models to emulate:

> Just being a mother is the main thing, like those old ladies. I love being a mother.
>
> You see some of the mothers being a mother and carrying a baby and you think about yourself having a baby and being happy all the time, playing with the baby instead of carrying another woman's baby.

The following statement from one woman, now a grandmother, suggests that, at least among women, there is some public recognition and reward for motherhood:

> I married the first son for [my husband's mother's clan]. I had all the [father's mothers'] first baby. That makes me boss of [that clan] because I had the first children for their sons. They remember me and treat me as really family. They give me anything I want. If we go out hunting together they will give me most of the food, lily roots, oysters. I had the first baby for the [father's mothers].

The use of the term "women's business" to signify activities associated with human reproduction suggests these carry a valance of interest and respect similar to that accorded the highly valued "men's business," that is, men's ceremonial activity. Chisholm's interviews with fathers—though focused on perceptions of children and fathering—also occasionally included statements indicating that men also value women's maternal role. For example, one man said: "Kids are the future . . . [It is] very important to have children." And then later: "It is your life and your wife's life to bring them on this land." Another father, when asked what he wanted for his daughter, replied: "I want her to get married so she can have a family." A third man described himself as a *wangulu* (orphan) (which also, perhaps not incidentally, is translated as "poor") because his mother had died when he was very young. His father was still living.

It is not yet clear how the lives of the single mothers at Mangrove will vary from those of their married peers. Some have already married and in doing so have become what women at Mangrove have long been expected to become—wives and mothers.[6] Whatever their choices may be, whether they remain single or marry, whether they work for wages or receive welfare, the value of the children they have produced and the appreciation of their mothering roles can be expected to support a positive self-concept and bolster efforts to move further into the adult female role.

DISCUSSION

Our analysis of the cultural construction of single pregnancy at Mangrove provides a means of exposing some of the assumptions behind Western constructs of "teen pregnancy" and a means of examining such component ideas as motherhood, dependence, children, gender, sexuality, and marital status to better understand the force these unstated assumptions have in shaping our experiences and research on adolescent behavior.

While it is difficult to characterize any facet of Western culture in the space we have here, our analysis of single pregnancy at Mangrove suggests that, in contrast, unwed mothers in Western society (whose children have only been regarded as "legitimate" in past decades), not to mention Western mothers in general, suffer because (among other things) a significant segment of this society does not value the children that they produce. Nor, by extension, is their role as mothers valued. There is much to suggest that children are greeted by American society at large with equivocation (Polakow 1993; Rossi 1987; LeVine and White 1987; Schepher-Hughes and Stein 1987). They are provided for, with schools and playgrounds, but these provisions almost seem to have been created to ensure that children keep their place. As for the children of young, single mothers, their "cost" to society is calculated, and they are seen as today's and tomorrow's social problems. The implications of such a perspective are seen currently in public policies that allow at least a fifth of today's children to grow up in poverty and necessitate such organizational opposition as a Children's Defense Fund (Bane and Ellwood 1988). As for motherhood, we came across this line in a publication on teenage pregnancy in California: "Expending time and energy on their children robs teenagers of the chance to continue investing in their own necessary growth and maturation" (Brindis and Jeremy 1988:64). In another society, "expending time and energy" on children might be considered an ideal way to grow and mature.

FOUR

Horticulture and Hierarchy

THE YOUTHFUL BEAUTIFICATION OF THE BODY IN THE PAIELA AND PORGERA VALLEYS

Aletta Biersack

for Mata

In the past, the Ipili speakers of the Porgera and Paiela Valleys in Enga Province, Papua New Guinea, cultivated youthful bodies through various magicoritual practices. Body cultivation is body beautification, and the practices described here ultimately promoted courtship and its romance, marriage, and reproduction. This chapter's scope can be summarized in its two key metaphors: planting (horticulture) and fencing (hierarchy). *Planting* refers to the symbolism of the magicoritual growth practices focused on informing ideas concerning the power of human agents. *Fencing* is a local metaphor for the hegemony male agents attain over female agents. Men fence the gardens that women cultivate; they also give bride-wealth to obligate their wives to "reproduce and give them children" *(andopane mandu mai),* thereby "fencing" *(ende pi)* their wives and planting them "in the middle of the garden" *(e tombeka).* Husbands encompass women's fertility, both as gardeners and as mothers, subordinating their wives' agency to their own in projects I have reported on elsewhere (Biersack 1991; 1995; 1996a).

Although this volume concerns adolescence in the Pacific basin, *adolescence* is a problematic term of translation in the Ipili cultural setting. The magicoritual practices I discuss spanned the period of late childhood and puberty but, for men, could include the early and even late twenties. They were begun when boys and girls *iwanaŋa* and *wanaŋa,* respectively, older children who have not yet gone through the growth spurt associated with puberty. Somewhere in the middle of the practices, boys and girls (as *iwana* and *wana,* respectively) began to court, and the various magicoritual techniques of self-beautification were abandoned once they married. Since traditionally males could be thirty years old or so upon first marriage, participating males were hardly adolescent. By the same token, since girls traditionally marry for the first time quite early, at around fifteen, *adolescence* is also problematic, though less so, for the females.

The chapter opens with a discussion of horticulture in the metaphoric sense of the term, specifically as a symbol for the cultivation of organic life. While I feature a ritual that young men participated in, the *omatisia* ritual (initially described in Biersack 1982; see also Biersack 1996a), I shall also venture into new territory: the parallel magical performances young Paiela women and young Porgera men undertook traditionally. The ethnographies of youthful growth practices in the two valleys is followed by a section placing these practices in life cycle perspective, the main claim here being that these practices created a bridge between childhood, sexless and sterile, and an adulthood centered on marriage and reproduction. While males and females, particularly as husbands and wives, are strictly complementary, they are also asymmetrical in the scope and prestige of their powers (Biersack 1995, 1996a). The subsequent section discusses male domination, as this is both reflected in and constituted by the magicoritual practices herein described. The tendency in Melanesian ethnology in recent years has been to set societies apart rather than to lump them together. "Big man" societies oppose "great man" societies; "high-density" societies oppose "low-density" societies; the highlands oppose the lowlands; and "heterosexual" societies oppose "homosexual" societies (see discussion in Biersack 1995). The pervasive, yet largely implicit, emphasis upon fertility in the Paiela and Porgera practices featured here affords insight into the commonalities among societies polarized in other frameworks.

HORTICULTURE

Traditionally, the pattern of youthful growth practices was the same in both the Paiela and Porgera Valleys. Girls and boys, *wanaŋa* and *iwanaŋa*, respectively, began cultivating their bodies when they were about nine or ten. As the procedures advanced, boys and girls began courting with the intention of eventually marrying and becoming parents. When they were ready to marry, efforts to cultivate the body were abandoned. In what follows, I shall detail these practices, first for Paiela and then for Porgera, the valley directly to the east of the Paiela Valley. The account opens with a framing discussion of the scope and powers of human agency as it was constituted and imagined in this part of the world.

Domesticating the Body

The power that the people of Porgera and Paiela assigned to human agents was truly extraordinary. Events were (and still are) divided between "random" *(ambe pene, me)* and "created" *(wa pene),* the intended and the accidental occurrence. The forest, which is not cultivated, is "random," for example, while gardens are cultivated and "created" (cf. Goldman 1993). Although the possibility of autogenesis was recognized, many organic processes that a Westerner would tend to classify as natural or wild were envisioned as the products of human effort. Body growth, including the transformations of puberty, were among these artifacts. Efforts to cultivate the body were metaphorically horticultural, a matter of domesticating (or planting) the body. This is the overriding concept underlying the plethora of growth practices I will describe in this chapter.

All organic growth, including body growth, was thought to take place during the darker and colder periods of the day, particularly at night when, for example, sweet potatoes "slept" or "lay" as well as "grew." Like plants, bodies required coldness, darkness, moisture, and invisibility to thrive. The conditions of organic growth were quintessentially botanical. Human agents cultivated the body by meeting the conditions for organic growth. The spells that were traditionally said to assure body growth had to be performed early in the morning, late in the afternoon, or at night, during the cold, dark, and damp margins of the day and in out-of-the-way places, wherever activities could be kept secret. The most spectacular setting for body cultivation was the *omatisia* ritual, in which boys grew their hair and skin by manipulating magical plants in a swampy and secluded mountain retreat. Many magical substances were traditionally moist if not liquid. Menstrual blood is a surprising example of the principle that liquids were essential to organic growth. A married woman deployed her menstrual blood as she deployed her breast milk—to grow a body, albeit her husband's and not her child's body. Being careful to observe the taboos that protected her husband against the negative side effects of menstruation, a woman collected her menstrual blood and stashed it deep in the forest, performing magic over it, "to take and make her husband large" or "to take and make his skin good" (Biersack 1987, 1995). The *omatisia* ritual centered on an analogous uxoral responsibility, one that was assumed, however, by a spirit wife rather than by a "real" *(enekeya)* wife (Biersack 1996a). In all of these examples, the human body was placed explicitly into the domain of objects produced by cultivation.

Growing the Body in the Paiela Valley

In the Paiela Valley, the hair of children, male and female, was clipped regularly, and the clippings were placed in the canopy of white pandanus trees so that the hair would be as "long" as the tree's canopy. To promote hair growth still further, a girl would use a wooden comb to stretch out each strand as she said a spell that visualized the desired outcome, a full head of hair, in montane imagery. She would also darken her hair with pig grease or a tree oil that Paielas imported from the Huli area to the south. A net of loose soil was placed over the oiled hair and the hair was covered with bark cloth *(tono)* to conceal it from view.

Before puberty, and as her first effort to grow her body, a girl rose at the crack of dawn and entered the cane stands that surround residential areas. Once among the reeds, she took the water that had collected on the leaves *(taiya)* and rubbed it over her arms, legs, back, and head as she said a spell that exhorted the water to "come sit" in the various body parts that she named and grow them. Among other things, the procedure was thought to enlarge the girl's breasts.

A girl might also have applied ochre *(ipakula)* to her skin to make it light and vibrant, in contrast to the hair, which had been darkened by grease or oil. The mud was applied without design to her upper torso, but on her face she traced a complicated pattern using the stem and leaves of two varieties of fast-growing banana plants, as she recited a spell filled with allusions to these plants. The stick with which the girl decorated herself was buried in mud after it had been used to prevent people from seeing it.

Mata, my Paiela mother, described these activities to me in the 1970s. Kongolome, a woman who belongs to the next generation and who learned some of her magic from Mata, described her own efforts to grow herself when I asked her in 1995. When she was still only a young girl, Kongolome smeared the water that had collected on leaves or pig fat on her hair, covered her hair with soot, and hid it with bark cloth. The word for fat, *ipane,* contains the word for water, *ipa,* the implication being that the body swells by encapsulating water, a notion that seems also to inform aspects of the *omatisia* ritual. The bark cloth hid the hair so that people and the sun would not see it; the hair should remain invisible. The cloth is made from the "skin" (or bark) of a species of fast-growing tree called *tono* (which is also the name of the bark cloth). Kongolome told me that when a *tono* tree is planted, a whole grove of *tono* trees springs up, the *tono* symbolizing the desired thickness of hair. As the hair grew, she combed it out, saying magical spells to enhance the effects of the pork fat.

As the girl matured, she promoted the growth of her skin and in particular her breasts by dousing them with the rainwater that collected on leaves at night. Kongolome's spell for this occasion evoked the strength of the cassowary *(eka angete,* the cassowary bird)—"Bird back / Girl, be strong / Cassowary wing . . . / Girl, have strong breath like that of a cassowary." The girl's breasts should grow and her arms and legs should become as strong as those of the cassowary. As her breasts matured and her pubic hair grew, a woman began to court, and the girl performed this magic "so that she would marry" *(akali peakale lo)*. The girl's breasts were erotic and useful, made to order for the core work of female adulthood, reproduction.[1]

Girls also grew magical plants to cultivate their body. A solid-colored, green-leafed plant called *omatisia* represented the hair, and a green and yellow stripe-leafed plant called *sialangai* represented the girl's skin; they were planted as the girl's breasts began to swell to promote body maturation.[2] The plants were grown in one or more gardens that the girl's father or brother had hewn but which the girl herself mounded. Around the plants, a ring of red-leafed cordyline was placed to conceal them and to notify passersby to look away. Ideally, only the girl herself saw these plants. As with ordinary plants, the girl weeded the plants regularly as she said a spell ("I weed the *sialangai* . . . / The sweet potato garden"). After she finished weeding, she might break off some leaves and place them in her net bag or rub them directly over her skin, reciting a spell that drew an analogy between her own personal growth and the growth of the plants.

Mata mentioned a third plant, a plant she called *tindali,* used for self-decoration, although when Mata described how a young woman decorated to attend courtship dances *(mali),* she almost invariably referred to the leaves that were stripped from the magical plants and rubbed over the skin as *sialangai* rather than as *tindali.* Kongolome's account of 1995 mentioned three plants as well. Two of these were planted to promote physical maturation, one symbolizing a girl's hair and the other symbolizing her skin. A third plant was planted "in preparation to marry" *(akali poyale).* This plant helped the girl get pigs, presumably bride-wealth pigs, and for that reason it is referred to as *yia kandolopa,* or pig bog iris (see note 2). Its leaves were put in the girl's net bag when she went courting in the hope of attracting a fiancé. Leaves of these plants might also have been wrapped around pork fat and rubbed on the skin, face, and hair to make these body parts grow, and they might also have been placed in the rafters of the girl's house in accompaniment to a spell designed to promote growth.

In discussing the contaminating touch of a menstruating woman, Mata sometimes emphasized to me the vulnerability of young courting women, whose hair and skin menstruating women should not touch. In addition to abstaining from intercourse, a young girl who wanted to grow avoided menstruating women (lest they touch her person or finery), especially her mother. The girl also did not touch or look upon corpses or have any contact with birds known for alighting on corpses, for fear that her plants would become "chilled" or "dead."

When a girl was trying to grow herself, she had to avoid heat, and she sat and slept away from the hearth. The same was true for boys. Warmth was thought to desiccate organic matter, and a boy who wished to grow his hair or body had to eat sweet potatoes that had been cooked for him lest he become exposed to the full heat of the hearth, and he slept far away from the embers, where it was cold. The boy spent the entire day, except for very early in the morning and late at night, out of the house and in the forest, where people were not likely to chance upon him. As a further precaution, the boy refused to eat burned sweet potatoes or indigenous (black) salt *(ipi)* or a certain variety of white pandanus, for these would dry out his body. Marsupials and birds (with the exception of the cassowary, the only "big" bird) were prohibited because they are "small"; so, too, snakes were forbidden because they have no fat, only bone; and pig intestines were proscribed because of their fecal stench. During this period, the boy's mother buried her food scraps in mud lest her son's skin dry out, and she, too, might have observed food taboos to promote her son's growth.

Like the girls, the boys smeared a liquid, the sap of the *yuma* tree (Guttiferae, Calophyllum [Ingemann 1997:85]), on their hair to grow it. The *yuma* tree is "long" and towers overhead: "If the foot is here where we are talking, then the trunk will be over there, a long walk away," one man explained hyperbolically. "The tree is rich in 'juice'," he added; "just cut it and the sap gushes out." In the spell for applying the sap, the boy used the massiveness and sturdiness of the tree as a symbol of his own body. The roots of the tree penetrate deep into the earth, anchoring it firmly, and the tree's canopy reaches high and spreads wide, as the hair ideally will. The boy had the bark of the tree cooked to render the sap, then coated his hair with it. The sap was cooked every one or two weeks, but was applied on a daily basis as a spell was said. In the spell that Lapu, a Paiela man, gave me, mountains were evoked as a symbol of the anticipated shock of hair. Lapu claimed that the boy could not cook his own *yuma* because that would require that he sit near a fire. Instead, he was helped by an older, less vulnerable boy who would cook for him. Pig fat was smeared over the *yuma* sap, and soil was caked on top. The hair was prepared this way multiple times, though informants differed as to how often and for how long. One man claimed that boys observed all the taboos and restrictions and continued to dress their hair over a four-month period, beginning on the new moon and continuing through the fourth month. Longer periods were mentioned, the differences in informant statements no doubt reflecting personal preferences and varying degrees of caution and fastidiousness.

A little later, or even concurrently, a boy began participating in the *omatisia* ritual. Although I have collected several accounts of this ritual from many knowledgeable males, I will restrict myself here to a summary of the information collected in 1995 from Nikolas, who attended the *omatisia* ritual of the Takali clan, which is based in the southern end of the Paiela Valley.[3] The ritual turned on the manipulation of magical plants and bamboo tubes. A spirit woman, who was the ritual wife of each boy who received bamboo tubes, was thought to "sit" in the bamboo tubes and to grow her ritual husband. Secrecy was the hallmark of the ritual. The boys stole away at night and climbed into the forest, taking care that no one saw them and the sweet potato provisions they carried. Ipili speakers name two kinds of forest: the upper forest, called *aiya anda*, a term that means "beauty house,"[4] and the lower forest, called *wapi*. Unlike *wapi*, which is hot and dry, *aiya anda* is cold and wet and therefore ideal for body cultivation. While in seclusion, the boys cooked only at night, lest people below spot the smoke and discover their location. To facilitate body growth, the boys observed certain taboos: they could not eat pig bone or burnt sweet potato, for example, and, although a boy began to court somewhere in the middle of his *omatisia* participation, he had to remain chaste lest his plants die.

A hierarchy formed among the all-male *omatisia* participants. At the lowest level there were the novices (*wene yo atene* ["those who put for the first time"]), boys who received magical plants but who had to wait until the second or third trip to the upper forest to receive their bamboo tubes. Newcomers might still be dousing their hair with tree sap when they started to attend *omatisia*. Old-timers (*ba yo atene* ["those who had already put"]) had participated at least once before and had already begun to grow *omatisia* plants, and, additionally, were tending bamboo tubes in the swamp. Finally, there was the male ritual leader, the spellmaster or *kamo anduane*, who taught the boys spells and procedures and who was a person who was old enough to have married and borne children but who had done neither, the type of person Ipili speakers refer to as *kinambuli*, an older yet still childless male or female.[5]

The first day of seclusion, and before the boys saw their plants or bamboo tubes, they washed their eyes, which had been contaminated by the "eye work" (as one person put it) they had done below. They had "seen bad things"—genitalia that had been exposed when clothing inadvertently swung aside, for example, or buttocks or feces or drops of menstrual blood that had fallen onto the ground—and had to be rinsed before they could gaze upon the plants and bamboo tubes (cf. Meggitt 1964). Unlike the residential area below, which was contaminated by coital couples and their activities, the upper forest was a pure zone, the preserve of chaste males. Nikolas's spell for this occasion emphasized the eyes of birds, omniscient and strong. "The bird flies everywhere / I wash the bird eye . . . / I cleanse the bird eye with water / . . . The bird flies everywhere / It divides the clouds / The bird goes everywhere and sees everything."[6] When the boys finally returned to the residential area, they said a spell as they looked at a pandanus tree, which was expected to wither and die, thus demonstrating the power of their purified gaze.

After he had participated at least once in the *omatisia* ritual, the boy received bamboo tubes (*uiyapa pene*) to prepare and place in the swamp. The tubes were ringed and roofed with the bark of the *makua* tree (Cunoniaceae, Schizomeria sp. [Ingemann 1997:44]), and the entire structure was ballasted with sticks, which were leaned against the structure and bound together at their tips. The tubes were the "house" (anda) of a spirit woman, the "omatisia woman" (omatisia wanda), or the "uiyapa [bamboo] woman" (uiyapa wanda). Each time the boy returned to the upper forest, he received a fresh batch of bamboo tubes, and he checked the batch of bamboo tubes that he had last placed in the swamp. If the water in any one tube was muddy or if there was a spider web in the old tubes, indicating that the spirit woman was menstruating and impure, the water in that tube was not discarded. Over the course of his participation in the omatisia ritual, the boy accumulated various batches of bamboo tubes, each batch surrounded and roofed by makua bark. The tubes were placed "so that the skin would grow" and presumably represented the encapsulated water that is fat.

Growing the Body in the Porgera Valley

Young Porgera boys began the process of self-beautification much as they did in Paiela: by coating their hair with the sap of the yuma tree and covering it with bark cloth or a cap made of white pandanus leaves. During the time that the boy was dousing his hair with tree sap, he avoided the heat of the hearth, sitting and sleeping away from it. In the morning, the boy hid in the upper forest, lest people see him. After ten months, the pandanus cap was removed and the hair was coifed using a rope to extend the hair out on either side of the head—in emulation, perhaps, of the well-known horned wig of the Porgera-Paiela region. As in Paiela, there was no clear break between the time when yuma sap was smeared on the hair and the period of omatisia participation. Kualata, a well-known cultural expert living at Porgera Station, in the heartland of the Porgera Valley, told me that the first time he went to the omatisia ritual, he did not receive plants but the sap of the yuma tree, which he smeared on his hair; and in the Paiela Valley, omatisia novices were sometimes described for me as "those who are smearing yuma" (yuma yangene).

Descent among Ipili speakers is cognatic. Since the omatisia ritual is a clan ritual, and since everyone is a member of more than one clan, it is possible for males to attend the omatisia ritual of more than one clan. Speaking for the ritual of the Maipangi clan, which is based at Porgera Station, and the Anga clan, based at Yuyan on the northwestern wall of Porgera Valley, Kualata provided a familiar enough account. The boys traveled surreptitiously to the upper forest, carrying with them sweet potatoes, which should not have been seen by married and, by implication, sexually active men and women. The boys' eyes were contaminated, and the first order of business was to purify them. The boys had seen their mothers' hips and legs, presumably at birth, as the spell used on this occasion stated, and consequently their eyes had to be purified before anything else was done. Legs is sometimes a code word for genitalia or a metonym for the organs of sexual reproduction, as it seems to be here; *hips* refers to the womb and to the vagina. The water was drawn to the eyes along a duct made out of various tree leaves, cordyline leaves, and moss.[7] The duct was held first in the right hand and toward the left eye, then in the left hand and toward the right eye, as a spell was said. The spell posited a metaphorical relationship between the water that cascaded into the eyes of the boys and the urine of several species of birds, named in the spell and also by implication: "Filthy legs, genitals / . . . I cleanse my eyes / With the piss water / With the piss water." The birds that were named in the spell all dwell in the upper forest (or "beauty house"), where they live off its abundant wild food. But these birds suck on rather than swallow the nuts they find there, so that they never do imbibe solids, only liquids. Relatively odorless, and a liquid uncompromised (as fecal matter is) by the presence of solids, the birds' urine represents the purities of the upper forest as well as, perhaps, moisture itself, which is required for body growth.

The two Porgerans who described the ritual for me, Kualata, who attended Maipangi's and Anga's *omatisia* ritual, and Koipanda, who attended Anga's ritual, spoke of two kinds of plants—the very plants, in fact, that Mata and Kongolome identified as critical to the traditional magical performances of young Paiela women. One was *omatisia,* a plant with a solid green leaf; the other was *sialangai,* a plant with a green and yellow striped leaf. Both of them, in Kualata's interpretation, represents the boy: *omatisia* represents his hair and *sialangai* represents his skin.[8] Later on, the boy would receive bamboo tubes, which, as in the Paiela variant, were walled and roofed with tree bark to create the "house" of the "bamboo woman" or the "*omatisia* woman" and placed in a swamp. Novices did not receive bamboo tubes, but those who already had participated in the *omatisia* ritual at least once before did. Upon returning, the old-timers checked their bamboo tubes to see if there was a spider web in them, an indication that the spirit woman was menstruating and impure. Every time the old-timer went to a ritual, he received new bamboo tubes, each batch walled and roofed with *makua* bark; they accumulated over time.

Kualata mentioned that preparing the bamboo tubes was arduous, and for that reason the bamboo tubes were being phased out, even before the missionaries arrived.[9] Koipanda, who is a generation younger than Kualata, never did receive bamboo tubes, even though some of the older boys attending the ritual when he participated did have bamboo tubes that they looked after. However, even without the bamboo tubes, the spirit woman retained a terrific presence in the Porgera version of the ritual. While traveling to the upper forest, the cult leader said a special spell to make the upper forest and particularly its precious female spirit invisible to the contaminating gaze of ordinary people (a practice followed in Paiela as well). Similarly, in weeding his plants, Kualata said a spell that addressed the spirit woman and told her to "sit" in the boys' calves, sides, back, shoulders, eyeballs, belt, hair, and so on. In one of Koipanda's spells, the spirit woman was asked to come and sleep in the boys' hair, making it round and full like the sweet potato mound.

The upper forest is pure because it is where the spirit woman sits and hides and because it is free of impure adults. In returning to the residential area, Kualata smeared a paste of charcoal from the logs of the *yambauwa* tree mixed with the eggs of various black-feathered birds found in the upper forests on his face. The eggs were greasy, and they symbolized the health and beauty that Ipili speakers associate with taut, "fat" skin. Mixed with charcoal, the grease was as black as the birds whose eggs were used, and the blackness or darkness of the face contrasted with and accented the whiteness of the eyes, now purified. "Little *omapo* bird, you've borne two eggs / . . . I break and smear / I break and smear them on my face / I decorate my face with stripes / My face will be beautiful."

My knowledge of comparable female practices in the Porgera Valley is far sketchier. What is clear from the little information I have is that girls grew themselves by rubbing rainwater over themselves and by planting cultigens. The leaves of these plants were stripped and worn during courtship to entice eligible men. Girls cultivated themselves individually rather than in groups, and they abandoned these practices once they married.

SELF-BEAUTIFICATION IN LIFE-CYCLE PERSPECTIVE

The purpose of the procedures just described were, as stated, to make the skin and hair of young men and women "large," to grow them. "Large" skin is "beautiful" skin, and to obtain it, boys retreated to the "beauty house" (*aiya anda*) of the upper forest and girls rubbed water and magical plants over their skin (see note 4). A young man's attractiveness was attributed to a spirit woman who "sat" in his skin and hair. When an *omatisia* participant journeyed to a homicide compensation payment gathering, a pig feast, a bride-wealth distribution, or a dance, girls would find him so irresistible that they would fight over him, a fantasy about the outcome of *omatisia* that more than one male divulged to me.

For both males and females, courtship began somewhere in the middle of the practices just described, and making the body alluring for courtship purposes was the explicit goal of these practices. That the body was cultivated to make it sexually attractive is more obvious in the case of young women, for the cultigens a girl grew were worn as decorative items or used as a cosmetic aid in courtship. A young woman might dip the leaves of her magical plants in the belly fat of pigs and rub them over her collarbone and chest while saying a spell to attract a fiancé, or she might put magical leaves in her armbands and net bag, especially when attending a dance, to heighten her allure. Some also put the leaves in their nasal septum to adorn their face. Mata told me that when she went to courtship dances she also magically prepared the skirt she wore. Although skirts are ordinarily made at night as females sit by the fire, heat impedes physical growth, and this skirt was made during the day as a spell alluding to various birds (the bird of paradise in particular) was said to make the young woman as spectacular in her appearance as these birds. Mata was the kind of woman who would spare no effort, and she took her preparations for courtship even further. Before attending a dance, she would arise early in the morning and slip into the reed stands to drink magically prepared water. This would be done four or five mornings running. On the last day the bamboo tubes would be buried in mud to conceal them from view. On these occasions Mata recited two spells, one for filling the tubes and the other for drinking from them. The tube-filling spell referred to the pandanus tree, often used as a symbol of strength and vitality. As she drank the water, Mata said a spell that referred to various body parts that the water should "come to" and grow.[10]

The thought of marriage was very much on the mind of those participating in the *omatisia* ritual. While boys tended their plants and bamboo tubes during the day, at night they sat inside the *omatisia* house practicing their spells. The most popular magic was designed to make one's girlfriend lovesick, the category of spell called "woman *kale*" *(wanda kale)* magic. The following love magic performance was described to me in both the Porgera and Paiela Valleys: First fern and tree leaves were wrapped around *omatisia* leaves, and these were jabbed with bat bones *(deke)*. The jabbing action represented a "shooting" of the fiancée's heart, her admirer's conquest of her. Everything was then cooked in the fire to engulf the boy's chosen with smoke and, as it were, asphyxiate or overwhelm her with feelings of love. A woman so smitten would be unable to wield her digging stick or do any other work. Kualata performed this magic every night he was in seclusion. On the morning of the day that Kualata returned to the residential area, all the boys gathered and said this love magic as they prepared a fire to signal their parents and girlfriends waiting below that they were about to return. A girl could indicate her affection for a particular boy by standing near his parents or by tossing him a cowrie necklace as he passed by. A girl who was growing magical plants also said love magic to attract the partner of her choice. Kongolome liked a man from Yokopia, and she recited a spell that alluded to him in the following terms: "I am a good girl / Those fellows from Yokopia / He should be delighted with me . . . / My skin should be beautiful like the skin of a pearl shell . . . / He should propose to me . . . / Tomorrow he should propose to me."

According to the folklore of both the Paiela and Porgera Valleys, a boy knew that he was ready to marry if a frog appeared near his plants or bamboo tubes or if a bird of paradise called *yange*[11] soared over him. A married woman is still symbolically referred to as "the bird of paradise feather" *(eka wambia itini),*[12] and the *yange* bird soaring overhead perhaps symbolized the future wife. Kualata explained that *yange* is also the name of a variety of grass skirt, perhaps the kind that Mata magically prepared as she said a spell featuring the bird of paradise, so that *yange* arguably symbolized not only wives but what the grass skirt covers, the vagina and its fertility. Both young men and young women abandoned their magic and their plants once they were ready to marry.

In beautifying the body, the procedures described above created an instrumental bridge between youth and adulthood. This bridge was embodied in the spirit woman, who was like a wife but who was not actually a wife. Traditionally, wives performed magic when they menstruated to protect their husband's skin (Biersack 1987, 1995, 1996a), and in growing her ritual husband, the spirit woman assumed a uxoral responsibility. The spirit woman beautified the boys specifically as their wife. In receiving bamboo tubes, the boy gave cowrie shells in payment for the magic while he was at the *omatisia* house, together with a pledge to give a pig later, after having returned to the residential area—a deal that both Paiela and Porgera *omatisia* participants struck. The cowrie shell payment was called *lu,* a term that refers to payment for magical and ritual services, and in this context it also was seen as a form of bride-wealth. Kualata said that, in Porgera, when a boy received magical plants he made compensation for them as well as for the spirit woman, who moved as bride with the plants. "I am reciprocating with bride-wealth, so that I can receive your woman *(Paini nimba waitapu geyo nimbana wanda namba meyo)."* That marriage was a pervasive subtext of the ritual is evident from the way the boys returned from the forest, at least as the Anga clan staged the return. According to Koipanda, just before returning to the residential area the boys decorated themselves and formed two lines, competing with each other for the spellmaster's accolades. The more beautiful line was deemed favored by the spirit woman, the other line to have been "divorced" by her. Similarly, in discontinuing participation in the *omatisia* ritual, a boy was considered to be "divorcing" the spirit woman.

While the similarities between the bamboo wife and the real wife are obvious, it is also easy to see the differences, the most important being that, unlike a real wife, the bamboo wife was virginal—never a mother, only a wife.[13] In "sitting in the boy's skin" and making him sexually alluring, the spirit woman promoted the goal of reproduction, but could not, in and of herself, consummate the process; for that, a real wife was required. The same is true in the case of girls, only more obviously so because no supernatural figure assisted them. By eroticizing the body with the intent of marrying, the procedures I have described prepared the young man or woman for the work of adulthood and its sexual reproduction, but they necessarily remained preliminary to that work. The play form of marriage at the heart of the *omatisia* ritual—the fact that the spirit woman sits in a toy house of her boy-husband's manufacturing and that he gives a modest bride-wealth of cowrie shells and a single pig rather than the standard bride-wealth of twenty-eight pigs—neatly identifies the ritual and its core relations as juvenalia.

The sterility of the ritual marriage between the young man and the female spirit in a context that explicitly anticipated marriage located the ritual and its main product, the eroticized body, within an overarching life cycle. In both the Porgera and Paiela Valleys, an elaborate battery of beliefs concerning the impact of heterosexual intercourse, childbearing, and menstruation and how it affects both sexes (Biersack 1987, 1995, 1996a) established that sexual congress undermined the health and beauty of the parties to it and that males and females would attain the heights of physical beauty *before* they married and would begin declining only *after* they married.[14] To achieve the social respectability that comes with marriage and parenthood, it was necessary to sacrifice the physical glamor of early manhood and womanhood for the more prestigious projects of adulthood (Biersack 1995, 1996a). That life's benefits could only be obtained at this cost was the key trade-off (see Biersack 1996b, 1998a).

HIERARCHY: SEXUALITY AND GENDER POLITICS

Despite gender complementarity, the relationship between husband and wife is a hierarchical one, bringing us to a consideration of the politics of the fencing metaphor. To give bride-wealth is to "fence" a woman, and a "fenced" woman is one who has been placed "in the middle of the garden"—girded and constrained, that is, by a fence. The "fencing" metaphor is masculine in its connotations, a reference to the fact that, while wives plant and weed gardens, husbands clear and fence them. These metaphors draw upon the language of horticulture to express the hierarchical relationship between spouses (cf. M. Strathern 1988:254), focused, as this asymmetry is, on the matter of fertility. A "fenced" woman is a woman who has been obligated by bride-wealth "to bear and give" her husband children, constrained to fulfill the conjugal duties her husband and his cocontributors to the bride-wealth have assigned her, not only or even particularly as a gardener and pig husbander, but as a mother.

While this is not the place to describe Ipili marriage in any depth, suffice it to say that Ipili speakers concentrate on marriage between clans for the purpose of organizing networks of kinship and affinity. To simplify, clan A might take its spouses from clans B and C, while clan B might take its spouses from clans A and C. Since Paiela descent is cognatic, the concentration of marriages among clans results in a cohort of people who are closely related through two or more descent ties—common membership in clans A and B, B and C, A and C, or even

A, B, and C. Paielas and Porgerans thus become related to one another through multistranded ties and embed themselves in dense and nucleated networks of kinship and affinity (Biersack 1995, 1996c). Developing tight-knit (yet, by virtue of clan exogamy, open) communities is a goal that Ipili speakers consciously strive after, and they do so through "woman exchange" *(wanda lawa lawa)*, the appellation Ipili speakers give this practice of marriage among clans. While women are the indispensable helpmates in this project of network organization and consolidation, the men, as leaders, encouragers, and supporters of strategic marriages, are its main instigators and overseers (Biersack 1995:233–47; 1996a). The male bias in this domain of activity is reflected in such local idioms as "woman exchange" and in the term for intermarrying clans, "woman suppliers" *(wanda atata)*, as well as in the fact that, instead of women giving groom-wealth and assigning men various conjugal duties thereby, men give bride-wealth, obligating women to reproduce in reciprocation. The relationship between husband and wife is a creditor-debtor relationship.[15]

In exchanging women, men organize women's fertility. A woman who is a member of the B clan but who is married to an A man will bear children who belong to both A and B clans, and these children, by virtue of the cognatic rule, will be closely related to the offspring of other A-B couples created through interclan marriage. Despite their womblessness, then, men achieve hegemony in the sphere of reproduction (see also Lindenbaum 1984, 1987), a political fact that the "fencing" metaphor, which alludes to the extraordinary powers that males culturally achieve, neatly captures.

The organization of sexual reproduction is most obvious in the remarriages of divorcées and widows, particularly if they have already borne children to their previous husbands. These women tend to remarry (levirate-style) their prior husbands' kinsmen to assure that the children that a divorcée or widow will subsequently bear will be closely related to the children that the woman has already borne. While the female spirit is a virgin, she circulates much as real women do and in fulfillment of the projects that not just one male but that a group of males undertakes. When a boy purchases his bamboo tubes from an older male, either the spellmaster or another boy, he gives *lu* valuables in return. Kauwambo, a Paiela man who attended Pepeyange's *omatisia*, implicitly referred to this exchange in his explanation of the payment given for the plants and the spirit woman: "When we are planting *omatisia*, our woman over there [the spirit woman] is a rich woman. She has made me rich. She should make you rich too. Give me pig and shell, and I will give you my woman. I will give her to you, and you will become rich."[16] The spirit woman therefore circulates among the boys much as divorced wives and widows tend to marry among males who are related to one another and who are, as a result, the ideal father of the widow's or divorcée's future children. While the union between the boy-husband and his ritual wife remains sterile, the spirit woman does perform the uxoral service of beautifying her husband. Much as with a real wife, the spirit wife's agency is harnessed to the husband's goals, a subjection that was alluded to in the spell for warning the spirit woman to conceal herself from interlopers as the boys entered the upper forest: "I want to come myself / I want to come, your male owner" (*Tane akali epokale / Anduane akali epokale*). This subjection is preliminary to the subordination of real women in adulthood, the one that follows from the creditor-debtor relationship between husband and wife engendered by the bride-wealth, which effectively subordinates the wife as a reproducer.

Insofar as the practices I have described transform youths into spouses, it prepares them to participate in interclan marriages and the exchange of women upon which the interclan marriage is predicated. In this regard, the social organizational dimensions of the *omatisia* ritual become relevant. Marriage is concentrated among clans, and *omatisia* was a clan cult. The boys who attended the ritual would later assist one another in assembling the bride-wealth that indebts women as wives and enables males to deploy women's fertility toward their own social organizational ends. While the *omatisia* ritual was a clan ritual, participation was not restricted to those who are members of the host clan. Boys who were related to one or more clan members through other clan ties might have attended the ritual as the guests of members of the host clan. Nikolas is a member of the Takali clan, but he told me that participants at Takali's *omatisia* typically included members of Eli clan (also based in the southern end of the Paiela Valley) as well, even Elis who were not also Takalis. (Nikolas himself is both Eli and Takali.) By the same token, Kauwambo is not a Pepeyange, even though he attended Pepeyange's *omatisia* ritual. The guests at the *omatisia* ritual were overwhelmingly (if not entirely) drawn from "woman-supplying" (*wanda atata*) clans of the ritual's host clan—that is, from clans with which the host clan exchanged women. Eli clan intermarries heavily with Takali clan, for example. The ritual therefore convened males who might sponsor one another's marriages in the aftermath of the ritual and who would be all the more likely to do so given their shared participation in a ritual whose purpose was to promote courtship through the beautification of the body and which involved a fantasy relationship with a common wife.

The *omatisia* ritual exhibited and constituted the power of males not as a clan but as a class, then. When a girl acquired magical plants from a mother or older girl, she reciprocated with a net bag, some pork, or a single strand of cowrie shells, but this was payment merely for the plants and their powers, not for a spouse. Of course, there is no groom-wealth in Paiela society. That men give a payment for the bride and not the other way around is a telling symptom of the patriarchal character of Paiela gender relations (Biersack 1995, 1996a). By the same token, that male youths gave bride-wealth for their spirit wife while female youths enjoyed no supernatural aid and acted individually rather than in a group reflected and perpetuated the asymmetry of gender relations in Paiela and Porgera society. As Bruce Lincoln has observed in *Emerging from the Chrysalis,*

> as has often been noted, women's rituals tend to be celebrated for individuals, while those for men are usually corporate affairs. And whatever immediate causal explanation or justification might be offered for either the practitioners or the analysts of these rites, the long-term consequences are all too clear. For whereas group solidarity, which serves men exceedingly well in the political arena, is ritually constructed for them in the course of their collective initiation, the corresponding rituals for women most often atomize the initiands, and provide them with neither bonds of solidarity nor experience in group mobilization that could be useful in later political action (1991:117).

CULTIVATING ONE'S OWN GARDEN?
IPILI SPEAKERS TODAY

Lincoln's conclusions are prefaced with a devastating critique of the Durkheimian notion that "society" is homogeneous and solidary: "society is hardly a monolithic entity, but is rather a tense and potentially volatile amalgam of various subgroups . . . , the members of which hold very different statuses from one another" (ibid., 117). If so-called society is pluralistic rather than monolithic, how much more so is it in times of rapid change?

By the very nature of this inquiry, those I talked to about the traditional growth practices of young men and women are now old. With missionization, the magicoritual techniques I have described have been abandoned. In fact, not every knowledgeable person has been willing to discuss them with me for fear of being compromised spiritually as a result. In keeping with the conjugal imagery of the *omatisia* ritual, the seventy- or eighty-year-old Kualata told me that young men are now "divorced," meaning that they no longer marry a spirit woman. He added, much as other old people in the Porgera and Paiela Valleys have commented, that he found the young men and women of today less attractive than they were in the past. Kualata still wears the traditional male apron (though he decorates his upper torso with sweaters), and in the landscape of faces and styles of present-day Porgera, where cloth long ago replaced traditional dress and where wigs are a rarity, he looks like—indeed, is—an anachronism. Young people today attempt to attract attention by donning, if they are male, trousers, shirts, and ideally shoes, flashy hats, and sunglasses and, if they are women, cloth skirts, blouses, and colorful scarfs and net bags. There is, in short, a clash of tastes and standards. But the heterodoxy goes much deeper still and concerns, yet again, "society" in its past and present manifestations.

Traditionally, work was always collectivized and, in any case, performed as a service that one person did for another (Biersack 1995), and wealth was public, circulated among a network of people who, by right and duty, shared wealth with one another. Giving bride-wealth created bonds and obligations between the groom's and the bride's kin. These ties were perpetuated in the next generation by the offspring of the union, who, in being positioned strategically "in between" patri- and matri-kin, perpetuated the obligations created through their parents' marriage as the consanguines of their parents' affines. Taken together, male and female practices of self-beautification represented a willingness on the part of men and women alike, first of all, to participate in the same gender hierarchy and, secondly, to promote the larger good by marrying in strategic ways and thereby enhancing the cohesion and peacefulness of the society (Biersack 1991, 1996b).

Today, while bride-wealth is still given, the prestation is no longer a foregone conclusion. A man may marry without giving bride-wealth, and he may also marry without regard to the organizational impact of the marriage. Increasingly, young folks appear to draw their spouses endogamously, from within their own clans, rather than exogamously, from "woman-supplying" groups. While clan endogamy sometimes did happen in the past—the couple compelling a begrudging acceptance of the union by eloping—in the 1990s it happens more and more frequently. In this context, a miscellaneous detail Mata gave me in the 1970s acquires significance. Mata told me that, after she weeded her magical plants, she avoided having contact with anyone who belonged to her own clans on the principle, as she put it, using the singsong form of Paiela maxims, that "she who weeds [sialangai] should not speak [to a man who is related to her]" (tani pene pi na lene), but "she who does not weed [sialangai] can speak [to a man who is related to her]" (tani na pene pi lene). Weeding magical plants made the girl attractive, and, to avoid a prohibited liaison, she would "look away" or "look to one side" if she saw a fellow clanperson.

What drops out of the picture with a loss of these practices is not just a magicoritual technology but, possibly, the very social order that the ritual was meant to construct and maintain. The loss of these practices could well be one of several symptoms that collective life in this part of the highlands is currently on the wane; that individualism, or some highlands version of it, may be on the rise, and no doubt one that depends as heavily upon redefinitions of sexuality, courtship, and marriage as the traditional collectivism did (cf. Errington and Gewertz 1996).[17] Lincoln's ruminations warn us that "society" may not be an unmixed blessing, for it may serve the interests of one gender at the expense of the other (1991:117; see also Buchbinder and Rappaport 1976). Underlying the collectivism of traditional Ipili society is the gender politics that accords the actions of men as a class their power (Biersack 1996a). Anything that erodes this collectivism could undermine those gender politics and lay the foundation for complementarity without asymmetry—for horticulture, as it were, without hierarchy.

HORTICULTURE, AGAIN

Under the rubric of "sexual antagonism," the literature on male initiation and other puberty rites has typically emphasized male fears of heterosexual congress and even hatred for women (see discussion in Herdt and Poole 1982). In the Porgera-Paiela area, women fear intersexual contact as much as—in fact more than!—men (Biersack 1987, 1995, 1996a), but like men, they actively pursue it through the practices I have described and through courtship and marriage. Offsetting any possible sexual antagonism is the sexual attraction between men and women, which was unmistakably revealed in the spontaneous glee male informants in particular exhibited when our discussions turned to romantic matters.

In actual fact, despite male and female fears of heterosexual congress, marriage, heterosexuality, and reproduction are culturally and organizationally focal (Biersack 1995, 1996a, 1996b). Their centrality is on display in the *omatisia* ritual, which was permeated with heterosexual symbols and relations. The most obvious of these was the union (albeit chaste) between the young male participants and the *omatisia* or *uiyapa* woman, the female spirit who "sat" in the bamboo tubes and who became the boys' ritual wife. Kualata spontaneously made the point himself, indicating that the bamboo tube was female-identified while the plants were male-identified.[18] The very division of labor upon which the ritual rested was inspired by the routines of conjugality. To supply the spirit woman with a house that was inviolate and private rather than public, a boy (the spirit woman's ritual husband) encircled the bamboo tubes with bark walls and put a bark roof over the structure, fashioning a "house" for her, much as a real husband builds a house for his wife. In return, and like a real wife, the spirit woman grew her husband (although without using the menstrual blood magic that a real wife uses [Biersack 1987]). There are other allusions to heterosexuality. In the procedure that some Porgera youths used to decorate and return to the residential area, the mixture of charcoal and eggs was sexual. The soot was obtained from charred *yambauwa* or *tato* wood (Facaea, Nothofagus [Ingemann 1997:68]) wood. The *yambauwa* tree is tall and is, like other tall trees, masculine in its connotations. Traditionally, wives stashed their menstrual blood at the base of the *yambauwa* tree, where they performed magic over it to grow their husbands (Biersack 1987), powerfully bringing together emblems of the husband (the tree) and the wife (the menstrual blood). So, too, did those Porgera males who decorated to return to the residential area by mixing female-associated egg with male-associated soot and smearing the mixture on their face.

I observed at the outset that the recent comparative trend in Melanesian ethnology has been to contrast types of societies and/or regions. For present purposes, the most interesting dichotomy is Shirley Lindenbaum's "homosexual" versus "heterosexual" societies (1984; 1987). The dichotomy opposes societies such as the Sambia, where males ritually donate semen to one another, on the one hand, and, on the other, societies in which heterosexuality remains an uncompromised norm. In so-called homosexual societies, women's fertility is "mystified" by males, who usurp women's accomplishments by initiating and ritually re-"making" men. In so-called heterosexual societies, these politics are in abeyance, but an equally pernicious politics of exchange unfolds as the products of women's labor are appropriated by prestige- and power-seeking males (ibid.). To some extent, this polarization between "heterosexual" and "homosexual" societies aligns with and draws its power from other dichotomies—between societies with high- and low-intensity production (Feil 1987), for example, or between societies with "big man"–style leadership and societies with "great men" (or ritual) leaders (Godelier and M. Strathern 1991; see discussion in Biersack 1995 and Knauft 1993).

Ritual homosexuality did not occur in traditional Paiela and Porgera society. Older boys gave younger boys plants, tubes, and spirit women as their brides, not semen. If to grow oneself was to beautify oneself, the outcome of these practices constituted an eroticization of the body whereby young males and females became mutually attractive and, given the coordinate activity of courtship, this glamorization resulted in marriage and reproduction. The purpose of male-to-male transfers, therefore, was to transform a sterile boy into, at first, a nubile and, ultimately, a fertile, male, the boy's body into an erotic tool, a goal that was consistent with the heterosexual symbolism and relations of the *omatisia* ritual.

Despite the alleged dichotomy between "homosexual" and "heterosexual" societies, the very same goal, the fertility of participants, can be found in the best-known case of ritual homosexuality, the Sambia. According to Herdt, through male insemination, the first two stages of the ritual established the boy's potential for fertility, the third stage enabled him to pass this fertility on to a younger boy, the fourth stage involved a marriage ceremony (1987:108), the fifth occurred after the bride's menarche (ibid.), and the sixth stage occurred when the male had fathered his first child. Moreover, like the *omatisia* ritual, the core symbols of the Sambia ritual belong to the world of heterosexuality. The flutes represent the penis but also the breast; semen is symbolically also breast milk (Herdt 1982:69–73); the flutes are always played in pairs, the shorter one being female and the longer one being male; and the flutes are said to be married (ibid., 75). Therefore, Sambia ritual homosexuality must be understood with respect to a wider sexual terrain in which heterosexuality, with its fertility, is still the ultimate, the standard, the adult sexual form. Thus understood, homosexuality, however conventional, remains marginal, a conclusion that effectively undermines Lindenbaum's dichotomy and motivates a comparison between Sambia and Ipili ritual based on their similarities rather than their differences.

In the concluding essay in *Gender Rituals,* Paul Roscoe notes how a number of the rituals that are described in the volume highlight amalgamations of male and female powers, and he wonders whether this emphasis has not been "overlooked or misinterpreted in studies of male initiation" (Roscoe 1995:223; see also Lutkehaus 1995:10–11), studies that emphasize misogyny, male fears, and "sexual antagonism" instead. Sambia male initiation is saturated with heterosexual symbolism, as is the *omatisia* ritual of the Porgera-Paiela region. Like the "female goddess" cult of the Melpa (A. Strathern 1970, 1979, 1994), moreover, there is the paradox that, whereas women and their positive powers are present symbolically in the male cult, actual women are prohibited from participating in it. Womanhood is simultaneously vilified and valorized, perhaps as a necessary evil. It is not the presence or absence of ritual homosexuality, which may remain incidental to the fertility goals of the various rituals, but this very paradox that requires explanation.

For Paiela and Porgera, I would explain this paradox in terms of heterosexuality's double significance: it brings death but it also brings new life (Biersack 1995, 1996c, 1998a; cf. Buchbinder and Rappaport 1976; Tuzin 1995). Among Ipili speakers, sexual reproduction is conceptualized and instituted as the relationship between death and regeneration. Through coitus, childbearing, and nursing, couples are fertile but only on the condition that they diminish, even extinguish, their own lives in the process. According to local perception, body growth, health, and beauty climax *before* marriage and procreation; afterward males, and even more so females, experience a bodily decline. That human life is poised between death and regeneration and that heterosexuality is the relationship between the two (see Biersack 1995, 1998a) explains the complex and perplexing attitude toward heterosexuality the *omatisia* ritual evinced. Participants secretly harvested sweet potato and carried it surreptitiously as they climbed high above, fleeing the residential areas below, where sexually active adults of either sex lived and procreated genital to genital. They left behind them all actual women and all actual fertility. Having shed a life that was premised on the link between death and regeneration, they nevertheless plunged headlong into a quasiconjugal partnership with a spirit woman, their ritual wife, and they cultivated their own flesh as sexual bait in pursuit of a fiancée and marriage. Not every Paiela or Porgeran married, and there were always boys who liked their spirit wife too much, who clung to the safer magicoritual practices of their youth, and who failed to mature as *akali* or men, growing to be *kinambuli,* infertile adults, instead. Such adults were expected to age more slowly, but the leverage they gained biologically was offset by the social and political handicap they acquire as superannuated juveniles. *Kinambulis* have no prestige. No doubt to avoid the stigma of infertility, most boys embraced their fate as human beings and married, fathered children, and lived shorter lives.

The ambivalence most if not all *omatisia* participants experienced is inherent in the ritual itself and its informing life philosophy. Like flesh, the cultigens the boys planted grew and regenerated. But also like flesh, they could wither and die—if the boy had intercourse, for example. In this context, horticulture symbolized not only the power of human agency but the perishability of human agents—indeed, the very relationship between death and fertility from which there was, and still is, no escape. To the extent that "sexual antagonism" is mitigated by a countervailing awareness of the inevitability and importance of heterosexuality—as happens among Ipili speakers and seems to happen among the Sambia—"(hetero)sexual antagonism" would give way to heterosexual ambivalence. Underlying this ambivalence—in the Ipili instance, in any case—is a certain outlook on life, a tragic view of it. Since the very telling paradoxes of the *omatisia* ritual are to be found in the ritual life of other Papua New Guinea groups, whether or not ritual homosexuality is present in them, Ipili speakers may not be alone in their ruminations and perspectives. In fact, these may be widely shared across a spectrum of societies that appear diverse in light of certain superficial differences (see Biersack 1996a; Tuzin 1995). In that event, ritual homosexuality would at best constitute an analytical distraction.

FIVE

Woman the Sexual, a Question of When

A STUDY OF GEBUSI ADOLESCENCE

Eileen M. Cantrell

Women's resistance to or contravention of male authority has been an important issue in Melanesian ethnography in recent decades. Following earlier studies of male-female relations and classic monographs by Marilyn Strathern (1972) and Annette Weiner (1976), Herdt and Poole (1982) discussed and critiqued the widespread notion of "sexual antagonism" in Melanesian ethnography. In the process, they called for more studies of the actual *experience* of gendered opposition in different Melanesian contexts. In subsequent years, a number of works refined our understanding of Melanesian women's participation in exchange, economic development, oral narrative, and their overall status, and have proposed general features of male domination and/or female resistance.[1] Despite some exceptions, however, there remains a surprisingly persistent need for nuanced studies of Melanesian women's experience in basic areas of socialization, sexuality, and marriage (cf. Herdt and Stoller 1990:chap. 6; Jenkins 1994). It is important to consider how these experiences affirm or deny gendered understandings. This approach resonates in Leavitt's (1991) analysis of experience and sexual ideology among the Bumbita Arapesh.

This chapter also attempts to go beyond the power-versus-resistance model to show how gendered, divergent experiences can lead women to distrust men's moral commitment to the very constructs and practices they hold in common. In looking at the relationship among cultural constructs, experience and practice as it gives form to adolescent female sexuality, this chapter proposes that Gebusi women see themselves not as "opposing men," but as opposing those excessive and transgressive areas of men's behavior that threaten gender harmony. Women's opposition to specific male practices is thus seen as prudent and protective of both individuals and collectively shared understandings. By considering this process, we can bring women's own lives more fully into view and move beyond models that take a simple or reified view of male domination, on the one hand, and women's resistance on the other (see Abu-Lughod 1990).

BACKGROUND

The ethnographic focus of this essay is the construction of meaning and practice as it applies to female adolescents among the Gebusi, a population of some 450 horticulturalists living on the East Strickland Plain in the Nomad district of the Western Province, Papua New Guinea.[2] Unlike most of the contributions in this volume, the present chapter does not have a "then and now" comparative base. This is not because Gebusi understanding and practice governing the transition from child to adult status are immune to historical processes. I assume that the Gebusi have always been and will continue to be both creators of and respondents to change, the antecedents of which lie both within and outside their own ethnically defined universe. A comparative historical approach to adolescence among the Gebusi is limited by the fact that, in the early 1980s, the Gebusi were still creating, interpreting, and enacting their lives within a primarily indigenous sociocultural framework. Except for the introduction of steel tools and a significant reduction of inter- and intra-group homicides, twenty years of highly sporadic exposure to "the outside world" produced few profound changes in the way the Gebusi thought about or lived their lives. In 1980–1982, cash cropping and missionization were absent. Participation in formal education and wage labor, within and outside the Nomad area, had been sporadic, brief, and available to only a few Gebusi. Opportunities to earn cash were limited and there were no stores within Gebusi territory in which to spend earnings.[3] Not dependent on store-bought food, the Gebusi diet remained the product of indigenous subsistence techniques, a combination of nonintensive horticulture supplemented by hunting and gathering.

For the Gebusi the primary effect of "contact" was a slightly less violent world in which they were left largely to themselves to pursue life along indigenous lines of thought and action.[4] In the early 1980s, this way of life encompassed a kin-based universe in which agnation was the basis for clan identity, and married male siblings formed core residential units which often included close matrikin and affines. Residential movement was fluid between garden sites and multiclan longhouse settlements, with longhouse sites changing every four to five years. Autonomy and self-sufficiency characterized both families and longhouse settlements. At the suprafamilial level, secular political leadership was absent, with neither big men nor councils of elders. Marriage was, ideally, constructed through the reciprocal exchange of sisters between men of different clans, though asymmetrical romantic unions were nevertheless quite common and subject to dispute. Transfer of wealth to compensate for the loss of persons through death or marriage was not practiced. However, cooked food was likely to be given as a gesture of goodwill and as an acknowledgment of grief.

In 1980–1982, the Gebusi were proud of their ritual enactments, their ability to communicate with the spirit world, and their ability to move emotionally "all who see them" in the upper, lower, and human worlds. They were avid sponsors and participants in séances, male initiations, and intercommunity feasts. Séances were held once every eleven days on the average, and feasts were attended about once a month. The construction of male bisexuality was central to Gebusi beliefs concerning social harmony and reproduction. Accordingly, men's homosexual as well as heterosexual relationships figured prominently in ritual contexts and emerged as significant aspects of personal relationships as well. Secondary to and derivative of the high esteem accorded male bisexuality, female heterosexuality was also lauded in ritual contexts. The positive regard for female sexuality was a critical feature in the way personal relationships were negotiated.

My analysis of Gebusi female adolescence will focus on tensions concerning the question of when female adolescence begins and ends. I regard these tensions as generated by and internal to indigenous sociocultural forms of representation, evaluation, and action. Methodologically, the analysis examines three discourses on the subject of female adolescence: (1) within the community of adult women, (2) within male-exclusive contexts, and (3) between men and women.

I shall begin by examining the discourse on female adolescence as adult women identify its commencement and completion and as they contextualize the significance of this period within larger gender constructs.[5] I will then examine how these understandings inform the relationship between adult women and "emerging women" (oifor elem). After sketching the salient elements pertaining to "emerging womanhood," "true womanhood," (oifor deb) and "manhood" (arl deb), I will then look at women's knowledge of practice as it appears to them in their own memories of adolescence, in ritual contexts, and in the formation of marriage. My aim includes but is not limited to rendering Gebusi women's constructs of female adolescence. Women, like all social actors, construct their understandings and interpret their experiences in relation to social others. Gebusi women's knowledge of female adolescence entails a reflexive interpretation of men's enactments and pronouncements. The present analysis therefore entails listening to men's voices as well as women's as part of an ongoing metacultural conversation. In this conversation, it is possible to discern areas of agreement, unequivocal adherence, ambivalence, and distrust concerning female adolescence.

FEMALE ADOLESCENCE: *OIFOR ELEM*

The Gebusi distinguish two broad age categories for all females beyond childhood: young women *(oifor)* and old women *(kogwasiop)*. Within the age/gender category of young woman, the most salient distinction is between "emerging young women" *(oifor elem)* and "true young women" *(oifor deb)*.[6] The root morpheme of *elem* means "to happen, to come into being as the result of transformative processes, to emerge." More specifically, *oifor elem* refers to a developmental phase attributed to females who are approximately between the ages of twelve to fifteen years, in which the transition from childhood to womanhood has begun but is not yet complete. *Oifor elem* (emerging young women) are set off from *oifor deb* (true or real young women) by visual assessment of breast size. Females whose breasts are "small but growing" are referred to as emerging women. True young womanhood is attained only when a "full and large breast" has developed. Most women are referred to as true young women by the age of sixteen and are said to remain in this age category until they have nursed two children, by which time breast shape is said to have changed again. Men as well as women recognize breast development as the key feature signaling the commencement of female adolescence. Neither menarche nor menopause emerges as a salient element in identifying female age categories.

Unlike men, whose sexual status is clearly celebrated in a major rite of passage that marks their entrance into adulthood, women have no social rites to mark their transition from immature to mature sexual persons. There is no female initiation, gift exchange, special clothing, adornment, scarification, songs, dances, seclusion, or the like that marks either the commencement or completion of female adolescence.[7] In the absence of such transition markers, there exists only the subjective visual assessments of breast development and a myriad of "little conversations" *(taw gamihe)* on the age status of individual females, conversations that also involve commentary on larger issues pertaining to sexuality, adulthood, and gender. At one level, there is agreement between men and women on how these elements inform the cultural category of emerging womanhood. Though adult women voice unequivocal support for such understandings, they portray men's position as ambivalent. This leads women to be uncertain and, ultimately, distrustful of men's commitment to a moral engagement with female adolescents.

WOMANHOOD EMERGING: THE NEED TO PROTECT

When a young girl's breasts first show signs of development, there is much gossip among the adult women of a longhouse community which communicates excitement, admiration, and nostalgia. Entrance into this phase of the female life cycle is said to be "very good" *(honui deb)*, making young adolescent females "very beautiful" *(do debe da)*. However, within the female community these attitudes are concealed carefully from virtually all males over the age of seven. Upon the approach of boys or men, women stopped their conversations about emerging womanhood in midsentence. Afterward I was told that, "Men are no good" *(arl honui mwi da)*, that thoughts of sex turn men's "heads upside down" *(ulkip helo fumda)*, and that men, indeed, had many sexual thoughts toward adolescent females.[8] Not only was direct sexual engagement with emerging women condemned, but public sexual joking, private teasing, and covert sexual propositions were disparaged also. Indeed, any social interaction perceived as compromising an adolescent girl's ability to refuse the sexual advances of a man was frowned upon.

Adult kinswomen, especially mothers, adopt a strong protective relationship toward Gebusi adolescent girls in regard to male sexual conduct, and girls entering puberty appear to appreciate rather than resist this relationship. The protective stance is, in part, generated by the contrastive elements through which Gebusi women understand and articulate manhood and emerging womanhood. When asked about their views, women said that emerging women are "not yet grown" *(giskawa he awf)* and scared *(abwida)* of sex because their knowledge of sex is small *(gamihe towe)*. They say that emerging women will become strong *(suskay de da)* in sexual matters only after they have become "true young women" *(oifor deb)*. Although *suskay* may be glossed as "muscle," its meaning extends well beyond the concept of biological strength. *Suskay* refers to an attribute of mind as well, namely, that which enables persons to conduct themselves in a powerful manner (for example, confident, bold, audacious, and so on).[9] In regard to sexual matters, emerging women are judged "not strong" *(suskay mui da)* in both mind (lacking in knowledge and confidence) and body (physically immature).

In contrast, women say that "all men" have a powerful sexual longing for women, and that men spend "a great amount of time" thinking of sex with women. Women also perceive men as being eager and unafraid *(abu he)* in pursuing heterosexual relationships. In turn, attributions of drive and confidence are linked to the belief that men have a "great understanding" *(gau towe)* of sex, such sexual knowledge being taboo or secret *(toym)* and highly inappropriate for women to discuss *(tau wala tu)*, especially in public contexts.

This belief appears self-validating in the enactment of spirit séances. Typically, participation in séances is exclusively male.[10] Gebusi men demonstrate the attributes of great sexual desire, knowledge, and strength through the aesthetics of séance singing and through their sexual repartee and behavioral displays in between songs. The power of men's sexual longing and sexual appeal is said to attract spirit women to the séance. Both men and women believe that spirit women must participate in the séances in order to communicate vital and otherwise inaccessible information. Although ordinary Gebusi women may not participate actively in the séances, they hear the entire proceedings through a thin sago leaf wall that separates their sleeping quarters from the room where the séances are performed. Typically, a séance includes more than one hundred narrative songs detailing the taunting and erotic adventures of the spirit women. In between these songs, men conduct highly salacious exchanges both with spirit women and with each other. Each eight- to nine-hour séance is, in effect, a discourse that validates the sexual vigor and sexual knowledge attributed to Gebusi men.

Not only do the attributes of confidence, special knowledge, and great desire weigh heavily in women's understanding of male sexuality, so does superior physical strength. The paired contrast most frequently cited by women to distinguish male from female is, "Men are strong (muscular); women are not!" *(Arl suskay de da; ulia suskay mwi da)*. In sum, women see men as both mentally predisposed and physically capable of exerting their will on women in sexual matters.

Gebusi women respond to this construct of manhood selectively. The prevailing opinion is that the appropriateness of being alone with a man (nonkin) varies with the age and marital status of the woman. While being alone with a marriageable man is an acceptable facet of courtship for an unmarried, young, adult woman *(oifor deb)*, the same is not appropriate for emerging women *(oifor elem)*. The disadvantaged terms with which female adolescent sexuality is portrayed (fear, inexperience, physical immaturity) relative to the superior attributes of male sexuality (confidence, knowledge, physical strength) easily lend themselves to predator-prey metaphors. Ever-married women warn that young, unmarried men, regardless of initiation status, are especially inclined to approach female adolescents at unguarded moments, scaring them with "sex talk." Such encounters are said to occur when an *oifor elem* is alone (for example, fetching water just outside the settlement) or in the company of only one other woman (for example, foraging in the forest or processing sago by a stream).

Although Gebusi women relish memories of first sexual relationships forged when they were true young women, they recall, with adamant disapproval, incidents in which young men disclosed a sexual interest in them during adolescence. Such stories point to a tension in Gebusi thought concerning the perception of female sexual status and its relationship to the emergence of womanhood. Although Gebusi men as well as women agree on the moral and conceptual elements that distinguish emerging women from true women, such consensus is belied by deeper tensions, manifest in practice, that appear, to Gebusi women, to undermine the *oifor elem/oifor deb* distinction. These practices point to an ambivalence in the way men view *oifor elem*. From a woman's perspective, this ambivalence makes men's commitment to proper behavior toward emerging women uncertain and undependable.

To understand why women are concerned with the distinction between emerging and emergent young women, one must understand the cultural value placed on true young womanhood. In the next section, I shall examine why differences in the construction of female adolescence and young womanhood are critical to attempts by Gebusi women to gain control over the sexuality for which they are acclaimed.

FEMALE SEXUALITY, AGE, AND CHOICE

Among the Gebusi, both men and women conceptualize the interval between birth and death as a process of growth, florescence, and decline.[11] Within this trajectory, the life stage of true young womanhood *(oifor deb)* represents the apotheosis of the female life cycle. The praise which true young womanhood elicits from men and women alike is cast in sexual terms. *Oifor deb* are attributed with and admired for a host of physical characteristics that set the standard for female beauty and sexual appeal. No other aspect of womanhood garners as much acclaim or attention. This sexualized understanding of womanhood is extolled in women's song, dance, and narrative as well as in men's séances.[12] Although genderized idioms of sexuality cast men in a superior position regarding confidence and sexual longing, women use these very same attributes to discern stages in their own sexual development, and these attributes make the emerging/emergent distinction so meaningful.

During the first few years of adulthood, the widely shared expectation is that all women, to varying degrees, become "strong" *(suskay de da)* in sexual longing. Depending on context, the strength with which women negotiate their own sexual relationships may be glossed as confidence, boldness, audaciousness, and courage. Power *("fawa")*[13] was the most frequent synonym given for strength *(suskay)*. Adult women who are not afraid to initiate sexual encounters with men, particularly illicit (nonmarital) sexual encounters, are said to be strong/ powerful. Women who lead the female chorus at all-night feasts, singing in a clear, evocative manner, are also said to be "strong" *(suskay)*, to "have power" *(fawa dasum)*. One woman described her husband's sister as strong/courageous because she never showed fear during her month-long incarceration in the subdistrict jail for an adultery conviction. The women who rendered these judgments communicated an unmistakable sense of pride and admiration for the women who acted in a *suskay*, or powerful, manner. In the lexicon of personhood, then, women are recognized as capable of acting with strength and courage while, in the lexicon of gender, the *suskay* attribute is strictly a masculine quality unequivocally opposed to femaleness (cf. M. Strathern 1981).

While emerging women are said to be "afraid," "not grown," and without "great sexual longing," both men and women regard true young womanhood not only as the period in which women become "bold and confident" but also as the period in which they develop "great sexual longing" *(fawfaw gau de da)* which causes their "heads to turn upside down." It is a time when women mirror, in female form, the sexual appeal, confidence, and longing of their ideal sexual partners, the *wa gisay:* men who are at the peak of the male life cycle, a period celebrated for masculine forms of strength, beauty, and sexuality.[14] In behavioral terms, true young womanhood is the life stage in which women attain the ability to negotiate their own sexual relationships with men. In fact, never-married, true young women do exhibit a high degree of autonomy in sexual relationships. True young women are renowned for their flirtatious behavior, for their enjoyment of sexual joking, for planning seductions, and for inquiring about and initiating sexual relations with men. Even true young women who describe their own behavior as shy demonstrate an ability to reject or encourage romantic relationships according to their own preference, even when it entails acting against the wishes of close kin.

Gebusi women do not object to the emphasis placed on sexuality in defining true young womanhood. Nor do they negatively value male sexuality. Typically, Gebusi women regard sexuality as a positive force in the formation of marriage—as long as such relationships are based on reciprocal sexual longing. What adult women oppose are practices that assume or attribute sexual longing, confidence, and knowledge to not-yet-emergent women. Given the important cultural linkage between true young womanhood and the acclaim accorded female sexuality, what adult women "protect" adolescent females from are the practices of men who prey upon the (culturally constituted) inability of female adolescents to negotiate their own sexual relationships. In comparative terms, true young women may be thought of as having relative parity with true young men in the development of sexual relationships, while disparity marks the relationship between adult men and emerging women. From a political perspective, women's autonomy (choice) in the development of sexual relationships is at issue in the *oifor elem/oifor deb* distinction.

Without rites of sexual transition for Gebusi women (or other symbolic forms marking their sexual status), there exists only a gradual continuum of female development against which understandings of age and sexuality must be negotiated on an individual basis. Countervailing practices push and pull at (affirm, challenge, deny) the way age and female sexuality are configured. In certain contexts, male practices cast doubt on conventional cultural understandings about when it is morally appropriate to regard females as mature sexual persons. Specifically, women's distrust of men's commitment to the *oifor elem/ oifor deb* distinction and women's subsequent protective behavior toward adolescent females are informed by (1) a cautionary lore based on specific incidents that women remember as salient in their own adolescence, (2) women's understanding of the sexual symbolism embedded in the discourse of men's séances, and (3) women's knowledge of child and adolescent betrothals, particularly as they configure this practice against the sexual meaning of marriage.

PERSONAL HISTORIES

Yob,[15] a married woman in her late twenties, spontaneously related the following story from her own adolescence, exemplifying the setting in which men sexually proposition emerging women, as well as the physical struggle, emotional experience, and social response that may ensue.

When I was unmarried, and my breasts were only just beginning to point, I was on a forest path with Mebay looking for the *kafis* plant near Sosbi.[16] Baya, a young unmarried man, came up on the trail. He was carrying his bow and arrows and surprised us. He asked where we were going. My breath flew out of me! Baya had strong muscles. He took my arm. I said, "No! Don't take my arm! I don't want to fight/struggle/have sex *(buala)*[17] with you." And I began to hit him with [the blunt side of] my bush knife.

[Yob lowers her voice] Baya is so ugly! He has bug eyes, a big nose and a fat stomach! [She uses her hands and face to mockingly imitate Baya's appearance and then breaks into a hearty laughter]

I said to him, "You're too old! I'm too young! We're not the same. You live there. And I will live here." Inside my mind I knew he was pleased at first because he thought he was going to claim me. I was afraid and ran away. I forgot my net bag.

Baya took the net bag and left with it. He went back to his house where his mother, Auled, lived.[18] He hung up the net bag there [at Sosbi]. Mebay and I went to Sosbi. Mebay spoke to her mother [Auled] and explained what had happened. She said that Baya had sex on his mind and that he was longing for Yob. Auled was extremely angry. Baya heard his mother's anger and fled the house. I took my net bag and left scared for Wasiobi where Luwob [a classificatory father's sister's daughter to Yob] invited me to sleep [spend the night]. I was really *kawsida* [upset, morally indignant, outraged].

This was not the only occasion in which a young unmarried man declared a sexual interest in Yob during her early adolescence. She and another adolescent friend, a little older than herself, were processing sago by themselves when Duwegaw, who was described as a handsome, strong, unmarried man, approached them and joked that he would really like to have sex with one of them. Yob said that she and her female companion "ran scared" *(bobgoi dida)* to their settlement where Lobas, a classificatory father's sister's son to Yob, intervened on the girls' behalf. Citing the fact that the girls' breasts "were not yet fully grown," he argued that it would not be right for either of them to marry at that time, even though Duwegaw was suggesting a sister exchange.

Almost all the women I talked to recounted similar incidents, coming from past personal experience or the life histories of other women. The recurring theme was that emerging women experience some form of pressure to engage in sex prior to attaining emotional or physical maturity. These biographical vignettes of early adolescence are part of a larger corpus of stories which describe how adult women, regardless of marital status, are also subject to various forms of pressure to engage in nonmarital sex. Again, the disquieting element is the narrator's assessment that Gebusi women are, for reasons particular to each incident, at a disadvantage in refusing such offers. The retelling of these incidents constitutes a cautionary lore, circulated among women, that informs standards of risk and propriety regarding male and female interaction. Such lore also constitutes a "knowledge of practice" that women interpret as consistent with the many boasts of sexual conquest made by men during séances, intercommunity feasts, and casual evening conversation.

Although adult women condemned covert declarations of sexual interest in emerging women, they recalled no incidents which concluded with a female adolescent forced or intimidated into having sexual relations. Indeed, out of fifty-two incidents of illicit sex in which the age categories of the participants were ascertained, none involved emerging women. The drama in these recollections is typically resolved when the young woman runs to the safety of kin.

This observation leads to a number of specific questions which deal implicitly with the relationship between event and meaning, or in this case, between nonevent and the interpretation of risk. First, what sociocultural considerations are likely to constrain the behavior of young Gebusi men such that pursuit of sexual relations with adolescent females does not result in sexual intercourse? Second, if sexual conquest of adolescent females is not the aim of such pursuits, what do young men gain by acting "as if" it is? Finally, if adolescent females are not, in fact, subjected to unwanted sexual relations, why do adult women feel compelled to protect them?

To address the first question, there are a number of considerations that influence young men to let *oifor elem* escape. First, should an uninitiated man engage in heterosexual relations, he risks losing the support of kin and community necessary for his initiation. Second, regardless of a man's initiation or marital status, sexual engagement with an emerging woman is likely to raise the ire of her close kin and increase the risk of a violent confrontation with them. While men claim frequently that illicit sex is the result of female seduction, such an argument is less persuasive when leveled at females in early adolescence. Third, young men do endorse the positive value placed on reciprocal heterosexual long-ing. However, young unmarried men are likely to have had little experience in negotiating such relationships. Communications of sexual interest or intent in isolated contexts to "not grown" women who are themselves likely to run away is a relatively safe way for young men to validate a different set of cultural un-derstandings in which men's "great sexual longing," "strength," and "confidence" are judged superior to women's. In spirit séances, at all-night feasts, and in pri-vate settings as well, conversations frequently refer to women's "shyness/fear" as both an amusing and exciting aspect of the way heterosexual relationships de-velop. Covert sexual propositions to adolescent females may be little more than an "amusing" way of confirming this understanding by young men whose confidence in sexual relationships may not be as great as cultural understand-ings make them out to be.

Gebusi women, on the other hand, are not amused. In early adolescence they are frightened, and as adult women, in a protective relation to emerging women, they are angered. Adult women remember themselves as escaping—not as being allowed to escape—from the sexual advances of young men. Adult women have other reasons as well to maintain disapproval of behavior that pre-sumes *oifor elem* to be sexually mature. First, although uninitiated men put their initiation into jeopardy by engaging in heterosexual intercourse, it is common for one or two young men from each initiation set to do so anyway. Although their partners are typically widows, sometimes young, never-married women and, occasionally, married, adult women do not assume that young men will re-main heterosexually celibate prior to initiation.[19] Keenly aware of this, adult women are not happy when young men, initiated or uninitiated, make sexual offers to adolescent females. Second, even though such behavior is likely to arouse community ire, visual assessment determines who is and is not in the *oifor elem* age category. This means that there may not be community consensus on the age category of the adolescent woman in question. Accordingly, assess-ments of her role, intentions, and responsibility may vary, necessitating stronger advocacy by concerned adult women.

Finally, although mutual sexual attraction is promoted widely in ritual con-texts and appears to be a significant understanding in the way heterosexual rela-tionships are negotiated, this construct of relative, age-based parity stands in an ambiguous relation to the more encompassing understandings of gender dis-parity in which men are attributed with superior strength, desire, and confidence in sexual matters. Young Gebusi men, having attended a hundred or more séances from early childhood on,[20] continue to be exposed to the taunting erotic images of spirit women. In response, séance participants shout, stamp the floorboards, shake the house posts, shoot arrows into the roof, and make boast-ful comments, all of which are intended to demonstrate the great strength of their sexual longing and capabilities. Proclamations of sexual conquest abound, sometimes employing images of violent force. In addition to the spirit séances, the initiation of young men is a celebration of manhood cast in sexual understandings. At no other time in the male life cycle are men as renowned for the attributes of strength and sexual appeal, drive and potency. Yet the ideal of voluntary heterosexual relationships based on mutual sexual longing is possible only with women who have attained adulthood. Covert communications of sexual interest by young, unmarried men, renowned for their sexual vitality, to adolescent females who are not, casts doubt on their commitment to the ideal of mutual sexual longing.

Gebusi women are aware of the ambivalence in men's behavior concerning the sexual status of female adolescents. They know that the same kinsman who affirms the sexual immaturity of an emerging woman on one occasion may, in another context, deny or test this understanding with a nonkin *oifor elem.* Women do know that men endorse a moral view regarding female sexual immaturity during adolescence. And yet they also know that these same men, in the collective setting of a séance, will, on occasion, cast a pubertal female in the role of spirit woman, the quintessential representation of adult female sexuality.

AGE, FEMALE SEXUALITY, AND THE COLLECTIVE MALE IMAGINATION

One of the mothers in our settlement had good reason to be concerned about her daughter's emerging sexual status. In the ritual context of an extremely bawdy, all-male séance, her daughter, Manwi, had become the object of intense sexual fantasy.

The séance took place in a another settlement about an hour's walk from where Manwi lived. Although neither Manwi nor the four women in her household heard the séance, the women living in the spirit medium's household did. From them came news of Manwi's "visit" to the all-male séance. There was little Manwi's widowed mother, her mother's sister, or the wives of her two mother's brothers could do except shake their heads, frown, and quietly express their disapproval of "men's talk."

Manwi's kinswomen, like all Gebusi women, had heard séance discourse and humor since childhood. Normally, the female voices who speak through the body of a male spirit medium are understood to be those of young spirit women *(todi ulia).*[21] However, on occasion, the soul *(fin)* of a living, human female *(ulia deb)* is portrayed as leaving its body during sleep and visiting a séance to talk and joke about sex with male participants. As a product of collective male imagination, these Gebusi females are, in effect, "spirit womanized"—reconstructed in the image of spirit women for the duration of the séance. While Gebusi women normally enjoy séance representations of female sexuality, I heard a flurry of condemnatory remarks when Manwi was inducted into the ranks of the spirit women. "Men are despicable! *[towa mwi da],*" "Men's sex joking is no good!" was the response to a séance whose humor and symbolism hit uncomfortably close to the real fears and protective feelings of adult women.

Manwi's mother's two brothers, both married and both in their twenties, attended the séance in which Manwi appeared.[22] Although one of these men dutifully promised to crush the chest of a fellow participant who threatened to have sex with (the séance persona of) Manwi, both men did so in a joking manner, with the stylized "Yei" concluding the interchange, each man thus disconfirming the intent to carry out his threat. Although Manwi's mother's brothers did not directly sex joke with her, they did sex joke with the other men in the séance frequently. They in no way put a damper on the raucous, lustful boasting that was directed at their sister's thirteen-year-old daughter. Manwi was in a *sawfu* relationship to a majority of the men attending the séance; that is, she was a nonkinswoman and, therefore, a potential sexual/marriage partner in real life.[23] Thus, her "presence" at the séance added to the extraordinary energy and enthusiasm displayed in the men's sexual repartee with her. It must be kept in mind that Manwi's remarks were entirely authored by the spirit medium, not by the real Manwi.

FEMALE ADOLESCENCE: THE LARGER CONTEXT

Before reviewing selected texts from the séance, it should be noted that the question of when emerging women become true women is itself embedded in larger issues and understandings pertaining to the changing nature of male sexuality and the relationship of heterosexual intimacy to gender. The development of and transitions to homosexual, bisexual, and heterosexual orientations over the male life cycle are involved deeply in the changing, sometimes ambivalent, regard with which men hold female sexuality. Although séances promote a positive ("exciting") view of female sexuality which affirms the value of heterosexual relations, the articulation of male and female in sexual idioms poses problems for the maintenance of gender distinctions.[24] Heterosexual relations are thought to deplete Gebusi men of that which endows masculinity with its superior strength and vitality: semen. Accordingly, there are many restrictions placed on heterosexual intercourse over the male life cycle (cf. Kelly 1976). Both a husband and wife are enjoined from heterosexual relations for at least the twelve to eighteen months encompassing the pre- and post-partum period. Incest taboos are extended to a wide range of classificatory kin. There is a ban on heterosexual intercourse prior to battle, raids, and hunting in addition to a month-long ban prior to the annual fish kill. There is a strict injunction on sex during mortuary and divinatory proceedings lest one be accused of sorcery. There is also a ban on sex for first-time widows, extending over a two- to three-year mourning period. Finally, there is an injunction against heterosexual relations for men until they are initiated, which is usually in their early twenties.

Competing against these injunctions on heterosexual congress is the young men's frequent participation in séances, communal events which intensively promote a pleasurable view of heterosexual relations and validate men's understanding that women are both desirable yet "out of reach." The spirit woman is the key symbolic representation of the sexually alluring female who, due to her incorporeality, is literally untouchable. The significant elements through which Gebusi understand female adolescence—the onset of sexual maturation, symbolized by breast development, in conjunction with the moral proscription against heterosexual union with adolescent females—creates for men a situation analogous to that of the spirit woman in which female sexuality is understood as erotic but inaccessible. Thus, while Manwi's adolescence makes her an excellent candidate for spirit womanhood, the issues posed by her age and sexual status are not unique when considered in the broader context of how Gebusi articulate gender and sexual practice.

The following quotes, excerpted from a séance which was recorded, translated, and transcribed by Knauft in 1981,[25] leave little doubt that the men of Gasumi village were capable of viewing Manwi as a highly erotic figure. What emerges as salient, however, is the ambivalence with which séance participants view her emerging sexuality. This ambivalence is represented in two sets of contrasting song images: one in which Manwi is not old enough, physically or emotionally, for sexual engagement; the second in which she is. These contradictory representations appear throughout the text.

Not only is Manwi's sexual status represented in contradictory images; ambivalence also marks the responses of the séance participants to their representation of Manwi. Sometimes they express outright rejection of Manwi as a suitable sexual partner, in preference for homosexual relations with each other. At other points in the séance, the men in the audience make great displays of their sexual passion for Manwi. Still, at other times, the response oscillates and encompasses both.

The age of the men who participated in the séance ranged from approximately age twelve to thirty-two, that is, males up to ten years on either side of their initiation. The spirit medium was a man in his early forties and the participants included never-married men, married men, and one widower. The most demonstrative participants were the recently initiated men of our settlement and the widower.

EMERGING OR EMERGENT? TWO IMAGES OF MANWI

In many songs, the spirit of Manwi, as voiced by the spirit medium, describes herself as "scared/embarrassed" *(abwida)* by sexual overtures from spirit men and séance singers alike. She repeatedly refuses their offers of sex. In the following lines, from song 25, she cites physical immaturity as the reason for her refusal.

Manwi:

My breast eyes [nipples] are not big and cannot be eaten.

A common sex-as-food metaphor in which sexual organs are "edible," implying a state of sexual arousal or maturity.

I don't want to [have sex].
My chest has not gotten big.

Elsewhere, in song 49, she says:

Breast has not come [developed] yet ... waistline is absent.

Image: still has a child's figure.

And again in song 55:

My breast has not come yet [developed] so I can not laugh [joke sexually] with you.

A few weeks later, a young man assisting Knauft with the translation of this séance confirmed that "when Manwi's breasts and vagina become big she will want to have sex but," he concluded, "this is yet to happen."

In contrast to the above portrayal of sexual immaturity, the predominant séance image of Manwi is that of a sexually active "true young woman" who is "lovesick" *(fayi wasi fala,* song 66).[26] She is represented as a female who is capable of sexual longing and of arousing sexual desire in men. She is seen as sexually assertive ("Come shoot me with your arrow [penis]" [song 69]), seductive ("My breasts sway in the water" [song 51]), and as wanting sex outside of marriage ("Your skin got tired [reference to postcoital relaxation] and you will leave. I don't want to marry you ... eyes want sex again" [song 51]).

In the following passage from song 53, Manwi's spirit asserts her sexual maturity metaphorically and alludes to a sexual encounter with an unnamed spirit man *(todi arl).*

Manwi to spirit man:
Breast is like a Dulo tree.   Metaphoric reference to large
Now we-two will [sex] play.   breast shape.

Spirit man to Manwi:
You are able to talk like that!   You (Manwi) are old enough to
Now we-two will wrestle/have   make a sexual proposition.
sex *(buala)*.[27]

Audience: Responds by yelling.

Manwi to spirit man:
You are done here. It [sex]   Rapids and white water: metaphors
is finished. I made your   for male orgasm.
white water rush [forth].

I am embarrassed/scared to
see you.
I was embarrassed/scared of
your long hardness [erection].

Audience: Lots of yelling throughout above three lines.

Manwi:
I ate but did not give you any.   Reference to heterosexual inter-
                                               course as an unreciprocated
                                               substance transmission, male to
                                               female. Eating refers to the general
                                               idea of incorporating substance
                                               (here sexual) into the body.[28]

Lodya (newly initiated, unmarried séance participant):
[Manwi's] vagina really has
gotten big!

In many songs, the audience responds to the heterosexual imagery surrounding Manwi with energetic displays of sexual desire for her. The following
two songs and subsequent audience response are excellent examples.

In song 51 below, Manwi's spirit is portrayed as having successfully seduced
her mother's brother. The song narrative describes Manwi swimming naked, her

eyes "turning big" with sexual desire, engaging in sex but refusing marriage, and enticing her mother's brother with still more sexual play. The audience conversation immediately following the song asserts that the men became so aroused by these images that they shook the house posts (behavior confirmed by Knauft, who attended the séance). There is an atmosphere of intense excitement and much sexual joking. In this context one man jokes about coming to orgasm as a result of listening to "talk of Manwi." This conversation is presented below.

Manwi:
Pig friend! my breast! jumped . . . startled!

"Pig-friend" is a term of endearment for a lover with whom she has shared pork. This lover, reaching for Manwi's breast, startles her.

Somiya (newly initiated, unmarried participant):
Vagina penetrate! It's become big!

Double reference: to breast in previous line and a joking reference to own penis.

Sawa (uninitiated man):
Your pubic hair has become like cassowary feathers [full, mature]. Is your bone hard? shaking?

Are you reaching orgasm?

Somiya:
The spirit (Manwi) has gone from the *du dugaw* tree. My hardness [erection] is gone.

The *du dugaw* tree is where the spirit women, in bird form, frequently sit when they join a séance.

Lodya:
The bird shelter up there was shaken down.

In bird form, spirit women are also said to sit on top of the center house post. The meaning here is that the men have shaken the house post (also a phallic symbol) so much that the spirit woman, Manwi, has flown off.

Somiya:
You were talking of Manwi and my bone (penis) got hard/shaky.

Lodya:
She went back to her house.

In songs 71 and 72 the séance participants respond to images depicting Manwi in various sexual situations with the spirit of a recently deceased initiate. Again, there is much enthusiastic yelling and rocking of the longhouse. These raucous displays of sexual desire continue in song 73:

Unknown spirit:
[Someone] comes across the Kum river. It's coming up.

Translator explains that Manwi's skirt floats up around her thighs, revealing her vagina.

Lodya:
[Yells in an intense display of excitement and shouts to Manwi]
Friend! . . .

Manwi to Lodya:
Small bag, you keep it.

Manwi refuses offer of marriage gift, implying that she will just joke and have sex without marriage.

Audience response: much stomping on the longhouse floor

Lodya (to Manwi):
Friend, come with me!

Manwi (to Lodya):
Are you telling me to come with you here? Or will I have to entice you?

Unlike the above, not all séance images of Manwi inspire acceptance of her as a sexual partner. The following example deals directly with the men's rejection of Manwi and their preference for homosexual relationships. The young man who interpreted song 69 for Knauft said that the line "scared of the child and left" meant that "the men [at the séance] were scared of the woman-child [Manwi] and left the longhouse to have sex with each other." Manwi's spirit reassures the singers that "it's all right" that they had sex with each other instead of her. To this, a newly initiated, recently married man named Iwah retorts, "I'd rather have sex with Lodya!" (Iwah's well-known homosexual partner). Knauft reports (pers. comm.) that séance participants indeed departed frequently for homosexual liaisons outside the longhouse during this particular séance.

In song 49, Manwi's persona has the same effect, galvanizing a range of homosexual/homosocial camaraderie among audience members. In the song, Manwi's spirit asks her mother's brother attending the séance to "tell your friends" (his fellow séance singers) that she is "not ready to eat," that is, she is sexually immature. In the next line, she reverses herself and says she will go with them for sex if they ask her secretly. This triggers an extraordinary amount of stomping, yelling, joking, and running around by the singers. Within the din, the following repartee was recorded.

Audience:
Get out of the way! Get out of the
way! [repeated many times amidst
much yelling and foot stomping]

Sawa (spoken coquettishly to Somiya):

Initiation mate!	Sawa and Somiya are members
Egret child!	of the same initiation set. Egret:
	clan name of Somiya.

Somiya:

I want a young sago just	Eating a sago shoot is a fellatio
becoming edible!	metaphor.

Lodya:

The W-clan child[29] might	"W-clan" child refers to Lodya's
leave the house [for sex].	homosexual lover, Iwah.

Somiya:

He's gone! [lets out a yell]	Confirms that Iwah has gone
	outside to have sex with one of
	the other séance participants.

Lodya:

W-clan child has laid down	The *igamor* is a tree, the stem
an *igamor*.	of which is said to resemble a
	penis. The metaphor's meaning
	was carefully explained to Knauft
	by a number of adult men.

Sawa:
You will see it?   Referring to an *igamor*, i.e., penis.
Is it open [uncovered]?

Noraw (newly initiated, unmarried):
It's all right. Don't be
stingy [with your genitals].

Sawa:
One of them [a testicle] is covered
up but the other one is open to be
looked at.

Noraw:
I'll take it!

Finally, songs containing sexual imagery are often followed by comments from séance participants that slip back and forth between assertions of both heterosexual and homosexual preference. At the end of song 49, Manwi's spirit says that she is leaving. The responses of three audience members, Sawa, Somiya, and Lodya, are an amalgam of alternating homo- and heterosexual preference. All three men were recently initiated; all were still unmarried.

Manwi:
Friends (singers), we all stayed
together. I'm leaving now.

Somiya (to Manwi):
Friend, I'll grab you!   Force you to stay for more sex/joking.

Manwi:
Sad longing or not, mother's   Regardless of whether you will
brother, I'm going now.   miss me, I'm leaving now.

Audience response: Much yelling

Somiya (jokingly):
My bone is shaking!   reference: nearing orgasm

Sawa (to Somiya jokingly):
I'll hold it and see [if you're   Knauft notes that this is verbal
telling the truth]. Mother's vagina!   joking only.
It is as hard as a squirming fish tail!

Sawa and Somiya:
Yei!

Confirms the joking nature of the previous verbal exchange.

Lodya:
My arm was heavy but now it's light. I'd like to shoot a bow [have sex]. I'll shoot you with my *warsok* [bamboo-tipped arrow].

The arrow head of the *warsok* is broad, more phallic in shape than other arrows used by the Gebusi. Such aggressive metaphors usually refer to heterosexual relations

Somiya (in a high, joking tone):
You shoot me and I'll cut off the arrow tip.

Threatens to castrate Lodya if he penetrates him sexually.

Sawa:
And I'll burn you in the back!

I.e., because of unfulfilled sexual longing. Reference here is to ritual burning of the dancer at all-night feasts for arousing great sorrowful longing among audience members. This practice, central to the Kaluli *gisaro* performance (Schieffelin 1976), is known but only rarely practiced among Gebusi.

You name the woman and I'll have sex with her!

This statement would indicate that the *warsok*/penetration metaphor refers to heterosexual penetration which Sawa rejects as appropriate homosexual activity but endorses, with boastful confidence, in regard to women. Gebusi homosexual relations entail masturbation and fellatio, but not anal intercourse

Opposing views on the sexual nature of early female adolescence are never resolved in this séance; contradictory representations of Manwi's spirit reflect the ambivalence of the men who have created this *dramatis persona*. This same ambivalence surfaced again, a few weeks later, during a translation session in which Knauft worked outdoors with several men who had attended the Manwi séance. Translating a passage that was particularly lascivious, the men laughed and joked loudly. Nearby, several settlement women, including Manwi and her mother, overheard segments of the tape and shouted inquiries as to the exact nature of the passages. The men suddenly became secretive, putting off the women's questions with a weak attempt at humor, finally shouting that it was none of the women's business, that their work was to continue cutting tall grass at the edge of the settlement. The men's enthusiastic reliving of the séance, the jokes, the laughter, all came to an abrupt end. Quieter, chastened, they returned to the translation process, informing Knauft that they were "embarrassed/afraid" to have the women, Manwi in particular, overhear the tape. They reminded Knauft (and themselves) that, "This is men's knowledge, not for women to hear."

Despite the men's best efforts, the women overheard snippets of the séance tape. This, in combination with prior gossip about the séance, made it easy to deduce what the men were trying to hide. However, there was little the women could do but grumble among themselves. Despite the fact that women know much, if not all, of "men's knowledge," they do not have social rights to publicly comment upon this knowledge. While Gebusi women may acknowledge the existence and attributes of spirit women, they may not respond openly to the sexual content of specific séance songs or the men's repartee.[30] While women find the majority of the séance material enjoyable, they are limited in their ability to communicate dissatisfaction when it arises. Sullen faces, indignant tones, rhetorical questions, terse comments made from a safe distance, may express occasional objections but do not ultimately challenge men's ability to portray female adolescents with the sexual imagery of spirit women. Thus, while women communicate their disapproval, Gebusi men can effectively ignore it.

Not only is there no forum for men and women to respond interactively to the sexual content of séances, the exclusion of women during séances denies them a direct generative role in the most widely praised and esteemed representation of womanhood. Put simply, women's voices are not heard in the contexts that create spirit women. The dispute between men and women over when female adolescence ends and "woman the sexual" begins is but one aspect of this exclusionary relationship.

To sum up thus far, the high value placed on female sexuality appears to be a factor in certain practices which, contrary to cultural understandings, promote or assume a view of adolescent females as persons in their sexual prime. Gebusi women interpret such practices by bringing into play a construct that ascribes innocence and immaturity to adolescent females and a predatory lustful nature to men, particularly young adult men. Women's knowledge of practice, based on incidents experienced in their own adolescence and the portrayal of emerging women in spirit séances inform their protective feelings toward *oifor elem*.

BETROTHAL: CONFIGURING SEXUAL LONGING
AND MATERNAL LONGING

Females enter the Gebusi marriage system as early as age four and as late as age twenty. Parental agreements regarding the future marriage of very young children are understood as secret information and are described as "forbidden talk" *(taw wala tu)* and as "taboo" *(toym)*. It is said that knowledge of these agreements is properly revealed only after the initiation of the groom. Mothers of young children are indeed reluctant to discuss such promissory understandings, particularly since the child who is not supposed to know about them is often playing nearby.

One hesitates to call such agreements "betrothals" as, in practice, they are difficult to enforce with the passage of time. Reluctance to forge or reveal such agreements is underwritten by their vulnerability to events which, over the course of fifteen to twenty years, undermine their binding intent. Mortality, sociopolitical realignments, and the unpredictable spousal preferences of the designated bride and groom can (and do) play havoc with distant parental promises. Of thirty-five ever-married women in the community where I lived, only four (11 percent) reported that their first marriage had been arranged initially while they were children (six to eleven years of age). Six other ever-married women (17 percent) reported that their first marriage had been arranged at the onset of puberty (approximately twelve to fifteen years of age). Of the ten women in these two categories, nine recalled their residential history and feelings during this period. Eight of the nine women represented this period as a time of great sadness and yearning for parents with whom they no longer resided. Although one of the nine women co-resided with both her mother and her future husband during her childhood, her situation was atypical. The other eight women associated early entrance into the marriage system with maternal loss, the degree of poignancy varying with the extent to which other close cognatic kin remained co-resident.

Not only do daughters prefer to live with their parents during childhood and adolescence, parents favor this arrangement as well. Among the Gebusi, the mother-daughter bond is particularly strong in affect and social interaction. Unlike a son who, after the age of four, increasingly looks to his father and other co-resident male kin as primary sources of trust, affection, and knowledge, mothers remain the primary source of these relational qualities for daughters. These aspects of female sociality are facilitated in same-sex work and sleeping arrangements. Long after both parents have died, it is the mother's death which a woman remembers as wrenching and poignant.

At the onset of puberty, daughters begin to visit kinswomen in other settlements for as long as a week without their mothers. The purpose of these visits is to assist female kin in subsistence tasks such as processing sago and clearing brush for gardens. For the mother left behind it is a time for the sentimental, if somewhat overstated lament, "My child! My child! She is growing up! She has left!" It is a time that evokes maternal feelings of *fawfaw dagemda*, "the sad longing for someone who is absent." The temporary absence of an adolescent daughter and her visibly emerging sexuality are also the symbolic harbingers of alteration in the mother-daughter relation, a transformation in which the primacy of the mother-daughter relation will be supplanted by the primacy of the conjugal relation. For the daughter, the poignant feelings of *fawfaw dagemda* will focus increasingly on sexual, not maternal relations (the term covers both relations), and the productive responsibilities of marriage increase the likelihood of residential separation from her mother.

While maternal feelings of "sad longing" are interwoven with pride in a daughter's transformation to womanhood, adult women do not assume generative agency in the processes of female adolescent maturation. Female maturation is thought to "just happen," gradually, without human intervention. As noted, although female adolescent maturation is understood in biological terms, epitomized by breast development, contrastive images of mind *(gor)* and social orientation also figure prominently in the discourse on female age categories. The metamorphosis from emerging to emergent woman is cast as a sexual transformation from shyness to confidence, from fear to yearning. It is a directional change that eventually takes newly emergent women outside the quotidian familiarity of female networks in order to explore and forge relationships with men whose sexuality "fills a true young woman's thoughts with sexual longing so that she thinks of nothing else." It is described as a transformation of mind so powerful that it affects other realms of practice. Sexual longing is said to make true young women unreliable workers because their minds are on men and not on work. Gebusi say that their waistlines are slim because thoughts of men make them lose their longing for food. They also say that young women "do not hear" their mothers' voices because "they think only of men." The transformation of girls into women is, indeed, viewed as a far-reaching affective and social reorientation.

The transformation of girls into women contrasts with that of boys into men insofar as male development, in mind and body, is seen as the product of human intervention. Both Gebusi men and women believe that boys will not grow into adults unless they are orally inseminated during adolescence. During this same period, adolescent males participate in séances with increasing frequency. These rituals encourage young men to verbally engage spirit women with confidence, promoting, through various symbolic displays, the self-perception of great strength in sexual longing. Finally, as part of the rituals that mark the commencement of adulthood, initiates receive "men's knowledge" about sex and gender. Transformation of the male body and mind is understood to be contin-

gent (see Worthman, this volume), the product of human agency, socially trans-
acted, culturally marked and celebrated.

While the primary duty (and achievement) of men is to bring forth manhood *through* social practice, the primary duty of women is to protect maturing
females *from* social practice, which is ill-timed.[31] This perspective on female development not only informs women's protective relation to emerging women
but also informs their dislike of the public betrothal of females during childhood and adolescence. Betrothal increases the possibility that mother and
daughter will live apart. Forty percent of Gebusi brides surveyed (fourteen out
of thirty-five) move away from their premarital kin network at marriage. The
general percentage holds also for the subset of brides discussed above whose first
marriages were negotiated publicly during childhood.

While a mother's "sad longing" for a newly married, adult daughter living
away is offset by cultural understandings that mark the transition as appropriately
timed, such is not the case with daughters who are "still growing," "shy," and "not
strong." In part, this is due to the fact that sharing, affection, cooperation, and
protection are key elements that give meaning not only to the mother-daughter
relationship but to the conjugal relationship as well. Within the conjugal relationship, sexual attraction is regarded as the initial catalyst for the development
of these qualities, a foundation from which elements of a broad-based, harmonious relationship may develop. To deny a daughter residential access to kin, especially female kin with whom she has cooperative, affectionate, protective ties
before she is of age in the local view and capable of establishing similar ties with
her future husband, is regarded by Gebusi women as a lamentable situation. It is
seen as the betrothed daughter's loss as well as the mother's.

But what about publicly acknowledged betrothals in which the bride's kin
and the groom's kin co-reside?[32] If residential separation is not involved, could
mothers still not go about the business of maintaining close ties and protecting
their daughters? They could. And yet only two women, one betrothed at the age
of eight, the other at the age of thirteen, reported maternal consent for their early
betrothal. Most Gebusi women still feel uneasy about child/adolescent betrothals. Among the Gebusi, marriage is first and foremost understood as a claim on
the heterosexuality of one's spouse. Formal betrothal prior to adulthood makes
this claim public and yet requires the betrothed to postpone sexual relations
until both have reached adulthood. The point at which an adolescent Gebusi
male reaches manhood is marked unambiguously and celebrated during his initiation. However, as previously noted, there are no equivalent rites or symbolic
markers of completed adolescence among females. And adult women, based on
their own personal adolescent experiences and their ability to hear the discourse
on female sexuality in the men's séances, perceive an underlying ambivalence
regarding the age at which men view females as appropriate sexual partners. The

uncertainty over men's commitment to withhold sexual claims until the designated bride has reached adulthood, in conjunction with the ill-defined, unmarked commencement of true womanhood, make public betrothal an unpopular marriage practice among women, with or without mother-daughter coresidence during the betrothal period.

Gebusi women do not object to promissory marital agreements made while a daughter is still a child, per se, as long as these agreements are kept secret. It is the public form of early betrothal that Gebusi women do not like. Public betrothal not only increases the risk of mother-daughter separation at an age when the daughter is judged not yet ready to leave, it also places the "not yet ready for marriage" bride in a tenuous position where moral notions conjoining sexual propriety and sexual maturity are at odds with the very emphasis placed on marriage as a sexual relationship. Both adolescence, with its emphasis on breast development, and betrothal, with its emphasis on marriage as a sexual claim, call attention to female sexuality. Yet neither resolves the question of when adolescence (sexual immaturity) ends and true womanhood (sexual maturity) begins. As with covert propositions in the forest and nubile girls womanized in spirit séances, the practice of revealing early betrothal highlights the ambiguity within Gebusi thought and practice concerning adolescent development and sexuality in females.

If both parents prefer to keep marriage promises secret, and if mothers are especially resistant to being separated from their nonadult betrothed daughters, how is it that such marriage agreements are made public at all? As noted, 29 percent (ten out of thirty-five) of the women surveyed said they were claimed publicly for marriage either as children *(wasink)* as young as six years old or upon entry into adolescence *(oifor elem),* about age thirteen. These betrothals were made public in one or both of the following ways: through gifts of meat to the bride's closest uterine and agnatic kin and, in six of ten cases, through affinal coresidence, usually between the bride's closest living agnates and the groom's agnatic kin.

The public betrothal of nonadult females is linked strongly to parental mortality. Of the ten women publicly "claimed" *(hup)* for marriage during childhood or adolescence, nine had a father who was deceased and eight had a mother deceased at the time betrothal was negotiated. None had both parents living at the time of their betrothal. In nine of ten cases, the betrothal was arranged by an adoptive male guardian: a father's brother, an elder brother, a mother's brother, or a senior male in the clan of the mother's second husband. And in seven cases the betrothals of adopted, nonadult females were politically expedient insofar as they enabled male guardians to cancel existing marriage debts or create new marriages through reciprocal exchange. An eighth marriage eventually served this function as well.

It appears, then, that there are two understandings of marriage which ulti-mately pull at the question of female adolescence and its relation to sexual de-velopment. First is the understanding of marriage as a relation of reciprocal sexual longing between spouses; second is the understanding of marriage as the reciprocal exchange of women between clans.[33] The former understanding leads parents, mothers in particular, to favor postponement of the public negotiation of a daughter's marriage until she is between the ages of sixteen and twenty (an *oifor deb*). However, when women in this age category are not available for mari-tal deployment, interclan obligations to exchange women lead to the deployment of females in child and adolescent age categories. Under these conditions, the most likely candidates are not true daughters, but adopted daughters whose marriages are arranged under the authority of male guardians. For 26 percent (nine out of thirty-five) of all women surveyed, the adoption/betrothal pattern characterized first marriage.

In sum, the practice of public child/adolescent betrothal, driven by men's obligations to reciprocate for in-marrying women, renders male commitment to women's protective interest in nonadult females undependable. In most cases, a true father will wait to reveal and/or negotiate the marriage of a daughter. In many instances, close agnatic and uterine male guardians will also wait, but not always. Women know that when male guardians have no other means of fulfilling their exchange obligations their thoughts turn to emerging women *(oifor elem)* and female children *(ulia wasink)*.

BETROTHAL SUMMARIZED: CONFIGURING PROTECTION AMID UNCERTAINTY

Gebusi men and women appear to agree on a number of vital cultural tenets regarding the sexual immaturity of adolescent females, the value of reciprocal sexual longing in the conjugal relation, the formation of marriage through the interclan exchange of women, and the right of parents to arrange the marriage of nonadult children. However, there is no higher order understanding on how to weigh, prioritize, or implement these tenets in specific instances, particularly concerning the public betrothal and subsequent residential transfer of nonadult female kin. At times, male practice seems to support the way women articulate these understandings; in other instances it does not. For Gebusi women, the is-sue of male equivocation is not limited to the negotiation of adolescent betroth-als but, as discussed previously, occurs in other areas of social practice as well, namely, in the covert expressions of sexual interest men make to adolescent fe-males and in the representation of adolescent females as spirit women in séances.

In a world where ambiguity and uncertainty may lead to premature claims upon (or representations of) female sexuality, Gebusi women respond by shunning all practices that assume, forecast, or publicize sexuality in females who are, in their view, "still growing." As a future claim on a female's sexuality, public betrothal calls unwanted attention to the "emerging" sexuality of adolescent females. As claims with ambiguously defined rights of commencement, secret promises (or no promises at all) are what mothers prefer. As a claim that entails the risk of mother-daughter separation, the betrothal of nonadult daughters is something mothers eschew.

Regardless of the fact that some betrothed adolescent females remain resident with kin, the field of associations women bring to their assessment of betrothal, and the ambiguities within, make early public betrothal a situation to be avoided. Just as adult men shun publicity on homosexual practices that promote male adolescent development, so too women shun practices that call attention to the "naturally" emerging sexuality of adolescent females. For these reasons, even women who remained co-resident with nonparental kin and did not experience great difficulty adjusting to their own public adolescent betrothal did not wish early public betrothal for their own daughters. They too saw early public betrothal as a "sad" situation, despite the assessment that it was "all right" for themselves. Within this conversation one also hears the voices of women who associate their early betrothal with complete residential separation from kin. Theirs is the dominant voice in this female discourse, one that laments the public betrothal of "not grown women" without qualification.[34]

GOVERNMENT INFLUENCE

In 1980–1982, the Gebusi were well aware that the national government upheld the view that women should not be forced into marriages against their will. They also knew that the subdistrict administrators objected to the public betrothal and residential transfer of nonadult females. However, national laws and local adjudication had little effect on the way Gebusi contracted marriage until the mid-1970s. Six of the ten brides in my sample were women between eighteen and twenty-eight in 1981. Their betrothals were contracted and made public between 1966 and 1976.

Although the national government's legal position in 1981 supported the interests of Gebusi women, it played no role in generating such interests. Gebusi women's knowledge of adolescent betrothals, of covert sexual offers by young men to emerging women, and of the sexual discourse in men's séances informed their protective stance toward adolescent females in 1981. Gebusi women understood these practices as undermining the otherwise shared cultural view that females between childhood and adulthood are not yet ready for sexual relationships. Without rites of sexual transition to mark a girl's entry into womanhood, without the ritual equivalent of a séance to encourage female confidence in negotiating sexual relationships, adult women saw adolescent girls as shy, inexperienced, and physically immature. Visual assessment of secondary sexual characteristics alone did not effect a consensus between men and women on the issue of age and female sexuality. In the future, the position and authority of the government may be a source of support for women who wish to oppose the public betrothal of adolescent females. Whether this possibility is realized remains to be seen. However, it is highly doubtful that national laws will have any effect on indigenous values and concepts governing adolescence and sexuality in females. Until nonindigenous forms intersect more deeply with Gebusi understandings, it is far more likely that Gebusi men and women will continue their consensus on the moral and conceptual underpinnings of female adolescence while, at the same time, men's practice—in certain areas—will continue to convey ambivalence toward this area of "cultural agreement."

CONCLUSION

This chapter attempts to move beyond a simple "power versus resistance" model of gender in New Guinea (e.g., Godelier 1986; Josephides 1985). It approaches discourse and practice concerning gender relations as a negotiated process whereby men and women take positions in an effort to make sense of dominant, culturally encoded ("shared") understandings of gender, constructs which are not in dispute when abstracted from concrete situations. Analytically, positions may be identified by examining social differences in the way meaning is assigned to practice, positions revealed by differences in the interpretation, significance, and application of "shared understandings" (Ortner and Whitehead 1981; Ortner 1990). The Gebusi case illustrates that positions may be enacted by men and women with ambivalence as well as unequivocal adherence. Furthermore, to the extent that gender constructs are both shared and simultaneously involved in differential access to prestige, autonomy, authority, and influence, gender discourse and practice will entail the dynamics of both affirmation and denial, maintenance and change, trust and "betrayal," uncertainty and the ongoing need to negotiate. Such a view of gender relations is preferable to one that assumes either uniform male dominance, on the one hand, or a parallel culture of female autonomy or resistance, on the other.

III

ADOLESCENCE AND SOCIAL CHANGE IN THE PACIFIC

SIX

Coming of Age on Vanatinai

GENDER, SEXUALITY, AND POWER

Maria Lepowsky

INTRODUCTION

The people of Vanatinai, an island two hundred miles from the eastern tip of the island of New Guinea, participate in an elaborate series of interisland exchanges of shell necklaces, ax blades of polished greenstone, pigs, and other valuables. These are close cognates of the ritual exchanges known to anthropologists as *kula*. When the men and women of Vanatinai go to visit an exchange partner, they make themselves beautiful by decorating themselves with magically enhanced scented coconut oil, flowers and aromatic leaves tucked in their hair and their woven armlets, and fine shell disk necklaces. Augmented by powerful magical spells, their appearance dazzles their exchange partner, male or female, who becomes overwhelmed and hastens to give away any ceremonial valuable the visitor requests, even against his or her conscious will.

This sexually charged power, expressed in the idiom of seduction, is the key to gaining renown and influence over others through a reputation as a person successful in exchange. These people are mature adults of both sexes who become known as big men and big women, accumulating valuables and then publicly giving them away in elaborate mortuary feasts.

The power to seduce others into doing what you want, through your personal aura of beauty and desirability, is first learned during youth, the stage of life in which Vanatinai individuals first become fully gendered persons. Postpubescent boys and girls use their newly acquired physical, mental, and magical powers to incite desire in potential sexual partners. As mature adults they not only refine their skills of seduction and magic to attract and retain lovers, but extend their skills to the metaphorical seduction of exchange partners, to the building of their reputation, and to increasing their influence over others.

This chapter explores Vanatinai constructions of gendered personal identity during the culturally marked life stage of youth, and looks at how these constructions relate, through the development of sexualized powers to influence others, to the building of social success in adulthood. In this island culture, youth is the first life stage that is explicitly genderized, both in name and in the expectation that the young person will develop strongly gendered identities and powers. These, paradoxically, are much the same for young women as for young men. Youth is a life stage of gradual, continuous transition from the irresponsibility and dependence of childhood to full adult responsibilities and potential influence over others.

I focus particularly in this chapter on indigenous beliefs and practices pertaining to sexuality and the courtship behaviors of both sexes, which are strikingly symmetrical. Youthful lessons in how to incite desire are transferrable to an array of adult activities that build the prestige, wealth, and renown of adult men and women. These include the building and maintenance of strong interlineage marriage alliances; mortuary ritual exchanges honoring ancestors; interdistrict and interisland ceremonial exchanges; and human relations with the supernatural world through the practice of magic, ritual, and sorcery.

I discuss the significance of cultural changes in the precolonial and colonial periods, particularly the impact of warfare and pacification upon the lives of young people. I note the changing contexts of youth in an outer island culture that is part of a postcolonial nation, an island where the influence of missions, the school system, and national government is only slowly growing. But I also argue that a distinctive "youth culture" is traditional on Vanatinai, and was so long before the advent of schools or migrant labor.

Similar "youth cultures," subcultures, or life stages have long been found in many societies of the Pacific Islands, and they clearly seem to have predated missionization, schooling, and the cash economy. These Pacific Island ethnographic examples, first comprehensively documented by Margaret Mead (1928) and Bronislaw Malinowski (1929), contradict recent assertions by cultural theorists, most of them not anthropologists, that youth cultures are relatively new epiphenomena of modernity or postmodernity, associated with industrializing or postindustrial societies, global and regional mass media, consumer economies, and rapid social change.

RANK, IDEOLOGIES OF MALE DOMINANCE, AND YOUTH

Vanatinai is one of the world's most gender egalitarian societies (Lepowsky 1993). There is no ideology of male dominance or female inferiority. Vanatinai also lacks any distinction between chiefs and commoners, superior and inferior lineages, or any other forms of rank. Herdt and Leavitt, in the introduction to this volume, contrast two traditional social forms in the Pacific Islands: Polynesian-style ranked hierarchies and the "egalitarian, achieved-status societies" that predominate in Melanesia, Micronesia, and Aboriginal Australia. Even granted that such a contrast has long been overstated in anthropological writings—there are chiefs in the Trobriand Islands and elaborate ranking systems in many Vanuatu societies, all part of Melanesia (cf. Thomas 1989)—there is a further crosscutting distinction of enormous significance for making sense of adolescence and constructions of personhood in Pacific Island societies.

In both the ranked societies of Polynesia and the "egalitarian" societies of the New Guinea Highlands, where big men earned leadership and influence through their economic success or ritual knowledge, there are ideologies of male superiority, and distinct hierarchies of gender. These vary in degree among the Polynesian islands and are often overridden by privileges of rank. Ideologies of male dominance and female pollution are most pronounced in much of interior New Guinea, where male superiority and male privilege, ritually marked and enforced, are often central to social life and personhood (see, e.g., Meggitt 1964; Langness 1967; Herdt 1982; Godelier 1986). Such a high degree of gender differentiation—in societies that traditionally placed a high value on male roles as warrior and military leader—almost by definition demanded a high degree of separation of the sexes in daily and ritual life, and thus very different processes of socialization toward youth and adult gender roles.

The sex segregation characteristic of societies organized around religiously validated ideologies of male dominance, combined with their elaborate, often years-long sequences of male initiation rituals, links together many of the egalitarian, big man societies of interior New Guinea with some ranked, hierarchical Melanesian island societies such as those of Vanuatu, the islands of the former New Hebrides (see, e.g., Allen 1967), and with Aboriginal Australia.

Still other ranked, hierarchical societies, such as those of traditional Polynesia (while some formerly had male initiation rituals such as penile superincision or tattooing) did not generally segregate either young people or adults by sex. They were organized primarily around the principle of chiefly rank, also religiously validated, rather than the principle of male superiority. High-ranking women could and did hold sacred and temporal powers (see, e.g., Linnekin 1990; Weiner 1992).

Adolescence in Polynesian societies, as famously documented by Margaret Mead in Samoa (1928), involved, for all but the highest ranking young women, a great deal of social contact between young people of both sexes, sexual experimentation, preoccupation with the beauty and power of one's own newly mature body and those of others, and a socially recognized period of relative irresponsibility concerning adult affairs of work and politics (see also Levy 1973 for

Tahiti; Linton 1942 and Kirkpatrick 1983 for the Marquesas).

Malinowski's (1929) portrait of Trobriand Island youth, the "flower of the village," is strikingly similar, in a Melanesian ranked society, but one without a central organizing principle of male superiority or a tradition of sex segregation or initiation (cf. Weiner 1976). What is more, there are remarkably comparable reports of youthful freedom, beauty, sexual experimentation, and irresponsibility from Micronesia. The Micronesian islands vary in their cultural focus on rank and hierarchy, but they too lack a central organizing principle of male dominance and female inferiority, with relations between the sexes more accurately characterized as forms of gender complementarity (see Schneider 1953 for Yap; Gladwin and Sarason 1953 and Marshall 1979 for Truk; and Burrows and Spiro 1953 for Ifaluk).

On Vanatinai—a genuinely egalitarian society without ideologies of male dominance or of rank—the life stage of youth is startlingly similar to that described for these Polynesian and Micronesian societies and to descriptions of the relatively nearby Trobriand Islands. Lack of a ritual focus on male superiority and female pollution, and thus of social preoccupation with residential and ritual gender differentiation—found in much of interior New Guinea—overrides the contrast between ranked and unranked Pacific Island societies, and crosscuts the larger culture areas of Melanesia, Micronesia, and Polynesia. The Trobriand Islands and Vanatinai—one organized around chiefly ranked lineages and the other a militantly egalitarian Melanesian society—share a similarly constructed life stage of youth with each other and with many Micronesian societies (which vary in their attention to rank) and with the chiefly societies of Polynesia.

VANATINAI, THE MOTHERLAND

Vanatinai, which means "motherland," is the indigenous name of the remote island usually labeled Sudest or Tagula on maps and nautical charts. It is part of the Massim culture area, a region distinguished by matrilineal descent in most of its island cultures, a markedly high status of women, elaborate series of mortuary rituals, and extensive interisland exchange systems, including the *kula* ring made famous to anthropologists by the writings of Bronislaw Malinowski on the Trobriand Islands (Seligman 1910; Malinowski 1922; 1929; 1935; Fortune 1932; Lepowsky 1983; 1989a; 1990a; 1990b; 1993; Weiner 1976).

The people of Vanatinai display a marked cultural conservatism and resistance to externally induced changes to their way of life. A century and a half after their ancestors first encountered European traders, whalers, and explorers, they still have little involvement in the world cash economy, with some families having no cash income at all in a given year, and per capita income well under

$20 per year in the late 1980s. At the time of my first fieldwork in 1977–1979 there were no whites living on the island. The first white missionary ever to live and proselytize on Vanatinai did not take up residence until 1984.

The islanders extract sago starch from the palms that grow prolifically in the swamps, cultivate yams, sweet potatoes, manioc, taro, bananas, and other crops in their swidden gardens, fish and collect shellfish in the enormous lagoon encircling the island, gather a variety of wild foods in the rainforests of the interior, and hunt wild pig, monitor lizard, crocodile, and small marsupials. They raise pigs to be exchanged and consumed at feasts. They are still involved heavily in regional systems of barter and ceremonial exchange for foods, locally manufactured household goods, and ceremonial valuables, sailing long distances in their outrigger canoes through dangerous seas to visit exchange partners on distant islands. A large proportion of this wealth eventually changes hands during a series of mortuary feasts marking the death of each individual.

Vanatinai society lacks political leaders and has a strong egalitarian ethic which disapproves of the accumulation of wealth without redistribution of goods to those who request it. While cooperation among individuals is extolled, and indeed is necessary for continued existence in a small-scale subsistence society, the culture's egalitarian outlook is revealed by its strong emphasis upon the principle of personal autonomy and an ethic of respect for the will and the idiosyncrasies of the individual. This respect extends from the care of infants to the treatment of the aged and enjoins tolerance of a wide range of character traits and behaviors by women and men of all ages.

Respect for others is enforced not only by the need to cooperate in daily life or have neighbors choose to live elsewhere on the island, but by strong beliefs in the destructive magical powers of others that take the form of sorcery and witchcraft. Virtually all deaths, serious illnesses, and other misfortunes are attributed to the malevolent actions of sorcerers or witches, and more rarely to a person's deliberate or inadvertent violation of a taboo.

VANATINAI YOUTH

The basic fact that small-scale societies categorize persons primarily by sex and age, but in widely differing ways cross-culturally, has long been noted by our anthropological forebears (e.g. Lowie 1920; Linton 1940; 1942). This is true in gender egalitarian societies such as Vanatinai as much as in societies characterized by ideologies of male dominance. A crucial way to document the degree to which a small-scale society really is gender egalitarian, then, is to evaluate and compare the powers, restrictions, values, and expectations for males and females at each point in the life cycle (see Lepowsky 1993).

On Vanatinai, young girls have virtually the same degree of control over their own actions as do boys the same age. In addition, both have almost as much personal autonomy as mature adults of both sexes. I outline the potential limits of young people's autonomy below. The principle of comparable personal autonomy for each sex at the same age holds true throughout the life cycle, from infancy to old age.

There are neither male nor female initiation ceremonies on Vanatinai for either boys or girls to mark the transition from childhood to adolescence.[1] In other words, the process of becoming a fully adult, gendered person does not require human ritual practice or spiritual intervention, as it does in many other parts of Melanesia. Parents and maternal kin on Vanatinai sometimes perform secret growth magic rituals for babies and small children to keep them healthy, well formed, and growing properly. But the only magical and ritual attention focused on youths is love magic, which they practice themselves, and which their maternal kin may assist them with at key times such as feasts. Mature adults of all ages may secretly practice love magic as well, so that while it is most identified with youth and courting, it is not exclusive to this life stage.

The period of youth on Vanatinai begins at about age fourteen, or when the signs of puberty or its imminent approach are visible to onlookers. For a girl, this is when her breast buds are noticeably "the size of betel nuts," and for a boy when his voice begins to change and as he begins his adolescent growth spurt. The term for young males is *zeva,* and for young females it is *gamaina,* which translates literally as "child female."

The life stage whose gender-marked terms I translate as "youth" continues significantly longer than the Western social categories of the adolescent (a biological term that is now a label for a social category) or "teenager." Youth on Vanatinai lasts through the middle twenties, or to the point at which a person has established what seems to be a stable marriage. This is a society in which people generally marry in their early twenties, but where early marriages often end in divorce.

It is significant that youth is the first life stage in which terms of reference distinguish between persons on the basis of sex. There is no separate term in the Vanatinai language for "infant" or "toddler" as distinct from "child," and a child is called *gama,* a gender-neutral term, from birth to puberty. The relative lack of age-grading on Vanatinai is in strong contrast to many other Melanesian and Pacific Island societies. It reflects the island's overall egalitarian ethic and nonhierarchical social structure, which includes not only relations among adult men but those between men and women and young and old.

Mature adult males and females from about their middle twenties are also referred to by gender specific terms, *ghomoli* and *wevo.* These mean both man and male, woman and female, respectively. In addition, the terms that mean old man and old woman—*amalaisali* (or the Papuan Pidgin term *olman*) and *laisali* or *mankwés*—are gender marked (unlike the Anglo-Saxon term *elder,* for example), and may be used to address people as young as about thirty years of age as a mark of respect. They are more commonly applied to people of an age to have adult children, or about fifty and above.

Gender identity in the sexually egalitarian culture of Vanatinai is formed primarily after puberty. Children of both sexes live substantially similar lives. As one woman explained to me, "The work *(kaiwa)* of children is playing *(mwadiwa)."* Children are greatly indulged by adults except when they must defer to the wishes of even younger children. They play in mixed-sex groups, fishing and foraging on the shore and in nearby tracts of forest. They are occasionally drafted as baby-sitters for younger siblings: this is more often true of girls beginning around the age of seven or eight, but older brothers the same age are frequently visible lugging their baby sisters and brothers around the hamlet or down to the shore.

Children occasionally accompany their parents or a grandparent of either sex during all subsistence tasks except hunting trips. They may wander about the garden or sago camp, playing with other children, care for toddlers while parents are weeding yams or beating sago pith, or try, without being asked, to help with simpler tasks, such as weeding, gathering shellfish or firewood, or fetching water. The efforts of younger children to work in this way are elaborately praised by adults.

A girl who is called *gamaina* performs the same tasks as an adult woman, except that she is unmarried and working with her parents and maternal kin rather than making a separate garden—in her matrilineage lands—with a husband. Unlike her mother, she is not "the owner of the garden" *(tonuwagai),* with the burdens and rewards of its successful management. She is also freed from the pressure of all the affinal obligations that married women face: to labor in her husband's matrilineage's yam gardens and sago camps for part of the year, and to contribute garden produce, coconut leaf skirts, clay pots, and other goods to help satisfy her in-laws' ritual obligations as they host or contribute to mortuary feasts.

Young girls work alongside their mothers and sisters in gardens, they care for their families' pigs, sometimes, like young boys, beginning to own and care for their own piglets, which will grow up to become ceremonial valuables exchangeable for shell necklaces or greenstone ax blades, or contributions to feasts. Young girls, like adult women, are somewhat more likely to forage in the forest or collect shellfish on the fringing reef than are young boys and men. This is generally considered by both sexes to be a more pleasant form of subsistence labor than the tedious weeding of yam gardens in the hot sun. Adult women, who are called "the owners of the gardens"—even though men actually own them as well, communally with mothers and sisters—do more garden work than men, boys, or young girls. Young girls and adult women also hunt marsupial fruit bats and other small mammals by climbing coconut trees, and they occasionally lay traps for monitor lizards, which may be four feet in length. It is taboo on Vanatinai for women to hunt with spears—one of the few taboos to restrict women's activities.

Collecting clams on the reef is fun—and to do so is even called *mwadiwa,* or play—though wading shin deep in sulphurous smelling mangrove swamps to grab blue mangrove crabs by their enormous front claws is risky and difficult, as is gathering razor-edge mangrove oysters. But collecting wild nuts, legumes, and fruits from rainforest trees, wild mustard *(Piper betle)* for chewing with be-tel nuts, roots and scented leaves for use in magic, and fishing for freshwater shrimp and eel in upland streams are all opportunities for girls and women to go off by themselves or with a friend or two, work at their own pace, eat little delicacies, put flowers in their hair, bathe and relax on a shady streamside after getting hot and muddy, possibly meet lovers, or arrange assignations away from the curious gaze of kinfolk and neighbors, or the hostility of a spouse or rival.

Girls, like adult women, sometimes remain in the hamlet to weave coconut leaf skirts, baskets, or mats, cook the evening meal, sweep the dirt of the central plaza with a coconut rib broom, and care for young children. Younger siblings, nieces, and nephews as young as five or so may trail along after them to reefs and gardens, learning subsistence tasks by watching and trying to help. This kind of childcare often gets delegated to girls who have not yet reached puberty, some-times as young as six or seven, in order to free older girls for subsistence tasks.

From the age of about eight, boys too are expected to care for younger chil-dren when their parents and older siblings are away from the hamlet. By the time they reach fourteen or fifteen, and especially as they reach their full size and strength, they are expected to form parties to hunt wild pigs with spears and sometimes with dogs in the forest, occasionally staying out overnight, and to work hard in family sago camps chopping down the mature female palms and sluicing out the starch with water. Along with experienced adult men, they hunt crocodiles with spears at dusk or at night. Youths also forage in the forests dur-ing the day—a good way to run into parties of young girls and women, as well as to collect the ingredients for love magic—and fish and gather shellfish on the reefs. Male youths are less likely to be seen in the hamlet during the day than young girls, and they are somewhat less likely to be in a work party directed by parents or maternal kin, a fact which occasionally is commented on irritably and publicly by an adult who wanted full use of their labor power in sago camp or garden, or in cutting or erecting house posts.

When I asked young people of both sexes what they thought was the most important quality in a spouse, they were unanimous in stating that it was some-one who works hard. I have to admit that I was surprised at the practicality of their "good provider" answer, which of course is an essential characteristic in a subsistence society. But this is because I had been watching and listening for a year as young people appraised each other's physical beauty, beautified themselves through magic and adornment, and declared themselves overcome by the power of someone else's love magic.

This last of course was the local explanation for why certain less than hardworking young men and women had attracted a series of lovers or a new spouse, sometimes one of the young people who claimed to be most influenced by the industry of a future mate. On the other hand, a husband's or wife's alleged laziness was one of the main reasons people gave me, and their relatives and neighbors, for divorcing youthful spouses, the other being adultery.

Young girls and young boys, then, are expected to work almost as hard at the same subsistence tasks as mature adults, although without the added burden of obligations to in-laws. By doing so they contribute their labor to the parents and maternal kin who grew them and fed them as children, fulfilling the basic moral covenant on Vanatinai between children and parents, the living and ancestor spirits. A young person's productivity and diligence should also demonstrate to other boys or girls, and to potential future affines, that she or he is a desirable future spouse. But at the same time, both the young people and their elders recognize that youth is a period in which a person is distracted easily by erotic adventures and the intrigues of friends and rivals, and by a preoccupation with beautifying her or his own body. As a result, there is a culturally marked tolerance for persons in the life stage of youth for a degree of irresponsibility, self-absorption, and certainly of sexual intrigue, that would be, and often is, the subject of disapproving talk in a supposedly mature and well-married adult.

MENSTRUATION

A girl's first menstrual period, which occurs at about the age of fifteen, is not publicly acknowledged, and it is treated no differently from her subsequent ones. Menstruation is called *wakinie,* also the adverb meaning "behind," and probably related to *waghena,* or "moon." Girls and women do not work in their gardens or go near a garden while they are menstruating. I was told that if a woman violated this taboo, wild pigs, birds, or other animals, attracted by the smell of blood, would eat the garden.

The menstrual taboo is particularly strict at the planting of a new yam garden, a communal event involving an elaborate public ritual petition to ancestor spirits by either a male or a female garden magician. Yams are the most important cultigen and the only annual one. Significantly, along with menstruating women, both men and women who have had sexual intercourse within the last couple of days are barred by taboo from participating in the yam planting. This can lead to interesting comments in the hamlet beforehand from parents, aunts, and uncles to young people (and more rarely, to adults, who are supposed to control themselves enough to abstain in preparation): "Why aren't you coming to help us?" (Embarrassed mumble from the boy or girl.) To a girl: "You can't be menstruating—you just did!" To both: "What do you mean, you don't feel well?" and so on. Garden workers then discuss who has not shown up to help, and the also absent person with whom the delinquent one probably indulged sexually.

Both male and female genital fluids contain the essence of human fertility. They should at this ritually sensitive time be kept out of the garden, an area being publicly consecrated to the fertility of cultivated plants, as they would endanger the fertility and future growth of yam seedlings. Later, while the garden is growing, married couples are expected to have sexual intercourse in the yam garden, their human fertility now enhancing that of the yam plants. This is one reason, besides fear of another's envy and subsequent destructive magic, why it is highly improper to visit somebody else's yam garden after the seedlings are planted.

In contrast to these taboos, women and girls may have sex during their menstrual periods, and there is no belief at all in any kind of supernatural danger befalling them, their lovers or husbands, or children, if they cook or touch food while menstruating. This is, of course, quite unlike most societies of interior New Guinea which are characterized by strong religious beliefs in the polluting power of menstrual fluids, and which bar menstruating women from contact with food or sexual contact with men and from visiting a variety of sacred locations or male cult houses (see, e.g., Meggitt 1964; Langness 1967; Brown and Buchbinder 1976; Godelier 1986).

YOUTH AND SEXUALITY

The work of young people, they and their elders agree, is sexual intrigue and self-beautification. Young people are more likely to trudge to the garden or the reef after a sleepless night—for which they will be thoroughly teased—and to be distracted by flirtations and the excitement of spending time with hamlet visitors.

As in the Trobriand Islands (Malinowski 1929; Weiner 1976), Vanatinai adults take pride in the beauty—and thus the power over others—of the youth of their hamlet, and they enhance the beauty and attraction of their young relations by offering magical assistance. Beauty magic, love magic, and the magic of exchange work on the same basic principle of seduction. The person who practices magic—rubbing magically enhanced scented coconut oil all over the body, tucking charmed, decorative leaves in one's armlets, and chewing secret rainforest roots while reciting spells—becomes dazzlingly beautiful. The objects of the magic, the persons whose bodies or whose valuables are desired, become *negenege,* dizzy with desire, and obsessed, unable to stop themselves from giving their bodies or their *kula* valuables away.

Sexual activity on Vanatinai is regarded as a pleasurable activity appropriate for men and women from puberty, around the age of fourteen or fifteen, to old age. It is not believed to be dangerous or depleting of vital essence for either men or women, unlike in many parts of Melanesia where an ideology of male dominance is prevalent (Meggitt 1964; Langness 1967; Herdt 1982; 1984). Although children engage occasionally in sexual play, it is quite rare for a person who has not yet reached puberty to engage in genital sex. If their elders hear about it, they disapprove strongly, attributing it to the predatory and powerful love magic of a mature adult male who has selected an inappropriate object for his desires.

I have never heard of a mature or elderly woman seducing a very young boy (at or about puberty), although older youths in their late teens and early twenties may well have affairs with mature women. One woman, then a widow in her fifties, taught me a particular procedure for preparing coconut oil with secret botanical ingredients and spells, and said, "If we use this scented oil, we can sleep with youths *(zeva)."* Youths are teased about such alliances if caught, but these are not disapproved of unless they are adulterous.

I found the same disapproval of male magical predation expressed in comments on the early sexual initiation of a young woman, then in her twenties, who had been seduced at about age fourteen by the powerful magic of another friend's widowed grandfather, with whom she maintained a relationship for a couple of years. He was perceived by other adults as something of a "dirty old man" who should have directed his attentions to a mature woman, such as a widow or divorcée anywhere in age from her twenties to her sixties. It was not his sexuality or love magic per se that was objectionable, but the extreme youth of the girl, and thus her lack of magical defenses against him.

If she had slept with a youth a little older, her mother would have scolded her, as I heard in the case of a fifteen year old who was about four feet nine inches, with small breast buds, that she was "too small" to have a lover. In this latter case, the mother disapproved of the lover, an eighteen year old who was a hard worker, but an orphan without strong relatives to help support him or a future wife. But she was also, I found, quite literally afraid that her daughter would become pregnant, give birth before she reached full physical maturity, and die in childbirth. Significantly, the young woman ignored her mother, continued to meet her lover secretly, became pregnant at about the age of nineteen by the same youth—after a number of sexual adventures by both partners—and married him. They remain married.

It is an island sport, as in other small communities, to figure out who is sleeping with whom. Young people try to hide their affairs from adults, particularly close kin, and feel ashamed to have their love life discussed or observed. Brothers and sisters especially must scrupulously avoid verbal or visual contact with the sexual affairs of their siblings.

Since it is hard to find privacy, there is a lively network of gossip both among young people and their elders about the ongoing romantic dramas in each district of the island. Girls as well as boys can and do proposition the objects of their desire. The direct approach, by either sex, is often successful: "I want you." The desired one can either say, "I don't want to," or agree to meet on the shore or in the forest after everyone else has fallen asleep, although this puts the couple at risk of sorcery attack.

It is more risky to meet in the girl's house after her family falls asleep, or to waken a sleeping girl and proposition her. She could cry out and shame the boy, as the neighbors will laugh about it for days, or he could be caught by the girl's mother or uncle (mother's brother) during the night. The girl's mother or uncle would then have the right to "put out the basket"—that is, to place a coconut leaf basket filled with ceremonial valuables at the head of the couple asleep on the girl's mat. When the boy wakes up, he must take the basket, slink off before dawn, and ask his own maternal kin to put an equivalent number of valuables in the basket, then return it to the girl's mother and uncle. If he does—and some boys cannot manage this—he can return to sleep with the girl as long as it is agreeable to the couple. People say this custom, *buwa*, pays the girl's kin for growing and feeding her. They state adamantly that it is not a marriage or betrothal payment. Having sex on the beach or in the bush avoids the *buwa*, which is called a payment "to the house."

Another common seduction strategy is to employ a friend of the same sex, or a cross-cousin of the opposite sex—either another young person or an older child—to act as a go-between and make the proposition: "X wants you." This avoids having to deal with the shame of a direct rejection. Using a third party to make requests is a common strategy as well in ceremonial exchange (see Lepowsky 1993). This, like direct verbal and magical seduction, is an instance where love affairs are good practice for building the social skills necessary for success in exchange through the ability to request valuables—here explicitly perceived as the prospective lover's genitals—from an initially unwilling partner.

Successful seduction, by girl or boy, man or woman, is not due to a person's intrinsic beauty or charm, according to my Vanatinai neighbors, but to the potency of the love magic she or he has learned from relatives or friends. As one might expect, there is an enormous variety of complicated and secret magical spells. These often include the use of some kind of personal leavings of the desired one—hair, discarded betel nut skins, or expectorant—and elaborately metaphorical spells (such as evoking the image of the butterfly) that cause the future lover to dream about one or become obsessed in their waking thoughts. Love magic frequently involves the use of scented roots or colored leaves that have been charmed by secret procedures. Charmed leaves and flowers are worn in armbands, leglets, and hair.

One of the most widely used techniques is the boiling of *bunama,* a magically enhanced scented coconut oil, with an intoxicatingly spicy fragrance produced by its secret botanical ingredients. The most potent *bunama* is made by adding a relic—a piece of bone or tooth belonging to a deceased ancestor or hero—to the clay pot as it boils, with the recitation of special spells known only to a few. One young woman, then aged about eighteen, who had a whole series of sexual partners at successive mortuary feasts we attended together, explained to me later the reason she was so successful in attracting all those lovers: her mother's brother had prepared special *bunama* beforehand using an ancestral piece of skull. This was clearly a mark of the interest of the maternal uncle, a senior member of his matrilineage, in this young woman's future fertility.

MARRIAGE

When the man stays for breakfast on Vanatinai, the couple is married. Making love quietly in the young woman's house, and then remaining until morning, instead of the lover skulking off just before dawn, is something that usually happens first when the couple is about twenty or so. The new husband must then immediately "go to work for his mother-in-law," doing the heavy labor and the tedious weeding in her garden, and whatever else she demands. This period of bride-service lasts for several months while the couple lives with the bride's parents.

Divorce is common, especially among young people, and is equally easily achieved at the desire of either party. Many youths are unable to adjust to the added demands of married life, which include sexual fidelity and a whole set of obligations to labor for a spouse's in-laws and contribute valuables to their feasts, toward their garden land, canoe purchases, and so on. A young married person is also expected to be a more diligent and consistent worker than a single young man or woman. With easy divorce, a young person can quickly return to the unmarried state, even with a small child, and can also reject a partner who turned out to be a more desirable lover than he or she is a steady worker. Parents also contribute their opinions on this latter point and may have an influence over whether a marriage succeed or fails, usually based on the young spouse's industry and willingness or ability to solicit valuables and labor from kinfolk toward affinal projects.

Vanatinai women rarely give birth before the age of about twenty, despite having been sporadically sexually active for four or five years before this time.[2]

A youth's matrilineal kin do not normally give bride-wealth to his wife's kin until it looks as if the marriage is going to last, often shortly before or after the birth of the first child. Her kin will give an approximately equivalent amount of child-wealth to the husband's kin to thank him, people say, for siring a new member of the wife's matrilineage. A stable marriage involves an elaborate series of affinal obligations to contribute labor and valuables as requested, obligations that children of the marriage inherit and should fulfill in the mortuary ritual exchanges honoring the deaths of their parents.

YOUTH AND FEASTS

The *zagaya*, or climactic mortuary feast, which is the last in a series of three or four feasts, normally takes place several years after a death and celebrates the public renewal of alliances among lineages and among individual exchange partners (Lepowsky 1989a; 1993). Death threatens these alliances with dissolution or enmity, due to prevalent suspicions or sorcery and witchcraft. The *zagaya* lifts remaining mourning taboos from a surviving spouse, who is ritually beautified by heirs of the deceased and henceforth permitted to dance, take lovers, and remarry. *Zagaya* rituals also celebrate the social rebirth of mourners and the enduring fertility of the living in the face of death. The feast is marked both by exchanges of ceremonial valuables and by sexual license. Young people are expected to be especially sexually active at feasts. There is generally dancing all night long either to traditional drums and songs or occasionally, in recent years, to guitars and ukeleles. The young—and some of their elders—slip discreetly away into the darkness to keep their rendezvous. Many marriages trace their origins to meetings at these feasts. The new marriages among feast participants who represent the social relationships of the deceased renew or initiate new alliances of affinity and exchange among matrilineages (Lepowsky 1989a).

YOUTHFUL SKILLS AND ADULT CAREERS

Persuasive skills—oratorical, interpersonal, and magical—developed during youth, for the clearly compelling purpose of seducing desired lovers, are the same skills necessary for a successful career as an adult on Vanatinai. This is a society with no hereditary category of chiefs and—before the intrusions of colonial and national government—therefore no one with the power to tell another adult what to do. In order to keep a spouse, attract the labor to help put in a communal yam garden, put up or reroof a house, purchase a canoe, pay a bride-wealth, host a feast to honor the dead, or make an honorable contribution to such a feast, you have to persuade other people—spouses, in-laws, neighbors, and exchange partners (actual and potential)—to do what you wish. If you are particularly successful in accumulating and then giving away valuables at mortuary feasts and to exchange partners, and in mobilizing the labor of others over a period of years, you gradually become known as a big man or big woman, or *gia* (see Lepowsky 1990a; 1990b; 1993), a gender-neutral term. The *giagia* are men and women, mostly in middle age and late middle age, with exceptional verbal abilities, both in public speaking and in private conversations, and exceptional knowledge of matters of custom, both practical and religious. Since all success in subsistence, exchange, or health is attributed to the actions of ancestral spirits and place spirits, or to the mobilization of spiritual forces for positive or negative ends by living individuals, there is no clear boundary between *gia* and *giagia*.

The *giagia* are the people who know the most about how to petition ancestor spirits and place spirits, and what customary practices will please or displease them. They begin to acquire this knowledge in youth. Everyone at that age is interested in love magic, and that is where the learning begins—from peers and, for the more ambitious or uncertain, from elders, usually maternal kin or fathers. Some individuals are content to know a few love magic techniques plus some basic gardening, fishing, or healing magic. Other young men and women apprentice themselves to specialists and gradually, as they mature, become known as healers or sorcerers (almost always a male role) or experts in exchange. This draws others to them, out of either respect or fear: almost all healing is countersorcery or counterwitchcraft, and a person who is expert in garden magic could blight one's garden by malevolent magic if she or he chose to.

YOUTH AND HISTORICAL CHANGE

Social life on Vanatinai has changed little in many respects despite six generations of contact with Europeans. In the islanders' perspective, the most significant change is the cessation of warfare and raiding. The last raids were as late as 1943, although the colonial government thought the archipelago was completely pacified by 1888, when gold was discovered on Vanatinai, triggering a rush of hundreds of Australian miners and precipitating the long-delayed annexation of British New Guinea (Lepowsky 1989b).

During the precolonial period, young men could gain renown and power by becoming known as an *asiara* (champion fighter), a term applied to exemplary and now legendary warriors, both aggressors who are alleged to have preyed cannibalistically on their own people and defenders who repelled invaders from other islands.

Becoming an *asiara* was a completely separate avenue to prestige from that of becoming a *gia,* or giver. The loss of the role of *asiara,* and the role of warrior more generally, reflects a lessened opportunity to excel for older youths, or young men in their twenties. Vanatinai women traditionally participated in decisions to make war and peace and accompanied brothers onto the field of battle. Nevertheless, pacification and the loss of the warrior role has probably contributed to a greater opportunity for women to achieve power and influence through other traditional means (Lepowsky 1993).

There is probably no Melanesian society where becoming a big man through wealth redistribution was the only traditional way to achieve power and influence (cf. Godelier 1986). In many societies, one avenue for becoming a big man was through prowess in warfare, derived not only from physical ability and intelligence but from the active intercession of ancestor spirits or other supernatural beings. In Vanatinai, becoming *asiara* was one such avenue. Although Vanatinai women were not excluded from councils of war or diplomacy or from the battlefield, the role of *asiara* was available only to men. The role of *gia,* the big man or big woman, could only be filled by a mature and knowledgeable individual of either sex. There are other kinds of powerful men and women in Vanatinai society—powerful sorcerers, renowned healers, and highly successful gardeners—but again, these are mature adults and not youths.

The colonial era left Vanatinai people only marginally involved in the cash economy and little controlled by British or Australian law. The first missionary activities on the island did not come until after World War II; a mission primary school was established on nearby Nimowa Island by the Mission of the Sacred Heart, and there were three United Church (conservative Protestant, with heavy Methodist influence) primary schools along the Vanatinai coast. But as late as the early 1980s, the majority of children did not attend any school at all. This changed with the establishment of the first government primary school, along the south coast, long sought by parents and elders, even culturally conservative ones. As one big man told me, "The mission schools only teach them how to read the Bible, not how to speak English or about the knowledge of Europeans." Parents also wanted closer schools so that they could see their children on weekends instead of once a year at Christmas.

By the late 1980s, most of the local children were attending primary school, as were a number of sexually active adolescents with no previous schooling, who began first grade alongside their small siblings. This development clearly has the potential to dramatically alter the lives of young people in the coming years. There are still almost no Vanatinai girls and boys attending high school on the mainland, although many would like to. Their parents fear the girls will return pregnant (as one girl did in 1978), and that the young people will marry spouses from elsewhere and never return.

The island has had a historically low out-migration rate during the colonial and postcolonial eras, especially compared to nearby islands such as Rossel and Goodenough (Armstrong 1928; Young 1971). During the 1970s and 1980s the rate was only about 3 percent. A dozen or so youths worked as laborers at the government station at the western tip of the island, and a few more at an expatriate-owned coconut plantation until it closed down some years ago. A few girls at a time work as house servants in the Sacred Heart Mission. It is likely that a few young men will, in the future, obtain jobs at the large, open-pit gold mine on Misima Island, but to date Misima people have closely held these jobs, along with a few more sophisticated and ambitious married Vanatinai men in their thirties, who already have some English skills and labor histories.

The rest of the local young people continue to remain in their home communities. They gradually become more responsible about subsistence tasks, and they enter the exchange system by raising a pig and giving it to a new exchange partner, through offering their labor at a feast and being rewarded with a greenstone ax blade. They also begin as older youths by requesting a valuable from a kinsperson or affine, or by contributing a valuable, obtained from a parent or mother's brother, at a mortuary feast for a deceased favorite relative or neighbor. They learn from their elders the magic and ritual petitions to ancestor spirits and other supernaturals necessary for success, health, and prosperity. And eventually, often in their early or mid-twenties, they enter a lasting marriage and become parents themselves, growing into mature adults: people who feel the desire to work hard and share generously to benefit their children, kinfolk, and neighbors, to gain the respect of others, and to avoid shame, or the retribution of sorcery and witchcraft.

YOUTH AS A LIFE STAGE

Youth on Vanatinai, as in much of the Pacific Islands, is a life stage with blurred boundaries. There is a gradual transition from childhood, with its play, irresponsibility, and self-absorption, to the slow and partly reversible assumption of the qualities of responsibility, stability, hard work, and generosity that are characteristic of mature adulthood.

During youth, gender differences and gender identity are culturally marked on Vanatinai for the first time. The stress on gender difference does not indicate socialization to gender hierarchy. In this sexually egalitarian society, maleness is not more highly valued or privileged over femaleness. The same personal qualities are valued in both women and men; these are strength, referring to hard work and productivity; wisdom, including intellect, experience, and knowledge of the overlapping human, natural, and supernatural domains; and generosity, the demonstrated willingness and ability to share the fruits of one's labor and knowledge with others. Again, these are all qualities typical of mature adulthood, not of youth.

Youths of both sexes lead essentially parallel lives. The opportunities, freedoms, and responsibilities of the young of both sexes in work, courtship, and personal autonomy are largely symmetrical. The new stress on gender difference during this life stage emphasizes the power of both male and female sexuality. This power remains part of the person through mature adulthood and into old age, but it is most strongly marked during youth, the age at which physical beauty and desirability are perceived to be at their peak even without the enhancements of love magic and supernatural intervention; the middle aged are the ones who have to rely especially heavily on love magic. Male and female youths experiment with their new sexual powers, practicing their verbal persuasive skills, spending hours in teasing one another, and acquiring new magical techniques from friends and sympathetic adult kin. They preoccupy themselves with love affairs and self-decoration. Their elders take pride in their beauty, identify with their sexual adventures, and expect them to be pleasure-seeking and a bit irresponsible.

Youths still manifest some of the selfishness of children who have not fully learned the value of working hard and sharing with others. They also, like children, either do not yet understand or, more likely, do not yet care that working and sharing enable a person to accumulate and give away goods and valuables, leading to renown and to power over others, even sexual power. But individuals vary greatly in the degree to which they accept and act on this simultaneously altruistic and selfish cultural valorization of working and sharing. Some young people are early admired for their industry, productivity, and willingness to contribute. And some mature adults refuse to participate in ritual exchanges beyond the bare minimum expected of everyone in their social position, a minimum enforced by the ever-present threat of punitive sorcery.

Vanatinai culture emphasizes throughout the life cycle both personal autonomy and the power of individual will. This is reflected in a culturally mandated tolerance for personality differences and idiosyncrasies and the usually unquestioning acceptance of the statement, "I don't want to." It accompanies a fiercely egalitarian ethic that refuses to recognize rank or formal authority or the right of any adult to tell another what to do. There are often several big men and big women in one settlement, and their influence over the behavior of others is limited and impermanent. The primary form of social control and coercion, fear of sorcery, also emphasizes the power of individual will. So does the extreme permissiveness of the Vanatinai child-rearing philosophy, with its stress on the child's desires and the danger to health of frustrating them.

This power of individual will is first fully exercised during youth. Young people are expected to be focused on themselves and to learn about themselves as males and females, their likes and dislikes, and their ability to influence others through attempted seductions. The sexual power of beauty and seduction first learned and practiced in youth is extended and transformed in mature adulthood to the more general power to persuade and influence others. Adults use the potency of words and appearance, the force of their personalities, and the strength of their magical and ritual knowledge to shape the actions of others to what they desire or think right.

YOUTH CULTURES AND PACIFIC ISLAND SOCIETIES

The Vanatinai life stage of youth is part of a widespread regional cultural pattern of gendered identities, ideologies, and behaviors that contrasts with both childhood and adulthood. Extending through much of the island Pacific, this particular culturally marked life stage of youth has been documented by anthropologists for nearly a century. The existence of this cultural pattern, and of a cultural category of youth in traditional Pacific societies, contradicts a great number of works in sociology and cultural studies. These have contended that "youth cultures," often loosely defined, are products of industrializing or postindustrial societies undergoing rapid social change, associated with age-based segregation in schools, and most strongly manifested in mass media, distinctive dress and adornment styles, and other appurtenances of consumer societies.

The term *youth culture* was first used by Chicago sociologist Talcott Parsons in 1942, and referred to "a set of patterns and behavioral phenomena which involve a highly complex combination of age grading and sex rule elements," which he found to be "unique and highly distinctive for American society" (Parsons 1942:607; cf. Wulff 1995).

Anthropologist Ralph Linton (1942:589) published his essay on age and sex categories in *American Sociological Review* the same year. An editor's note asks at the outset, "Do age groups have separate cultures?" Linton remarks on the cross-cultural variability of societal recognition of adolescence "as a distinct category." Turning his Marquesan field experience to good use, he remarks,

> Thus in Polynesia adolescents are sharply differentiated from both children and adults. They are relieved of most social and economic responsibilities and left free to pursue their courting and tasks of personal adjustment. Their primary social functions are those of providing amusement, by their organized dancing and singing, for the age groups above and below their own, and of cementing the friendly relations between villages by their reciprocal group visits. . . . Trends toward the development of a somewhat similar system are to be seen in at least the upper classes of our own society. The social roles of undergraduates in a coeducational university have much in common with those of the Polynesian *Kaioi*.

Linton further comments that, in societies without a "formal recognition of adolescence," the young person is incorporated either into the "child status" of "submission and dependence" or the adult status of "social obligations" (595–96).

Linton's anthropological and comparative article has been largely over-looked. Parsons's sociological usage of the term *youth culture*, explicitly identified with adolescence in America, came into wide usage, marking off what James Coleman (1961) more precisely referred to a generation later as "the emer-gence of an adolescent subculture in industrial society." Significantly, Coleman's own research focus was on the American public school, the age-grading institu-tion par excellence of industrial societies, one which has only had a major im-pact on Papua New Guinean young people in the last generation or so, particu-larly since independence in 1976 (cf. Herdt and Leavitt, this volume).

Since its origins in the American sociological literature, the term *youth cul-ture* dispersed to the Euro-American public and was used both in mass media and public discourse during the late 1960s to refer to what was also called "the counterculture." This was supposed to be an amorphous, transnational, overlap-ping set of youthful subcultures comprised of post–World War II baby boom adolescents and young adults, conspicuously marked by dress styles, music, sexual behavior, choice of intoxicants, and often by a rejection—temporary or ostensibly permanent—of adult work roles.

British sociologists of the Birmingham School further developed the study of disparate congeries of urban working-class youths in what Hebdige (1979), for example, labeled a "subculture." The Birmingham School has in turn been influential in the interdisciplinary and transnational cultural studies movements of 1980s and 1990s academia, involving literary and media critics, historians, so-ciologists, and, less often, anthropologists.

These cultural studies scholars too have often focused on the consumption patterns and personal styles of urban working-class or middle-class European or American youths—usually white and male—or on the mass media or cul-tural productions that supposedly appeal to youth and reflect their values and sentiments. The theoretical focus of these studies is most frequently on resis-tance, deviation, and consumption. Their unfounded underlying assumption, not always explicitly stated or placed in cultural or historical context, is gener-ally that youth cultures, or subcultures, are products of urban, or urbanizing, industrial or postindustrial consumer societies.

Despite the pioneering research of Margaret Mead (1928) and Bronislaw Malinowski (1929), anthropological studies of adolescence, or youth cultures or subcultures, have been surprisingly sparse over the last sixty years (cf. Schlegel and Barry 1991; Schlegel 1995a; 1995b; Herdt and Leavitt, this volume), leaving largely unchallenged quite a number of allegedly global generalizations that are based on observations of Western urban white youth and the cultural produc-tions they consume. More recently, anthropologists have again begun publish-ing ethnographically informed studies of youth in a variety of societies, Western and nonwestern. They have done, I believe, a significantly better job of analyzing larger cultural and historical forces as they affect youth, and in placing their findings in cross-cultural and comparative perspective (see, e.g., Condon 1987; Burbank 1988; Davis and Davis 1989; Amit-Talai and Wulff 1995).

It is obviously true that youth subcultures and their distinctive styles, argot, and consumer products—often transnational in scope—are most visible to local adults and to social scientists and cultural studies scholars when the young people in question live in urban industrial societies and where video cameras, radios, and other mass media are plentiful. These often are local youths' reactions to and representations of an ongoing absorption into the global economy, national education systems, worldwide religious movements, and the transnational flow of consumer products and media.

But small-scale, non-European societies, such as those in the Pacific Islands, often have their own indigenous, traditional youth cultures. Anthropologists today need to continue the disciplinary tradition, begun by Mead and Malinowski, of describing and analyzing these indigenous youth cultures and life stages, and of offering them—both within and beyond our disciplinary boundaries—for cross-cultural comparison and cultural critique.

Recent anthropological studies of adolescence have, understandably, heavily emphasized the social contexts and consequences of rapid cultural change and their accompanying generational conflicts. These often include increasing age segregation through formal schooling and migrant labor, greater access to transnational commercial media, and a loosening of parental authority. This last is particularly significant in the choice of marriage partners, control of female virginity and sexuality, and adult supervision.[3]

A point worth considering in comparing the cross-cultural impacts of rapid social change and the increasing influences of a cash economy, wage labor migration, schools, and national and transnational media on the lives of young people and their elders is that the young in some "traditional" societies are significantly more satisfied with their lives than in others where their activities have customarily been more restricted. For example, in societies that traditionally permitted, and expected, premarital sexual activity or allowed young people free choice of marriage partners, youthful sexuality and daily freedom of movement are generally not major points of conflict, and the cultural break with what the young person may perceive as an oppressive home village or urban neighborhood may not be as dramatic as in, say, Morocco, Egypt, or Nepal. In a similar fashion, increasing articulation with the global political economy raises some aspects of women's status and increases women's autonomy in traditionally male dominant societies, while it often restricts the influence and autonomy of women in gender egalitarian societies (cf. Lepowsky 1993).

This satisfaction with personal autonomy and quality of life at home may be one reason Vanatinai youths migrate significantly less often in search of work or schooling than do young people from many other parts of Papua New Guinea. It may also explain why even Trobriand youths, from islands with alarmingly dense and growing populations, and with relatively high rates of primary school completion compared to the rest of Papua New Guinea, are less likely to migrate than other young Papua New Guineans who have completed primary school. As an illustration, one young Trobriand man I met in Port Moresby, highly educated and with many potential career opportunities, told me that urban life was significantly less exciting in most ways than village life back on Kiriwina (although he enjoyed going to the cinema), and that he and his friends had definitely had a much more active and satisfying sexual life back home. He held a series of challenging government and commercial jobs for several years, but eventually returned to his home village.

By contrast, young unmarried men from Rossel Island, just east of Vanatinai—traditionally a male gerontocracy where marriages were tightly controlled by male elders who jealously accumulated and hoarded the necessary "shell money" bride-wealth—were observed as early as 1920 by anthropologist W. E. Armstrong (1928) leaving the island in search of work on plantations or coastal vessels, returning several years later with cash to exchange to male elders for *ndap,* the local ceremonial shell currency, so that they could marry. Young men from Rossel Island continued to migrate in much greater numbers than those from Vanatinai through the 1980s.

Rapid social change anywhere in the world clearly has a disproportionate impact on the young, often diminishing the perceived and the actual authority of their elders, and offering alternative visions of future life courses and possible routes to wealth, power, and satisfaction. Young people are the ones who are segregated by age in primary schools, high schools, and colleges—as well as in factories, back offices, and plantation fields—and who are socialized into the distinctive age- and cohort-based styles, values, and customs that characterize these educational institutions and workplaces. Nevertheless, there are behavioral styles and customs distinctive to the life stage of youth in many preindustrial or culturally conservative small-scale societies.

The cumulative weight of ethnographic evidence from the Pacific Islands, as well as corroborating accounts from other small-scale, nonindustrial societies, clearly indicates that "youth cultures," or more precisely, youth subcultures—consisting of clearly defined ideologies, values, expectations, and actions appropriate to the life stage that begins around the time of biological puberty and ends with the establishment of a stable, socially recognized marital union—are a distinctive and traditional aspect of many small-scale societies. It is appropriate to point out here that, just as the term *culture* is increasingly recognized in the 1990s to refer to systems of knowledge and practice with notably blurred boundaries and locations that are replete with contradictions, a subculture of youth need not be fully discrete or separated from those of the life stages that precede and follow it. Thinking of these small-scale societies, for the sake of analysis, as having indigenous youth (sub)cultures dramatically extends the universe of comparative cases for examining youth culture phenomena in global perspective, particularly given the attention to date on industrial societies, rapid social change, male urban youths, conflict and resistance, and patterns of consumption and style.

Verrier Elwin (1947), in his study of the Muria of Central India, uses the evocative phrase, "the kingdom of the young," which comes from the Muria themselves, to refer to the semiautonomous lives of young people of both sexes in this "tribal" horticultural and foraging society. Muria unmarried boys and girls past puberty live together in their own communal house, or "village dormitory," the *ghotul*, often for six or eight years, preoccupying themselves with beautification and sexual intrigue, and forming serial relationships. They finally leave the *ghotul* when they marry, moving out to start their own families and join the adult world. Adult Muria look back on their youth with enormous nostalgia, as a period of romance and play. As Elwin (1968:viii–xii) notes, there are similar institutions in other "Austro-Asiatic cultures," such as among the Naga of Assam.

Elwin's descriptions of the Muria young people's lives and associations are strikingly similar to Malinowski's (1929) portrait of the *bukumatula*, the Trobriand bachelors' house, where young people slept at night and relaxed during the day, carrying on their sexual affairs without bothering adults, and avoiding the shame of conducting sexual relationships in front of parents and cross-sex siblings. Elwin's and Malinowski's accounts, minus only the youths' special sleeping and meeting houses of the Muria and the Trobriand islanders, are also remarkably parallel with my own observations of the life stage of youth on Vanatinai, and with those of numerous other anthropologists working in Polynesia and Micronesia, as I noted earlier.

A distinctive life stage of youth may be particularly common in small-scale subsistence societies that lack a strong, religiously validated, central ideology of male superiority, and where young people are generally free to engage in sexual activity before marriage. After all, that is what generally happens in all societies when youth are left unchaperoned by adults and able to devise their own activities. In some cases, as on Vanatinai and among commoner Samoans, for example, young women and young men are free to choose their own spouses rather than being subject to the control of elders who arrange their marriages. In other cases, as among the Muria, marriages are arranged by elders. In all of these societies, though, there is a significant lack of control of the sexuality and fertility of younger, unmarried females by elder males—although adultery is forbidden for married people. Male control of female sexuality, and thus the suppression of female autonomy over her own person and actions are defining characteristics of cultural ideologies of male dominance. And in virtually every human society it is the sexuality of girls and young women that is the focus of the most intense cultural attention.

Youth cultures or subcultures in small-scale societies reflect larger forces of social change, and they are the locus of much creative innovation and cultural syncretism by young people. Vanatinai male youth, like Trobriand islanders and many other young Papua New Guineans, have taken up playing guitars and ukeleles and composing soulful "string band" songs of love and homesickness in their own and neighboring languages. As in youth cultures in developing countries, this reflects the influence of youth migration to cities and towns as well as national and global technology or media productions.

The specific sources here include Western musical instruments that gradually spread in popularity, along with musical genres, across the Pacific from Hawaii beginning in the 1920s; youths from other parts of the country, observed in towns, government stations, and distant plantations by the small number of young Vanatinai who have left the island and returned, or who have worked at the station or district office with off-islanders; acquisition of cassette tapes of music produced or pirated on the mainland; and the popular music broadcast on shortwave Radio Milne Bay, part of the national radio network. Young men who are good musicians and singers are called by the English loan word *cowboy*, a term of admiration derived in part from the still popular radio broadcasts of music by the singing cowboys Gene Autry (American) and Slim Dusty (Australian). Note that these famous singing cowboys often are accompanied by Hawaiian-influenced steel guitar. Vanatinai cowboys wear ragged shorts, a couple of meters of flower-printed cotton tucked around the waist, or a pair of blue jeans bought off-island at a secondhand store.

In quite a different vein, I have infrequently seen parties of courting young people gather in a house at night to sing Wesleyan hymns for hours, with breaks for chewing betel nut, smoking, and flirting. I have never seen mature adults sing hymns at social events or work parties. Some of these young people attended mission schools as children.

Adults consider the singing and playing of "*gita*" an amusing part of youthful high spirits and courting behavior, but generally are unmoved by the music that stirs youthful emotions. Elders compose new songs in traditional musical styles. Occasionally, though, string band music substitutes for the all-night drumming and singing at mortuary feasts, and elders dance gamely to it in honor of the ancestor spirits.

But some young men have learned how to drum, all young people know and perform traditional dances, and many know a repertoire of traditional songs, continuing to find them emotionally moving and satisfying. The new styles and consumption patterns do not seem to be perceived on Vanatinai by either youth or adults as resistance or opposition, but as amusing and innovative things that the young have introduced, and that are "something of theirs." Here, even in the face of social change and innovation, youth and adult subcultures are complementary and interpenetrating.

The life stage of youth in subsistence societies—all currently under pressure from external economic systems, material goods, religious beliefs, and cultural ideologies—is an excellent place to look for the vanguards of cultural syntheses, innovations, and changes. As the customs and ideologies of youth are inevitably more deeply affected by school attendance, mission activity, government control, wage labor, and migration, young people in societies such as Vanatinai, where they are traditionally granted a great deal of freedom and license, deal creatively with external pressures on their bodies and beliefs and synthesize new patterns of action and consumption.

SEVEN

Youth in Rotuma, Then and Now

Alan Howard

INTRODUCTION

The island of Rotuma is located at 12° south latitude and 177° east longitude, some three hundred miles north of the Fiji group, with which it has been politically affiliated since 1881. It is a similar distance to the south of Tuvalu, while Futuna, its nearest neighbor to the east, lies 240 miles distant. The closest islands to the west are in Vanuatu, approximately 500 miles away. Rotuma is therefore somewhat isolated, a factor that helps to account for its unique characteristics. The Rotuman language, for example, has peculiarities that distinguish it from others in this part of the Pacific. Although it shows heavy borrowing from both Tongan and Samoan, linguists do not regard Rotuman as a Polynesian language, and its classification has been a matter of debate (Biggs 1965; Churchward 1940; Grace 1959; Pawley 1979). Physically Rotumans show a considerable amount of variation, but in general they resemble the Polynesians to the east rather than their Fijian countrymates. The culture of the island also has a distinctly Polynesian cast to it.

When I first arrived in Rotuma to begin dissertation research in December 1959, I was not much beyond adolescence myself. I found it relatively easy to make friends with the young men in my village. They were as curious about young people in America as I was about what interested them and how they spent their time. When my younger brother arrived to assist in my research—he was only nineteen years old at the time, and unmarried—it made investigating the subculture of youths all the easier. He quickly became part of the young men's group and accompanied them on their various adventures. They instructed him and gossiped in his presence. Much of what I have written about courtship and other aspects of adolescence on Rotuma is based on his experiences and what his Rotuman friends told him.[1]

I did not return to Rotuma until 1987, when I was in my mid-fifties. Much had changed.[2] Whereas Rotuma had previously been governed as part of the British Colony of Fiji, it is now part of an independent Fiji. A wharf had been built in the 1970s and an airstrip was opened in 1981, lessening the island's isolation. In 1960 two-thirds of the Rotuman population were resident on the island, with the remainder in Fiji. In the early 1990s only a quarter of all Rotumans lived on Rotuma. The rest were mostly in Fiji, although substantial numbers now reside in Australia, New Zealand, Europe, and North America. The economy of the island, once almost entirely dependent upon copra exports, now is buoyed by remittances from relatives employed abroad. Money is more plentiful and the material standard of living has improved considerably. Concrete houses have supplanted thatch structures. Refrigerators, motorbikes, pickup trucks, indoor toilets, power lawn mowers, and other appliances are now commonplace.[3]

The subculture of youth has changed as well, in more ways than I am able to relate. Researching adolescence was much more difficult for me in the late 1980s than it was in 1960, for Rotuman teenagers were less interested in talking to a middle-aged man about their activities than they were to a twenty-five year old. As a result I had to rely on information provided by their parents (many of whom were teenagers during my first visit). Nevertheless, some changes are rather obvious, and I will focus on them in this chapter.

Life Cycle Categories

Rotumans divide the life cycle prior to adulthood into three stages corresponding to infancy, childhood, and youth. Nursing infants are called *lā riri' susu* (milk children); *lā' riri'* (without the modifier *susu* [milk]) is applied to children past weaning until they finish school, or reach the age of about sixteen if they remain in school. Those who have left school, or are past the age of sixteen, are referred to as *haharagi* (youths). The term *haharagi* means fat, stout, or plump; in good physical condition; youthful; and unmarried, in addition to adolescent (Churchward 1940:212). In all its meanings it has a distinctly positive connotation.

These categories specify social roles and expectations rather than physical stages. Since children begin school at age five or six and may continue into their late teens, and since the term *haharagi* is applied to unmarried men and women well into their twenties and beyond, there is no direct correspondence with the English category of "adolescence."[4] My focus in this chapter is on the period of youth, as defined by Rotumans, rather than on a period defined by age or physiological development.

I begin by describing the subculture of youth in 1960. This is followed by an account of continuities and changes as I experienced them during my recent visits.

THE SUBCULTURE OF YOUTH IN 1960

In 1960 Rotuma was governed by a district officer appointed by the British governor of Fiji and advised by a council of chiefs and elected representatives. The district officer was very much in charge and ruled over the island with a firm hand. His orders had the force of law behind them, and although Rotumans are masters of passive resistance, on the whole they followed his orders. The district officer saw to it that roads were maintained and villages kept clean and sanitary. This meant organizing labor, much of it done by young men. Communal labor was also used to repair thatched houses, in the preparation of feasts, and for various church-related projects. Again, the young men provided the core of labor in most communities. Though not formally organized, they worked as teams, usually under the direction of a district chief, or subchief.[5]

The economy of the island was based on typical Polynesian subsistence crops, including taro, yams, breadfruit, cassava, bananas, and various tropical fruits. Pigs and chickens supplemented fish as main sources of protein. For those not employed by the government or one of the trading companies operating on the island, copra was virtually the sole source of income. When copra prices were high, money was relatively easy to come by; when prices dropped, it took long, arduous hours of work to earn only a few shillings. Copra cutting and drying was a prime occupation of young men.

Of the seven schools on Rotuma in 1960, three (two primary and one secondary) were Catholic and four (three primary and one secondary) were under government control. All the schools, with the exception of the Catholic secondary school for boys only, were coeducational. The secondary schools went up to Form 4 (grade 10), after which students desiring further education had to emigrate to Fiji. Approximately two-thirds of Rotuman children had left school after completing eight years or less, and slipped into the role of *haharagi*. The period of "youth" thus began for most at about age thirteen or fourteen.[6]

While in school, children were generally excused from doing serious work such as gardening, fishing, mat making, and food preparation. They might take on light chores around the house, but spent most of their time out of school playing with friends or studying. Youths, however, composed the mainstay of community labor. During this period they learned proficiency in performing adult tasks—the boys to plant and fish, to build houses and make canoes, to prepare food for feasts; the girls to weave mats, to keep house, to fish, and to prepare everyday meals. Since employment was scarce on the island, youths spent most of their time engaged in subsistence activities and copra cutting.

Historically young men on Rotuma have taken every opportunity to travel. In the eighteenth century, for example, Rotuman men eagerly sought employment aboard European vessels and sailed to all parts of the globe (Allardyce

1885–1886:132–33; Bennett 1831:77, 480; L. Forbes 1875:226; see also Howard 1995). In 1960 the main destinations for Rotuman youths were urban centers in Fiji, where they could obtain employment and experience city life. Many left Rotuma, some for brief excursions, some for several years, some permanently. On Rotuma itself, however, motorized transportation was limited to only a few trucks, two automobiles, and a handful of motorbikes, limiting mobility. For the most part, pedal bikes (difficult to negotiate on roads that vary from sandy to rocky), horses, and walking had to suffice. Youths were therefore largely confined to their home communities most of the time.

Social Relations

The most important relationships for youths in 1960 were with members of their own age group. Boys in particular did not spend much time with their families. As soon as a lad left school he began to associate with the older boys in his village, initially in a somewhat marginal way. During this socialization period no one pressured him to participate in events; the degree to which he got involved was mostly up to him. He might form a close alliance with another boy his age, or perhaps several other boys, thereby establishing a separate subgroup within the larger group of youths in the community. By the time a boy was seventeen or eighteen, however, he and his age mates were usually absorbed into the core of the local contingent. By then they had learned expected behavior by listening to the older boys, by helping them perform various tasks, and by imitating their actions.

During this stage males ordinarily slept away from their parental homes, although each customarily continued to eat with his own family. This was not a formal arrangement. For sleeping houses young men often commandeered structures in temporary disuse, or they would go to the home of an agreeable bachelor or widower. In only a few villages did the boys build their own structures, none of which projected an image of permanence. Likewise, groups were not formally organized, nor were hazing or initiation rituals prerequisite to participation. Membership was unspecified, so it was difficult to determine their composition. Relationships within the groups were generally egalitarian, although older boys frequently asked younger ones to do things for them and the latter ordinarily complied.

Restrictions were much greater on adolescent girls, who did not form peer groups of the same intensity. They slept at home and contributed to household activities more regularly than did males of the same age. Nevertheless, girls formed close friendships with peers and, provided their parents were not too strict, spent some time in mixed groups. They spent most of their time at home with their mothers, grandmothers, and aunts, however.

Modesty in demeanor and dress was required of young women. They were obliged to be fully covered when appearing in public. Wearing shorts, or a bathing suit, was unthinkable. When bathing in the sea, or spending time away from home, they donned a *ha' fali* (one-piece cloth wrap-around). At special events they wore neat, clean dresses, *ha' fali*, or skirts and blouses, but avoided wearing anything that would draw special attention. They wore little or no jewelry, used no lipstick or cosmetics. The object was to look respectable but not to stand out.

Same-sex siblings generally acted warmly and affectionately with one another, and if close in age participated in many of the same activities. When performing serious work older siblings had the right to give instructions and direct activities, and their juniors generally complied. Between siblings of the opposite sex a mild avoidance taboo was the rule. Brothers and sisters rarely would go to the same dances or other youth-oriented social functions. They said they would feel overly shy in one another's company and would not have a good time. At home they were restrained and respectful to one another, and did not participate in the raucous joking that characterized interaction between same sex siblings and friends.

Activities

Although young men formed the nucleus of communal labor they did not regard the obligation as an imposition, since most communal events involved feasting and fun as well as work. They relished the opportunity of working together with friends, even under trying conditions. For example, while discussing the preparations in progress following a hurricane warning, a young man of twenty exclaimed, "We [the young men] are really hoping there will be a storm. Then we'll all get together and go from house to house, tying things down, fixing roofs and doing whatever needs to be done. It's lots of fun." His elders, who stood to lose much in the way of copra (and hence money), crops, and property if the storm were severe, did not share his attitude.

Despite their importance as workers, young men were granted a great deal of license by their elders, who often turned a blind eye to youthful pranks and evasions. Young men were generally absolved from regularly contributing to their households unless there were no married adult males to carry the burden. In general, Rotumans saw youth as a time for fun and recreation, and for courtship—something of a golden age. The real burdens of responsibility came after marriage, when couples started families of their own.

Nevertheless, young men farmed and fished, and contributed, albeit irregularly, to their parental households. Often they maintained plantations that they farmed together, on ground requisitioned from one of the larger landholders in their locality. Typically, each boy developed a plot of his own and disposed of the produce as he saw fit. Some food was contributed to the household in which he lived, some was cooked and eaten on special occasions, and some donated toward community feasts. In the latter case the boys sometimes presented food as a group, rather than as individuals.

Sports—primarily soccer, rugby, cricket, and the indigenous sports of *hula* (wrestling) and *tika* (dart-throwing)—also preoccupied the unmarried men. For competitive events they trained in earnest, giving up smoking and holding team practices several times a week. During a "season," a soccer, rugby, or cricket team practiced for two or three hours every afternoon except Sunday, sometimes under the supervision of a teacher who had learned the finer points of the sport in Fiji or New Zealand. Most practice sessions consisted of playing an intrasquad game; little time was devoted to learning specific techniques, and strategy was rarely discussed. As a result, athletes tended to reach peak performance quickly, but did not improve beyond their gross abilities.

Sports clubs—ephemeral groups organized to play games of European origin—formed when a particular sport generated sufficient interest. A specific sport's season was usually initiated by a group, or groups, of young men who casually took it up. During 1960, for example, a number of groups formed for the purpose of playing table tennis and soccer. It all began when workers at the government station set up a ping-pong table. At first only a few government employees and their friends played in their spare time, but before long regulars began holding informal competitions. The idea caught on and tables were built elsewhere on the island—one at the Rotuma Cooperative Association headquarters in the district of Noa'tau, one at the Catholic Mission Station in Juju, and one in the main village of Motusa. These places became headquarters for sports clubs, which soon included most of the young men on the island (including many who were married). At irregular intervals the clubs issued challenges to one another, initiating interclub competitions. Interest in table tennis waxed strong for a while, and within a remarkably short time many young men who had never seen the game played before became excellent competitors. Equipment used met European tournament specifications and international rules governed the matches.

About six months after the table tennis craze began, an interest in soccer developed. Each club purchased uniforms and equipment and began regular practice sessions. Eventually cricket replaced soccer. Ultimately, interest in organized sports would wane to the point that the clubs would cease functioning. Girls' clubs, organized for the purpose of playing basketball and field hockey, emerged and dissolved in the same way.

The requirement for hosting feasts at interclub competitions contributed to the disintegration of sports clubs. At the very least clubs were expected to provide refreshments to visiting teams; initially this might include only beverages and cakes, but eventually one of the groups would invite others to share a meal as well. A multiclub competition that consumed the better part of a day, requiring a meal in between, might stimulate the escalation. Visiting clubs felt obliged to reciprocate, indeed, not simply to reciprocate, but to prepare a more elaborate repast. Each club escalated in turn until the demands became excessive, and members started dropping out because they could no longer afford to participate.

At the height of interest, club organization became quite complex. The Ahau club, to which I belonged, was perhaps the most elaborate. We elected officers, including a chairman, secretary, and treasurer, and meetings followed parliamentary procedure. The chairman assigned a committee to frame a constitution. When the club needed money to purchase equipment, we initiated three methods of raising it: (1) levying a subscription fee on each member, (2) holding European-style dances and retaining proceeds from admissions and refreshments sold, and (3) fining members for tardiness or missing practice sessions and meetings. Eventually our meetings took on a businesslike flavor, with a major portion of the time spent discussing finances. This contributed to making participation less enjoyable for most of the members, and to diminished interest.

Dart throwing *(tika)* and wrestling *(hula)*, two traditional sports still played in 1960, were differently organized. Spontaneous interest initiated competitions in both sports, but instead of forming clubs, formal matches were organized between the two sides of the island, the "sunrise" and "sunset" sides.[7]

A few youngsters in one of the villages would initiate *tika* competitions among themselves. The darts were made of straight reeds about three feet long, with hardwood tips; the object was to throw them as far as possible along a sandy stretch of road. Distances were calculated from the point at which the darts were thrown to their final resting place, a good proportion of the throw being a slide along the ground.[8] As interest mounted, more and more young men participated, and villages challenged one another to informal matches. Whole districts got involved, and eventually the men from one side of the island agreed among themselves to issue a challenge to the other side. They made their desire known to the chiefs of their districts, and if agreed, the chiefs negotiated a time and place to hold a formal competition.

A significant portion of the island's population attended formal *tika* matches, which involved a good deal of ceremony. The host side (the one accepting the challenge) prepared a feast to which each family contributed. All the chiefs attended and were afforded traditional courtesies. They in turn made speeches of thanks, appreciation, and apology.

Wrestling *(hula)* was also initiated by the casual play of young men and was similarly organized. As the seriousness of play increased, intradistrict and intrasectional competitions were held, and the best man selected. Then, as in the case of *tika,* the young men requested their chiefs to challenge chiefs from the other side of the island who, if agreed, organized matches to select their champion. The ultimate competition consisted of a number of individual matches, resulting from spontaneous challenges, but only that between the champions from each side counted in determining which side won. The mode of wrestling was similar to sumo wrestling in Japan; the first man thrown to the ground lost.

Sports competitions were taken seriously, especially between rival villages or districts, driven by an unmistakable will to win. Young men often responded badly to the frustrations of losing, and fights sometimes broke out toward the end of a hard-fought game. As a rule, the more important the game, the more frequent the flare-ups.

Although the nature of their tasks differed, the activities of unmarried women paralleled those of unmarried men in many respects. Just as young men formed the nucleus of male communal labor in their communities, young women provided the core of female communal labor. On any occasion when a village or district hosted visitors, the young men prepared and cooked most of the food, and the young women did most of the serving and cleaning up. The spirit of comradeship that pervaded boys' work gangs also characterized those of girls.

Young women were as enthusiastic about sports as their male age mates and were equally keen competitors, and equally temperamental losers. Major sports for women were netball (a version of basketball) and field hockey, both of which were taught in school as part of physical education (as were cricket and rugby for the boys). As with males, females sporadically held competitions between groups from different localities. Both males and females participated in track-and-field events as part of physical education at school, and once a year, on the day celebrating Rotuma's cession to Great Britain (May 13), they represented their districts in an islandwide competition held at the government station.

In their households young women assisted with cooking, washing clothes, cleaning the house, and fishing on the reef. They were also given much of the responsibility for taking care of infants and young children. This they did enthusiastically, providing as much indulgence as did parents and grandparents. Young women also learned to weave mats, a primary occupation for women at that time. Mats are critical items in Rotuman ceremonial exchanges, and fine white mats in particular *(apei)* are highly valued. Fine mats are a major form of wealth for Rotuman families and are produced exclusively by women. One of the main ways in which a young woman could enhance her reputation in 1960 was to become a skillful weaver of mats.

Church provided another venue for activities. The Methodist Youth Fellowship (MYF) periodically held special events and met regularly in most parishes. In the district of Noa'tau, for example, members held prayer meetings every

Tuesday, and on Thursday evenings they met to play table tennis, cards, and checkers. No age limit was imposed, and many individuals in their late twenties participated. This is but one indication of the flexibility of the category *haharạgi* at the time. The Catholic Church had comparable religious and recreational programs for their youths.[9]

When young men and women got together informally in groups they frequently played guitars, ukeleles, and sang Rotuman songs—songs they often composed themselves. They also adapted tunes from other Pacific islands or translated popular English songs. In order to overcome their shyness, young men sometimes had an alcoholic drink or two, but rarely got drunk. Since spirits and beer were expensive and not readily available, home-brewed orange wine was their main indulgence.

During the Christmas season opposite-sex youths had special opportunities to get together, in large measure because young women were allowed opportunities to stay out late. This period is called *av mane'a* (time to play); it is the hot season on Rotuma, when little serious work gets done. The period lasts for approximately six weeks, from the beginning of December until mid-January. A main activity of youths during this time is "going *fara*" (to ask or to beg), which involves mixed groups of young men and women going from village to village at night, entertaining selected households with song and dance in exchange for food and drink. Younger children are allowed to tag along in the early evening, but the youths and adults who join them often stay out until early morning.

Fara groups usually form spontaneously. Someone will suggest to his or her friends that they go *fara* one evening, and word is passed around the village. Groups vary in size from half a dozen to thirty or so participants. Anyone who wants to can join a group, which has no formal organization. During the course of an evening individuals, including some from other villages, might join while others drop out.

Typically, a group quietly approaches a house and sits down in a convenient place. Properly done, the first piece is instrumental only, played on guitars and ukeleles. Then the rest of the group joins in with a song. Anyone might introduce a song by starting to sing; the rest of the group joins in, and those with guitars and ukeleles provide accompaniment. Usually, however, participants discuss which song they will sing next after completing the last one. People make suggestions, one is agreed upon, someone commences singing it, and the rest join in. Most songs are accompanied by dancing, and one by one the merrymakers get up and choose a partner, dancing in Rarotongan style.[10] Everyone, except those playing instruments, normally dances at least once at each location.

After a short period of time, people inside the house make an appearance, often after aroused from sleep, and bring lanterns to light the scene. They douse the performers with sweet-smelling powders, perfume, and pomade in a show of appreciation. Host families sometimes bring out tins of biscuits, watermelon, pineapples, or other food and drink to reward the performers. They sometimes participate in the dancing, and youths from the household may join the group for the remainder of their excursion.

For boys and girls who are romantically interested in each other, *fara* presents opportunities to pair off prior to the conclusion of a night's activities and to spend some time alone together. A favorite pastime following *fara* is trying to figure out who has gone off with whom.

Another traditional form of entertainment during the Christmas season, more prevalent in times past but still existent in 1960, was *manea' hune'ele* (beach games). As the name suggests, they were played on the beach, away from a village. One game, *kau mo'mo'o* (to lie in wait or ambush), was a version of hide-and-seek, in which first the girls, then the boys, would take turns hiding. If a boy found a girl with whom he shared a romantic interest, or visa versa, they might linger a while before rejoining the group. Another game, *hil lea 'ou vārvāreag* (choose your favorite) was a version of spin-the-bottle, except without a bottle. Girls and boys would sit in rows, about ten feet apart, facing each other. The girls would begin by tying a kerchief over the eyes of one of their members, twirl her around several times, then face her toward the line of boys. The first boy she touched must kiss her, or the boys lose. Then it was the boys' turn, and so on until they tired of it and switched to a different game. Another game involving a blindfold was *he' tāe sạmuag he* (call out the nickname). In this instance the boys and girls formed a circle, with the blindfolded individual in the center. The circle moved around the one in the middle until he or she managed to touch someone. The circle then stopped and the blindfolded person tried to identify the person whom he or she had touched. If the one in the middle gave the correct answer the person touched became "it" and took his or her turn in the center. The fun of the game came from the fact that everyone's family has a humorous story *(tāe sạmuag)* associated with them. These are generally known, but if not, participants were obliged to tell something funny about themselves or their families before the game began. A word or two referring to the story became people's nicknames, which were chanted by the people in the circle. For example, one man's great-grandmother had reputedly rejected some gold coins as buttons without holes. When he was in the center the group would chant "buttons" over and over again.

Quite often the last game played was *'a papại* (to eat *papại*). In this game the boys and girls sit one behind one another in a line. The boy who sits at the front of the line is called the "king." The others, who are behind him, are called *papại* (large edible tubers, Cyrtosperma spp.). One person, usually a boy, is designated owner of the "plantation." He walks around his plantation carrying a stick. Another boy, sitting some ten or so meters away, is designated king of another land. He has a servant with him, usually one of the strongest boys. During the course of the game, the owner of the plantation tells the king at the head of his *papại* that he is going away, and asks the king to look after his garden. When the owner leaves, this is a signal for the foreign king to send his servant to the king of the plantation to beg him for a *papại* he might feed upon. The plantation king tells the foreign king's servant to pick any one of the *papại* he wants to take back to his master. Then the servant goes over to the girl selected by the foreign king, attempts to pick her up bodily, and carry her away. The boy immediately behind the girl in line is her "root," and holds her around the waist in an effort to keep her from being carried off.

If the servant is successful the foreign king gets to hug the girl (symbolically eating the *papại*). When the owner of the plantation returns, he counts his *papại* and, when noticing one missing, scolds the king at the head of the line. He then punishes him, usually by having him stretch out his hands and hitting them with the stick he is carrying. Different boys in turn are chosen to be the alien king, and if each one keeps his *papại*, the game ends with paired-off couples.

The Christmas season was especially important in 1960 since it offered Rotuman youths opportunities for courtship denied them during the rest of the year, when girls were far more restricted. *Fara* and beach games provided culturally structured frames for courtship which relaxed the prohibitions that ordinarily applied to romantic escapades. The message communicated was that courtship cannot be trusted to individual whims, which might result in a couple's defying the cultural order. By providing an approved, culturally ordered framework for courtship, Rotumans reinforced the sense of obligation courting couples owe to their kinsmen and their communities.

Courtship

In 1960 parents strove to groom their daughters as desirable spouses. Although this required that they learn to perform all the requisite housewifely chores, it also required, more importantly perhaps, learning the decorum of a proper Rotuman lady. This included modesty with a touch of shyness, consideration for others, and respectfulness. A subtle sense of humor and unobtrusive coquettishness were also assets, but should not be salient. Olfactory sensations were particularly stressed, and youths of both sexes made use of sweet-smelling flowers, oils, and pomades to enhance their attractiveness. Female socialization aimed at producing desirable wives because it was virtually the only role open to women who remained on the island. Success meant attracting a man who would be a considerate husband, a warm and loving father, and, most important of all, a good provider. The ways in which a girl learned the essential aspects of self-presentation and strategies for getting a desirable husband were varied and complex; some were overtly taught by parents, but much was learned by unconscious imitation of culturally approved models.

With regard to premarital sex, Rotumans maintained a double standard. Boys were expected to pursue sexual gratification whereas girls were discouraged and, in most cases, closely guarded. Restrictions on unmarried girls date back to premissionary days, when brides were required to undergo virginity tests at marriage. Control of premarital sex was more social than moral, however, and although missionary teachings have reinforced the moral dimension, social aspects of control remained salient. In traditional times virgins were more desirable as wives because they had demonstrated their submission to the cultural order and so were expected to conform to the rules governing proper wifely behavior. Virginity thus enhanced a girl's desirability and increased her chances of making a suitable match. Since the dominant residence pattern following marriage was uxorilocal (the husband coming to reside with his wife's family), this usually benefited her entire kin group, in some cases yielding economic, political, and military benefits.

Rotuman attitudes toward premarital sex in 1960 were rooted in a conception of sexual intercourse that involved a male taking license with a female. Whether or not she consented was not the issue. Sexual license was considered justified only when a young man accepted corresponding responsibilities, which meant, in effect, that he support her economically. To state this arrangement in terms of social economics, sexual license over women was a valued "commodity," and for a man to take it without paying the appropriate price (accepting responsibility for her economic support) was equivalent to stealing. As a result, social controls over sexual behavior were strong.

In precolonial times a girl's sexuality was "owned" by her local kinship group, and all its members benefited from a favorable marital transaction. Correspondingly, members of a girl's local kinship group took an interest in controlling her behavior; by taking sexual liberty with an unmarried girl, a boy was committing an offense against the entire group. Despite the fact that localized kin groups no longer operated as effective social units in 1960, and no other clearly circumscribed group stood to gain in a comparable way by a "good" marriage, premarital chastity was still valued for girls. Sexual transgressions were regarded as offenses against a girl's family and her close kinsmen. They implored her to remain virtuous and not to shame them, and attempted to control her movements so that she did not have the opportunity to do so. Brothers, in particular, monitored their sisters' behavior, for they were most likely to bear the brunt of ridicule if their sisters acquired a reputation for promiscuity.

This is not to imply that girls were merely passive players in the game of courtship. They certainly were not, and in fact sometimes took initiative and exercised control over budding relationships. But they were encouraged to display a submissive demeanor and were generally thought of as potential victims rather than as persons with strong volitional controls.

In order to understand the nature of Rotuman courtship behavior I found it necessary to relate it to the pattern of childhood socialization. Three child-rearing practices in particular appeared to play an important role: a high degree of bodily contact and physical demonstrations of affection, the association of affection with material indulgence, and discipline by ridicule (Howard 1970).

As an apparent consequence of gratifying physical contact in childhood, youths seemed motivated to express affection physically, frequently walking hand-in-hand with friends of the same sex. At first I found it rather strange to see husky young men walking holding hands, but the implication of homosexuality that might be inferred in San Francisco or London did not apply. I came across, in fact, no evidence of exclusive homosexuality at all.[11] It simply seemed that when Rotumans got to like each other, they expressed their fondness physically, regardless of sex. As far as courtship was concerned, this meant that romances were assumed to become quickly sexualized. Any hint of a romantic attachment therefore had sexual overtones.

The association of emotional commitment with material indulgence carried over into courtship with two important ramifications. First, giving became instrumental for the gratification of emotional needs. Thus young men, in order to express affection to their girlfriends, periodically gave presents bought with money earned from cutting copra. Girls were in a more difficult position. For a balanced relationship, each person was expected to give and receive gifts of roughly equivalent value. Girls, however, having less access to cash, had less to give; the main gifts they had to offer in reciprocation were sexual favors. They therefore experienced considerable pressure to sexually engage a boyfriend who regularly provided store-bought presents. Only disreputable girls had sex without regard for reciprocation, the implication being they wantonly enjoyed sex for its own sake instead of granting favors as a gift of love; such girls were regarded as fair game. Second, women with no economically productive males in their households sometimes sought to alleviate material deprivation by forming sexual alliances with men of means. This cannot be interpreted as prostitution, for the element of kindness was fundamental. A man who impersonally offered money or gifts in exchange for sexual intercourse would likely have been harshly refused. Sex, in other words, was clearly construed as the product of an intimate interpersonal relationship rather than as an appetite-satisfying indulgence.

Discipline by ridicule also shaped courtship patterns. As a result of relentless teasing for breaches of social rules, Rotumans learned to avoid situations that might expose them to ridicule, and since courtship behavior is a prime target for teasing and banter, they scrupulously avoided its public display. Affectionate behavior was particularly inhibited in public, since it was regarded as a form of showing off. As one young man put it, "If a boy and girl are affectionate in front of others, it would be just like they were saying they are the only people in the world in love." In effect, they would invite ridicule by tacitly suggesting that they cared so much for each other they were impervious to the taunts of their fellows. Few Rotumans are so insensitive. Even married couples took care not to express affection overtly, and often went separately to church or other community functions.

For these reasons courtship in 1960 was surreptitious, and lovers carefully concealed their alliances. Unrelated boys and girls avoided being seen talking privately to one another. If they were seen together, others might infer they were lovers, or in the process of becoming lovers. This would result in social pressure from their families, urging that the presumed affair either be legitimized through marriage or terminated. Indicative of such caution was the pattern of social intercourse at European-style dances.

The dances were usually held in a meetinghouse or a house temporarily unoccupied. Generally only unmarried man and women attended, but sometimes young married couples would participate. Guitars and ukeleles provided music, with a persistent Polynesian rhythm accompanying every song, although many tunes were recognizable adaptations of American pop hits. The girls sat around on chairs, and at the beginning of each dance boys trickled over and asked them to dance with a tap on the knee, usually while looking away. During the dance couples did not talk to each other. Their faces were fixed and rigid, with somewhat vacant stares. After each dance the boys escorted their partners back to their chairs, without at most a polite word of thanks. Between dances the boys went outside where they joked with their friends, discussed various girls, and gossiped. If some of the guys had brought a container of home brew, beer, or a bottle of liquor they kept it outside and passed it around. They said they drank because they were nervous and needed to gain courage to ask girls to dance. A boy rarely danced with the same girl more than two or three times in an evening, for fear others would begin to tease him.

Fear of ridicule did not suppress courtship behavior, of course; in fact, it sometimes had a reverse effect. A boy and girl might be seen talking innocently together, but when the gossip and joking started they might decide to go ahead and become lovers since people were talking about them anyway. Rather than suppressing courtship, social pressures led to an elaboration of the process, bringing into play all the ingenuity that youths could muster. A game of intrigue was continually afoot, with notes passed through trusted friends and clandestine meetings arranged on the spur of the moment. Boys usually made the first approach, although they were generally reluctant until they had some indication that their advances would not be rebuked. Often time was short, involving only a few seconds in which to make intentions known. In these precious moments a boy would profess his love and attempt to arrange a meeting, but if the girl was willing, if she had been waiting for his approach, a great deal could be decided very quickly. Meetings usually took place in a secluded spot to minimize chances of detection. Girls sometimes sneaked out of their houses at night for a rendezvous under the pretense of going to the toilet. More rarely, since it involved a greater risk of discovery, a boy would sneak into his girlfriend's house under cover of darkness with the expectation of leaving before her parents or brothers awoke. Other opportunities sometimes presented themselves when throngs of people returned from evening church services or other communal events. Partners would inconspicuously drop away from the group, then go to a prearranged meeting place where they would have a brief encounter before returning home.

This is not to suggest that most girls readily took partners in clandestine affairs. Even if a girl liked a boy who approached her, concern for family motivated her to avoid casual involvements. A good deal of seduction, coupled with convincing reassurances, was usually required to persuade a girl to grant sexual favors. Typically a suitor would proclaim the intensity of his love and promise marriage. The girl might respond to his overtures with the tactical assertion that he was not really sincere—that he only wanted to have his way with her and would then leave, making a fool of her. He would attempt to allay her anxieties by giving her presents to demonstrate his sincerity, and unless something intervened, negotiations would continue until the girl had extracted a sufficient demonstration of commitment to justify, in her own mind at least, her submission.

Sweethearts rarely joked in each other's company and on the whole acted exceptionally respectfully to one another. If a boy engaged in banter with his girlfriend, others (including the girl) might interpret it as an indication that he took the relationship lightly, that his promises were insincere. Getting involved in a romantic affair made a girl vulnerable to devastating ridicule, and her boyfriend needed to reassure her by demonstrating that he took her seriously. Only a disreputable girl permitted her lovers to joke without taking offense. If a girl and boy joked freely with one another, therefore, people assumed they had no romantic interest in each other. Correspondingly, a youth with a romantic interest in another likely reacted to certain types of joking—especially banter with sexual or romantic overtones—with embarrassment rather than reciprocation. Thus an embarrassed response to joking sometimes signaled romantic interest, and a girl wishing to rebuff a boy might purposely banter with him to indicate her lack of interest. A boy making an unwanted overture exposed himself to possible ridicule if the girl chose to treat it as a joke and make it public.

For these reasons courtship took on the quality of an intricate game based on subtle signals and attempts to interpret barely perceptible cues. Since restraint characterized relationships between unrelated boys and girls under any circumstances, one could not easily identify lovers, although in their anxiety to avoid suspicion they might appear *too* shy with each other in public.

Young men learned about sex and courtship predominantly from their peers, since parents rarely discussed such topics with their children. By listening to the older boys talk about their experiences, real and fantasized, they learned most of what they needed to know about the game of courtship. Young men generally confined their discussions to sexual encounters with disreputable girls. They generally kept secret affairs with a respectable girl, either because they had feelings for her and had honorable intentions, or because they considered it strategic to do so. At most they would inform close friends, whose assistance they might solicit in winning her over. Informing friends of an interest in a particular girl had the effect of declaring her off-limits. On the other hand, by indiscriminately publicizing an affair with a respectable girl, a boy risked public censure. He could expect adults in the community to demand that he either propose marriage or terminate the relationship.

Young men often experienced first coitus with an older woman, usually a widow or divorcée with prior sexual experience, or alternatively with a disreputable girl around his own age. An older woman would sometimes take the initiative in teaching the young novice the finer points of lovemaking. In return, her lover would provide regular supplies of food and other necessities. In some instances a young man might become sufficiently attached to an older woman to marry her.

When their initial experience was with a disreputable girl, older peers generally offered instruction and encouragement. Girls known for promiscuity, and there were not many, usually lived in households devoid of a dominant male; indeed, the absence of a father or older brother appeared instrumental in the development of promiscuity, for it was they who exercised the strongest controls over a girl's behavior. Households lacking a dominant male sometimes became hangouts for young men, where they often ended up spending the night. In exchange for sexual favors they helped to support the family by bringing food and doing masculine chores.

Young girls often had no knowledge of sexual physiology; in some cases they were reputedly so ignorant that they could be induced to sexual intercourse without realizing it. Feigned ignorance could also be an excuse for a girl, allowing her to skirt responsibility for her submission.

Since none but a few of the most educated persons practiced contraception, sexual liaisons involved a high risk of pregnancy, but an extensive analysis of demographic data indicates that only about 20 percent of the young women became pregnant before marriage (that is, gave birth to a child when single or in less than eight months after a wedding). Considering the commonly held stereotype of Polynesian sexual practices, this figure is strikingly low. Four out of five unmarried girls were not sexually active enough to get pregnant. Adolescent sterility might have been a factor, but effective social controls more likely accounted for this relatively low rate of premarital pregnancy.

When an unmarried woman learned that she was pregnant she would commonly confront her lover and remind him of his promises. If sincere and willing to marry, he would take appropriate steps, but otherwise would terminate the relationship. People then regarded the girl as tricked, provided she had not been promiscuous or previously gotten into trouble. Her family held the boy responsible in contempt, but would not otherwise harass him. If he formally apologized to the girl's parents, and accepted economic responsibility for the child's support, he could minimize antagonisms, but a young man who gained a reputation as a chronic philanderer became an object of scorn rather than a hero, even to his own kinsmen.

MARRIAGE

The golden years of youth abruptly ended at marriage. Even before the ceremony, people impressed on young couples the solemnity of the step they were taking, or in some cases, that was taken for them.

Three principal types of marital arrangement existed on Rotuma in 1960. Most prestigious was *sok fāeag* (to join through talk), characterized by formal negotiations between the boy's and girl's families. The young man, or members of his family desiring the match, initiated negotiations by sending a representative to the girl's family to speak on his behalf. A suitor often sent his father or an eloquent uncle, but if he wanted to add weight to the proposal, he would recruit a man of rank—a subchief, or even the district chief—to present the overture. According to custom the girl's parents could make the decision without consulting her, although that was rarely the case, but some marriages were in fact arranged between individuals who barely knew one another and had not courted.[12] An accepted offer initiated a series of gift exchanges, culminating in an elaborate wedding ceremony. Properly arranged marriages brought honor to the families involved for several reasons: they were premised on the presumption that the girl was virginal and hence untainted; they followed prescribed custom, therefore reinforcing it; and they involved feeding large segments of the community at a series of feasts. Following a *sok fāeag* wedding, custom called for the couple to stay with the wife's family, at least for an initial period.

A second type of marital arrangement was called *fu'u* (to stay). This took place when a boy went to stay at his girlfriend's house, amounting to a declaration of intention. In 1960, *fu'u* marriages commonly occurred between couples who had been lovers. When revealed, the girl's family usually accepted the boy's proposal, and he remained in their household until a legal marriage was arranged. Going *fu'u* could also be a strategic move, especially when the match was opposed by either family. In other instances boys were encouraged to go *fu'u* as a means of avoiding the expense of a *sok fāeag* wedding. This was more likely if the couple's sexual liaison were common knowledge, since under such circumstances the most important aspect of a *sok fāeag* wedding—the implication of virginity—would be absent.

The third type of marital arrangement, *taupiri* (to follow), involved the girl going to live in the boy's home. A rare occurrence in 1960, it was the most shameful, especially for the girl. If indeed a legal wedding ensued, people referred to it in disparaging terms, using the phrase *fita'ma a'ma'ma'ạkia iria* (just to make them clean). Such unions only resulted when a girl's family completely rejected her suitor, or when they had arranged a match in spite of her attachment to another boy. Going *taupiri* was therefore an act of outright defiance, for which a girl had to formally apologize in order to regain her family's good graces (Malo 1973:13).

Integration into the Community

On the whole, youths integrated well into their communities in 1960. Young women made significant contributions to their households by taking on important tasks like cooking, cleaning, and tending children. Their mat-making activities added both to their family's and community's status by providing prestigious items for exchange. They were valued for their potential to marry well and to bring home a husband who would enhance their family's and community's work force. Though young men were granted considerably more license they formed the core of communal labor and acted responsibly vis-à-vis their families and neighbors. They often contributed significant amounts of food for feasts as well. Though by no means submissive, their actions rarely caused their elders consternation. Occasionally they drank too much and slept too late, or stole someone's chicken to have a midnight snack, or failed to show proper respect to a chief, but these antics were considered typical of young men and were readily forgiven.

THE SUBCULTURE OF YOUTH IN THE 1990S

Following the termination of British colonial rule in 1970, when Fiji gained its independence, responsibility for governing Rotuma shifted to the Rotuma Council. District officers are still appointed to the island, but their powers are substantially reduced. Council politics has therefore replaced executive rule (see Howard 1989; 1991). No one is now in a position to give orders and command compliance. As a result, communal labor is strictly voluntary. Young men and women still supply the labor core for communal events, but only when it suits them. For weddings, funerals, and feasts they generally can be relied upon, but for repairing roads and cleaning up villages their participation is more problematic.

The economy of the island now depends more on remittances from relatives abroad than on copra sales. Although more paying jobs are available than in 1960, few are open to adolescents just out of school. From time to time, various business enterprises require help but the pay is low, and occasionally a major project, such as laying telephone lines, offers temporary employment, but for the most part cutting and drying copra remains the major source of income for young men. They may supplement this by raising pigs, goats, or cows which they can sell, sometimes to their own relatives, for feasts. They spend money on *kava* (a drink made from the root of the *piper mythisticum* plant) and beer, on music tapes, on transportation (especially if they own a motorbike), on clothes, and on various church activities. Young women have more difficulty obtaining money since there are fewer jobs calling for their services. They may sell *fekei* (native puddings) or baked goods and may hold fund-raising events for specific purposes, but otherwise remain financially dependent on their families.

The school system on Rotuma has not substantially altered, although the Catholic secondary school has closed; postprimary Catholic children now attend the government high school, which now goes up to Form 5 (grade 11). Today children remain in school longer, delaying their entry into the youth subculture. Approximately half of the children on the island between the ages of fifteen and nineteen, surveyed in 1989, had gone beyond grade 8.[13] As in 1960, school children are excused from contributing labor to the community.

On the whole, demands on youthful labor have lessened, with the preparation of feast foods the main exception. The shift from thatch to cement dwellings has resulted in less need for routine repairs—a task at which young men excelled. Nowadays house building requires more skilled (adult) labor, which is often paid for (Rensel 1991). Young women are much less confined to their houses, although they continue to assist with childcare and routine chores. In general, the youth of today are far more mobile. Many have motorbikes, some drive cars or trucks for their families, and all have access to public or quasipublic transportation. Whereas in 1960 going to another district was a major event, today it is routine. This means that youths have a much wider network of acquaintances than previously, spread over the entire island.

Social Relations

Despite increased mobility, youths still spend much of their time in the company of their village age mates. It is still commonplace, for example, for young men to sleep together in an empty house or other available accommodation. But I have the impression that peer group solidarity is not as pronounced as in 1960. Individual young men are more likely now to go off on their own, visiting friends or relatives elsewhere on the island. They also sleep at home more often, perhaps because recent house construction includes internal partitions that afford more privacy, making it easier for adolescent siblings of the opposite sex to stay at home together without embarrassment. Same-sex solidarity may also have lessened as a result of fewer restrictions on young women, leading to a greater degree of casual social mixing between the sexes. In addition, peers have become less important as sources of knowledge, since education (in the broadest sense) has become more publicly accessible.

Modesty still is required of young women, but the code has relaxed considerably. It is now acceptable for women to wear shorts around the village and to wear costume jewelry. Parents and brothers now exercise much less control over their daughters and sisters than before. The avoidance taboo that characterized brother-sister relations in the past is less evident, and cross-sex siblings more often co-participate in group activities. They appear relaxed in one another's company and joke more freely. In short, the rather noticeable division between the sexes that was so prominent in 1960 has given way to a much greater degree of gender integration.

Activities

Youths of both sexes still enjoy working together, especially during feasts. Characteristically, their interactions involve a good deal of light-hearted banter, singing, and horseplay. Young men still go on escapades together and often fish and garden in groups; as in the past, they make sporadic contributions to their families' food supplies.

Sports remains a major preoccupation for most youths, although the traditional sports of wrestling and dart throwing have all but disappeared.[14] Rugby and cricket have been the main interests of the young men in recent years. Rotuma now regularly sends a rugby team to participate in the annual pan-Fiji competition, and the young men look forward to the opportunity this affords them to spend time in Fiji, experiencing urban life and visiting relatives. The organization of these sports is now along district lines, with teams from one district challenging another on an irregular basis. In cricket, a championship team is recognized and when challenged must defend. If beaten, it gives up the "title" to the challenger, which must then defend when called upon. Table tennis experienced a resurgence in 1989, with a few tables scattered around the island, but formal competitions were not held. Track-and-field events are included in physical education programs in the schools, with formal meets held on special occasions.

A major change in young men's activities stems from the development of *kava* drinking groups in most villages. In 1960 *kava* was drunk almost exclusively at ceremonies. But with increased exposure to Fijian culture, in which social *kava* drinking is central, Rotumans have adopted the custom with gusto. Groups of men, ranging from youths to senior citizens, commonly get together in the afternoon, drink *kava,* and talk for hours, sometimes until the wee hours of the morning. Individuals may join a session at anytime and leave at anytime, but the hard core remains for hours on end. Youths often join these groups in an apprentice capacity, learning to pound *kava,* to prepare and serve drinks to their elders. They begin their involvement by sitting on the margins, listening to the conversation and banter. As time goes on they participate more and more, until considered regulars.

For many Rotumans the *kava* groups are anathema. Methodist ministers often rail against *kava* drinking in their sermons; they cite it as a primary cause for the neglect of Christian and familial responsibilities. Many people make comparisons with the past. In the old (pre-*kava* drinking) days, they say, men used to go to their plantations at sunrise and remain all day, working hard. They were extremely productive. Now they only go for a couple of hours, if at all, and spend much less time there. By staying up so late they are too tired to get up early to work, they say. Others complain that gossip is a main preoccupation at the drinking sessions, and that whereas women's gossip at mat-making sessions used to cause most mischief, now the men do more damage. Their critical tone contains implications of moral decay.

Alcoholic beverages are more readily available now than previously, and the young men get together for drinking bouts from time to time. Drinking liquor is especially prevalent on the Catholic side of the island (the Methodist Church prohibits alcohol consumption among its members), and home-brewed orange wine provides a low-cost substitute. Young women may also participate in drinking sessions, without the implications of moral looseness it would surely have had in 1960. Neither drunkenness nor drug use are yet social problems of serious concern, however.

The young women still play field hockey and netball, as they did in 1960. More interesting is the introduction of volleyball, which was played in our village (Oinafa) before sunset every afternoon, Sundays excepted, over a period of several months. Sides were composed of a casual mix of boys and girls, along with some of the older folks. Much high-spirited banter accompanied the play. This is another indication of relaxed rules governing cross-gender relations.

Although young women still perform a great many housekeeping chores for their families, they enjoy a good deal more autonomy than previously. Some take service positions for certain periods of time with prosperous relatives, or chiefs, in exchange for small payments and other benefits. A few have regular jobs with co-ops, government, or the National Bank of Fiji branch office. In general they are more mobile and less confined to their homes. Perhaps the biggest change in their activities, however, is the decline of mat making. Whereas in 1960 this was a prime occupation for young women, today very few take the time to learn. Mat making is regarded as extremely arduous work, and given their increased independence, few young women choose to engage in it. As a result, fine mats, still a vital commodity in ceremonial exchanges, have become more scarce and more valuable, a trend that is likely to continue as older women, skilled at the craft, die off.

Young women in some districts participate regularly in women's clubs, which were founded in 1961. Some were started in association with churches; schoolteachers initiated others. These groups focus on demonstration and practice of skills such as baking, cooking, and needlecraft. Many young women have developed expertise in such areas as a result. In the early 1990s a resurgence of interest in traditional crafts, including mat making and basketry, attracted some of the younger women, so there is renewed hope that these traditional crafts will survive into the twenty-first century.

Church-centered activities for youths have retained, even increased, their importance over the intervening years. The Methodist Youth Fellowship is particularly active and sponsors a number of events over the course of the year. At rallies, some of which are all-day affairs, dramatic skits are enacted, dances performed, and a variety of games played. Here, too, increased mobility makes a difference; it is much easier now for youths to attend events on other parts of the island. As a result there are more large-scale, interdistrict events at which youths can meet a broader spectrum of their peers. These activities provide important opportunities for youths to take responsibility and to develop organizational and leadership skills.

The addition of tape players to guitars and ukeleles has resulted in a significant change in the ambiance of youthful social gatherings. While in some villages youths still get together and sing Rotuman songs, in others one is more likely to hear tapes of Western, Fijian, and professionally recorded Rotuman songs. In the latter villages, active involvement in composing, playing instruments, and singing has given way to passive listening. Youths everywhere, however, continue to participate in traditional group dances *(tautoga)* that are performed on special occasions. At rehearsals the young men are often a source of irritation to their elders because of their propensity to clown around, but at actual performances they can usually be relied on to do their best. This is very much like it was in 1960. Youths today also participate extensively in the church choir competitions held with some regularity.

The Christmas *av mane'a* season retains its special role in the lives of youths. The custom of *fara,* traveling to other villages to sing and dance, remains in full force, and visits from Rotumans resident abroad, many of whom are taking their school holidays, add spice to romantic possibilities. *Av mane'a* is a time for picnics and beach parties, and little work. Beach games, however, have disappeared from the scene, perhaps because courtship has become more open. There seems to be less need to disguise flirtations and romantic encounters in the wraps of gamelike activities.

Courtship

Since the roles open to women today are more expansive than in 1960, grooming daughters to become desirable spouses is less emphasized. Seeing to it that their sons and daughters get good educations and well-paying jobs is now a priority for most families. This is not to say, however, that traditional female virtues of industriousness, modesty, and virginity have been forgotten. They remain important values, significant criteria for assessing marriageability, as opposed to a heavy emphasis on looks or glamour, for instance. But a family's fortunes now depend less on their daughters' ability to attract dependable husbands than they do on sources of income, to which their daughters may directly contribute. Both sons and daughters may add substantially to their family's income if they emigrate to Fiji or elsewhere, get a well-paying job, and send remittances home. Those who are admired most do just that.

As a result of this shift in emphasis, young women are under less pressure to publicly communicate their purity. They are freer to form romantic liaisons and are less compelled to hide them. Flirtations are more open, though still subdued by Western standards. My impression is that girls are now seen as exercising more volitional control over their bodies. They appear to be less under the direct control of their families and more personally responsible for their destinies. In short, they give the impression of being more autonomous in relation to courtship, as in other areas of social life.

One factor contributing to more female autonomy has been increased knowledge of birth control methods. Most young women are now aware of birth control, and at least know how to calculate their fertile periods. This reduces the likelihood of unplanned pregnancies, the most shameful consequence of premarital sex. As one young man put it, nowadays a boy may see his sister at a party drinking and acting silly, but he won't make her go home; he'll simply tell her to be careful not to get into trouble, that is, pregnant.

Despite increased freedom of movement, and fewer restrictions imposed by fathers and brothers, I doubt there has been any substantial increase in promiscuity, or that premarital sex is more prevalent than it was in 1960. On the whole Rotuman women manifest a strong sense of pride and are very much concerned about their reputations in the community. Teasing and ridicule still play an important role in keeping people discreet, and social penalties still exist for courting too openly. Couples, including married couples, still do not show affection in public, for example. But in general, controls over sexual behavior have shifted from overpoweringly social toward individual restraint. I must emphasize that all of these changes are matters of degree. Courtship behavior is still shaped by characteristically Rotuman child-rearing practices and social sensitivities. Although moving in the direction of Western models of courtship, Rotuma in the 1990s still resembles Rotuma in 1960 more than it does contemporary Chicago or Sydney.

Marriage

Arranged marriages, those in which bride and groom barely knew each other, are relics of the past. While parents may still get involved, couples now are granted the right to initiate plans for marriage. Whereas in 1960 the bride's prior consent was not considered crucial, today it would be unthinkable to begin marriage negotiations without it. *Sok fäeag* weddings, with all the obligatory rituals and ceremonial exchanges, still take place, but they are now admired more for their adherence to, and affirmation of, custom than as statements about the social respectability of the bride. Such weddings have become prohibitively expensive for many families, and they choose to have small ceremonies attended only by close family and friends. The reduction in pressure by parents to choose their children's spouses also means that lovers are less likely to have to escape to one or the other's home in order to avoid being trapped in an undesirable union. In general, the processes leading to marriage, including courtship, are less weighted with tradition than before.

Integration Into the Community

While youths remain well integrated into their communities, and are valued for their contributions to communal labor, they enjoy a greater degree of autonomy than in the past. This is particularly true of young women, who have largely escaped the confines of their parental homes. They no longer engage in mat making to any significant degree, nor are they relied on to bring productive husbands into the group. Mobility has greatly increased, both within Rotuma and between the island and abroad. Almost all youths leave the island for extended periods of time; many never return. Their parents are well aware of this, and encourage it, especially if they perceive their children as having the potential to succeed educationally or occupationally. Their own economic prospects are at stake. Everyone is aware of the dramatic success stories of parents whose children have done well abroad and sent back money and goods to substantially enhance the family's standard of living. But those youths who remain, or return, are valued for their contributions as well. Whereas their siblings abroad may provide money and goods, they provide much needed labor. They are counted on to help with subsistence activities and household chores, as well as with communal events. Without them, large-scale feasts would be intolerably burdensome, if not impossible. Without them, the vitality of social life, marked in so many ways by their humor and youthful antics, would be greatly diminished.

They have more choices now and can leave more easily if they wish. That some choose to remain, even for a while, is interpreted by their elders as a sign of their commitment, of their *hanisi* (love and compassion).[15] As a result households with youthful sons and daughters are deemed lucky, and envied. For youths, the knowledge that they can go abroad and try their luck, that if they fail or are dissatisfied they can return to a community that cherishes them, is a buffer that makes a potentially stressful period much easier to bear.

The Bikhet Mystique

MASCULINE IDENTITY AND
PATTERNS OF REBELLION AMONG
BUMBITA ADOLESCENT MALES

Stephen C. Leavitt

In recent years, the Bumbita Arapesh people of the East Sepik Province in Papua New Guinea have noticed an increase in disruptive and disobedient behavior by local adolescent males. The Bumbita use the Neo-Melanesian term *bikhet pasin* to refer to such misconduct, and they call the perpetrator a *bikhet*. People complain that young bikhet men now engage in theft, vandalism, slander, and sexual harassment. Local village courts, they say, have become clogged with cases of young men who refuse to comply with the law or to follow accepted norms of human decency. While it is prudent to be skeptical about such laments over the loss of a nobler, more virtuous past, the Bumbita view of the local rise in adolescent misconduct is consistent with recognized changes occurring throughout Papua New Guinea, from the rise of urban "rascals" to the increase in crimes committed by minors in villages and along the Sepik and Highlands highways (see Clifford et al. 1984; Harris 1987; Suvulo 1988).

It is likely that the dramatic social change occurring throughout Papua New Guinea contributes to these developments. One could point immediately to several possible social and economic factors—loss of tradition, unemployment, changing social roles. However, studies exploring adolescent responses to specific historical events and processes (Elder 1980) have noted that the effect of social change on adolescent behavior is highly context-dependent. Individuals respond to change differently according to how old they are (physically or socially) when the change takes place, what specific social and cultural conditions surround them, and how they themselves interpret the events that occur (Elder 1980:39). In a country as culturally diverse as Papua New Guinea, cultural differences probably have important effects on adolescents' varying responses to social change. To date, though, even comparative studies of delinquency and adolescent misconduct still tend to emphasize developmental and social themes and pay less attention to cultural factors. In this chapter, I examine how Bumbita adolescent bikhet behavior is shaped by local cultural constructions. I present the configurations of local concepts of "adolescent male" and *bikhet pasin* (misbehavior), respectively. I concentrate on adolescents' and postadolescents' own interpretations of bikhet behavior in the context of their understandings of what being an adolescent means in Bumbita.

DELINQUENCY AS REBELLION AGAINST SOCIAL NORMS

One initial problem in evaluating adolescent misconduct in different cultures arises when we begin to question some basic assumptions that we (and others) have about "delinquent" versus "normal" behavior. When the Bumbita voice their consternation over adolescent misconduct, they appeal to an immediate sense that the behavior stands in opposition to what decent and responsible people would do. Common sense tells them that good people normally act according to social norms, and that bikhet adolescents are rebelling against those norms.

Classic Western sociological and even psychological theories of delinquency also tend to dichotomize delinquent and normal behavior. In a discussion of the definition of delinquency, Caven notes, for example, that "even though we know that behavior falls into a continuum, nevertheless we tend to think in terms of dichotomies, . . . in terms of black and white" (1961:245) and that studies trying to relate delinquency to social structural patterns have "sometimes been obscured by the tendency to think of the social norms not as our workable expectations of behavior but as ideal or perfect standards" (1961:247). In fact, she argues, those "overconformers" who adhere strictly to social ideals are themselves unusual, and if one were to evaluate the important question, say, of peer response, one would have to conclude that "it seems very doubtful whether so much admiration is really accorded the overconforming group as some sociologists and researchers state or imply" (1961:248).

Caven's point is particularly relevant when looking at deviance in societies, like those in Papua New Guinea that once endured endemic warfare, where disruptive and violent behavior received positive sanctions in some contexts. One must be wary of applying Western views of delinquency and adolescent misconduct which contain assumptions—or assertions—that delinquent behavior is some kind of reaction against social norms. Such ideas lie at the heart of classic sociological theories of delinquency. For example, Cloward and Ohlin's (1960) application to adolescent gangs of Merton's (1938) general "social strain" theory states that delinquency occurs as adolescents band together in reaction against predominant values in a society that sets goals (like economic success) that have become unattainable. Cohen (1955) argues that the disenfranchised in fact develop a set of standards that is expressly contrary to prevailing values and develop delinquent "subcultures" that are part of a psychological "reaction formation" against prevailing middle-class values (133). Sutherland's "differential association" theory argues similarly that delinquency results from an overabundance of association with criminal behavior patterns that stand in opposition to law-abiding behavior (Sutherland and Cressey 1974). These approaches, by stressing the shared values or "subculture" of adolescents, successfully counter a view of delinquency as simply antisocial or anomic. They argue that adolescents have particular aims and concerns, but they also stress that these aims oppose the prevailing values of adult society.

Psychological theories reflect similar tendencies, emphasizing adolescents' "acting out" against the wishes of parental figures. Blos's (1967) psychoanalytic theory states that some adolescents who cannot master their "second individuation" from parental figures have to rebel or stand in opposition to them (168). Erikson's (1968) concept of "negative identity" refers to a delinquent's attempt to compensate for a failure to establish an acceptable role identity by choosing instead an identity "perversely based on all those identifications and roles which, at critical stages of development, had been presented . . . as the most undesirable or dangerous and yet also the most real" (174). These formulations all share a view of delinquent behavior as representing, for differing reasons, a pointed departure from, or opposition to, the accepted norms of the dominant sections of society.

Considering delinquency as a rebellion against social norms tends to underscore the behavior's reactive motives at the expense of its more constructive motives. Researchers are inclined to ask why adolescents need to rebel instead of asking what adolescents are trying to do when they act in disruptive ways. I make this point because in the Bumbita case, when one attempts to understand bikhet behavior by addressing the experience of individual adolescents, using the standard delinquency model may lead one to overlook important themes. In fact, for the Bumbita, bikhet behavior reflects, in important ways, disorganized attempts *to become men*. Furthermore, close examination of some of the characteristics of bikhet behavior reveals that they resemble attributes deemed appropriate for powerful and successful political leaders. Indeed, the most notorious Bumbita political leaders were known themselves for their bikhet behavior, and in that context the term connoted a ruthlessness to be grudgingly admired. Thus, when Bumbita adolescents told me that they actually aspired to become bikhet, I had to recognize that perhaps they were not so much interested in rebelling as in striving to emulate the most powerful and successful adults in their society.

These observations parallel what Kulick (1993) has reported from the village of Gapun, also in the East Sepik Province, just inland from the north coast.

Kulick argues that village representations of "rascals" stress their resourcefulness and their access to powers akin to those once reserved for senior men. He argues, in fact, that "there are a number of suggestive similarities between how rascal leaders are described and how Gapuners talk about now long-dead 'great-men'" (10). In local Gapun discourse, the boundaries between official authorities (police) and rascal leaders are blurred. As such, they represent a kind of progressive product of social change: "Rascalism seems to be not so much an identity as it is specific categories of activity conducted by individuals who have the same kinds of skills, education and power as those officials who uphold the law and the government" (12).

The effect of such discourse on adolescents is all the more striking when political leaders themselves appropriate images associated with delinquency to enhance their own reputations. Brison (1996) has argued, in fact, that among the Kwanga, a society neighboring the Bumbita, village leaders regularly use "images of a savage past to reinforce their authority" (6). In the view of one Kwanga man, "New Guinean big men of the past were so strong that Europeans were like mere powerless boys in comparison" (12). Illustrations such as these from Papua New Guinea show effectively the dangers of assuming that disruptive behavior represents a simple rebelling against authority.

By looking at adolescents' interpretations of their own behavior, one can access the cultural contributions to Bumbita adolescent bikhet behavior. However, one should not simply accept the adolescents' statements as true. On the contrary, I hold that whenever people talk about themselves, they are making an argument, or asserting a particular identity, which may attempt to deny some unacceptable (and usually unstated) alternative (see Leavitt 1995a). When a young adolescent says, "I want to be a bikhet," he is cultivating a certain kind of self-image, but he is also implicitly trying to avoid associating himself with other unacceptable alternatives. Because the statements involve the assertion of a certain identity, Bumbita notions of self, adolescence, and manhood must all play a role in the explication of the bikhet concept. But one must consider both what people say about themselves and what they implicitly deny.

The local concept of the bikhet is associated not only with the behavior of adolescent males, but also with a host of other behaviors thought, in some contexts, to be appropriate for men. Bumbita ideals for male sociality contain contradictions. On the one hand, powerful men are expected to be assertive and aggressive leaders, defeating their rivals in competitions. At the same time, though, truly wise men respect and follow the wishes of fellow villagers, and competition must be closely controlled. Young adolescent males, because of their particular preoccupation with establishing themselves as men, tend to favor, however, the more aggressive model of masculine identity, and their bikhet behavior reflects their preoccupations. Young men may be particularly worried about this aggressive aspect of their masculine identities because the initiation system that tradi-tionally cultivated the bikhet aspects of men is no longer in place. Preoccupa-tions with bikhet behavior now tend to dominate adolescent interactions out-side the ritual sphere. Material from personal interviews with a young Bumbita man supports that interpretation.

BUMBITA SOCIAL CHANGE

The Bumbita Arapesh number some three thousand persons and occupy fourteen villages on three contiguous ridges in the hinterland foothills of the Torricelli mountains in the East Sepik Province of Papua New Guinea. I con-ducted twenty-six months of fieldwork from 1984 to 1986 in the village of Bumbita (pop. 189). During the fieldwork period, subsistence crops of yams, taro, and sago were supplemented by cash crops of coffee in plots owned by in-dividuals. At that time, sales of coffee generated between one hundred and two hundred dollars (USD) per household per year. Traditional social organization featured competitive exchanges of yams among men. Men marshaled their spiri-tual, magical, and labor resources to produce both abundant crops and tellingly long individual specimens. The construction of large, circular bins of yams dis-played a representation of individual prowess, as did conspicuous prestations to exchange partners. Many yam exchanges occurred in the context of the male ini-tiation cult referred to as the *Tambaran*. In Bumbita, the Tambaran cult com-prises three grades (cf. Tuzin 1980) corresponding to different stages of male physical and spiritual maturation; the second grade, called *Maolimu*, ostensibly marks a transition from adolescence to adulthood. In recent times, however, the Bumbita performed Tambaran initiations so rarely that the actual age of initiates varied considerably at each stage.

In their short lives, young Bumbita adolescents in the mid-1980s had already seen some significant social developments. While the South Sea Evangelical Mis-sion had established in the 1950s a station and school at Brugam on the north-eastern periphery of Bumbita territory, the mission had an uneven influence on Bumbita villages. The southeastern villages (those covered during fieldwork) were too far from the mission for children to make the daily walk to and from the school. Consequently, few people from these villages had any schooling and few converted to Christianity during the first three decades of the mission station's presence.

Things began to change, however, after Papua New Guinea independence. In 1978 the government established a community school in the center of Bumbita Arapesh territory, so that by the time of my arrival in August 1984 the first cohort of school children had just finished school after completing grade 6. In the same year, the religious situation changed dramatically. A Christian revival, sponsored by the indigenous affiliate of the mission, swept through a large area that included the Bumbita and adjacent language groups (Leavitt 1995b, 1997; Tuzin 1997). Scores of people, including most adolescents, took church-sponsored crash courses in the fundamentals of Christian theology so that they could be baptized. Many believed Jesus' arrival to be imminent. Children refused to go to school for fear that when they returned home their parents would have been taken away by Jesus in the Second Coming. The most significant event of the revival was the revelation of the men's cult secrets during church services. Many said that the men had been so shamed by the public airing of their cult activities that it was utterly impossible to conduct initiations. The Tambaran, they said, was dead.

Bumbita adolescent males, at first glance, seemed to take these changes in stride. In casual conversation few lamented the loss of the traditions, saying that the ordeals of the Tambaran and accompanying taboos were onerous. While most found the Christian prohibitions on smoking and betel chewing irritating, church services offered opportunities for socializing, and many young men enjoyed singing hymns. All looked forward to participating in the larger world they had learned about in school, either by traveling to find work at coastal plantations or by trying their hand at running trade stores or organizing work projects in the village. By the end of 1985, each village had formed a youth group as part of the nationwide youth group program. These groups raised money by hiring themselves out for labor and sponsoring community events such as dances and string band contests. But there was also a sense among youths that they, as villagers "from the bush," would never really be able to make significant contributions to the new social world. No one from the village of Bumbita had ever done well enough in school to be admitted into high school, and that situation seemed unlikely to change. Youth groups were unable to sustain profits. Furthermore, the traditional domain for demonstrating male skill and spiritual energy, the cultivation of yams, had lost its luster, for yam competition had been associated with the Tambaran cult. Older men lamented that now it was a "woman's world," meaning not so much that women were in control but that now only women retained their "proper place" in the order of things.

THE BIKHET MYSTIQUE

Within this social context, adolescent males were gaining a greater reputation for being bikhet. Their ill-behaved and disruptive acts—thefts, vandalism, sexual harassment, fighting—are, for the Bumbita, part of a behavioral pattern that reaches far beyond the particular irritations of adolescent insubordination. The Tok Pisin term *bikhet* has wide application: it is used as a synonym for "heathens," for those recalcitrant in spurning Christianity and retaining traditional customs; has become a gloss for a certain type of notorious political leader; and has sometimes been used to describe male behavior in general. One village in the adjacent Urat language group even adopted the term as a generic label for themselves, cultivating the reputation for being "a bikhet village" (Eyre 1988). Use of the term as a label suggests that *bikhet* denotes a set of personal attributes, marking a potential icon for identity. The Bumbita even prefer the Tok Pisin term *bikhet* to their own expression, *"naneh nama'"* (to act badly), a verb with a temporary action marker *(nama')*, best glossed, perhaps, as "you're at it again."

Identifying the broader cultural assumptions behind the bikhet mystique is essential to understanding what motivates an adolescent male's provocative or disruptive acts. In the following occurrences, one can begin to delineate a pattern that is regarded by the Bumbita as indicative of adolescent bikhet behavior. One incident involves a conflict over marriages between two villages. In 1985, tensions between Bumbita and the adjacent village of Buter had been high for some time. The two villages had a long tradition of close ties of marriage, but over the past couple of generations a disproportionate number of women had married into Bumbita from Buter. The Buter people's irritation over the imbalance was compounded by the fact that while both villages recognized the need to redress the asymmetry, the Bumbita men, both married and single, had annoyingly redoubled their efforts to acquire even *more* Buter women.

Bumbita adolescents staged parties on the road between the villages to encourage rendezvous. At one point a brawl broke out between the two villages over the nightly excursions by Bumbita adolescents to Buter and the continued harassment of Buter women. It was decided that henceforth Bumbita youths would be forbidden to enter Buter after dark.

Several months later a Bumbita teenager, using love magic, convinced a Buter woman to accompany him back to his hamlet to be married. One of the boy's subclan "brothers" berated the young man for being a "bikhet," apparently concerned about his subclan's growing reputation for contracting objectionable marriages. Others counseled forbearance, saying that if anyone were to be angry, it should be the girl's father. The following night, a party of Buter adolescents retaliated by vandalizing several gardens they mistakenly thought belonged to Bumbita. The gardens, in fact, belonged to the people of Sa'unes, innocent bystanders, as it were, to this dispute. The boys' actions had complicated the situation considerably.

When the young woman's brother arrived the next day to take her home, he was greeted with a tirade by a Bumbita man:

> You are just a little village that wants to test the strength of Bumbita now! We're not afraid of you—you're afraid of me! You want to play rough, be rough! . . . You Buter people are shits! You are Bumbita's shit!

The young woman returned home, and the Buter adolescents eventually paid a small compensation (forty dollars) to the owners of the damaged gardens.

It was generally agreed that the situation had gotten out of hand because all of the principals in the dispute had acted in a bikhet way. The Bumbita teenager had disregarded the agreement between the villages. Purchasing love magic just prior to his visit, he had actively sought out the young woman, even though he knew that bringing her home with him would lead to trouble. While the village of Buter had a legitimate grievance, it was not appropriate for their adolescents to take it upon themselves to rectify matters by (rather indiscriminately) vandalizing gardens. They were, as the Bumbita man who derided them said, "testing their strength." And this man himself was bikhet for trying to heighten tension by launching into a tirade that framed the incident in terms of manly competition. In spite of the general disapproval over these behaviors, the three parties— the seducer, the vandals, and the taunter—all indicated to me later that they were quite pleased with how they had comported themselves. They were able to feel that way about themselves because the bikhet acts they perpetrated were not simply rebellions against social norms or lapses in moral conviction; rather, they involved behavior deemed, in principle, appropriate for men—in some contexts.

In fact, far from being seen as an unambiguously negative thing, bikhet behavior evokes an ambivalent reaction. People disapprove of it, but at the same time they think it is an appropriate way for men to act. Bikhet behavior points to a series of moral tensions that not only animate notions of masculine assertiveness and power, but also shape political careers. Seen in this way, adolescents aspiring to be bikhet are staking out a position on the community's moral landscape.

Let us turn once again to each of the bikhet acts from the vandalism incident. What precipitated the conflict was the suspicion that the young man had magically seduced a Buter woman. The seduction and harassment of young women is a central component of being a bikhet, as the Bumbita see it. Their concern is less with the dynamics of the young people's relationship (such as whether the young woman was charmed, seduced, bullied, or threatened) than with the fact that the two initiated their relationship on their own, without support or approval from their respective kin. Bumbita marriages establish and maintain strategic relationships among villages and clans. One is bikhet for ignoring those relationships, for putting individual desires ahead of what is best for the group. At the same time, the prevailing ideology of male sexual domination regards any form of seduction as the result of the male's power to manipulate the will of women (see Leavitt 1991), and for that reason, too, it is considered a type of bikhet behavior. The individual's style of seduction (whether callous or violent or not) is of lesser significance—in some sense, all seduction implies a violation of women's autonomy. But such seductions are also admired to the extent that they indicate masculine prowess. Thus, in pursuing young women, especially against the wishes of kin, an adolescent male exhibits the stubborn resolve that marks bikhet behavior while at the same time he enacts Bumbita definitions of what it is to be a male. The social tension here lies in the conflict between, on the one hand, a man's assertion of masculine competence and power through manipulating the wills of women, and on the other, his disregard for the possible problems he will cause his group by failing to negotiate a prudent marriage.

In addition, the young man's continued efforts to obtain a woman from a place where there was already an imbalance exemplifies one of the basic assumptions of systems of competitive exchange: make all efforts not only to beat your opponents but to trounce them. In true bikhet fashion, the Bumbita young men, upon sensing Buter's frustration over their failures to contract marriages with Bumbita women, strive to exacerbate the situation by attracting even more Buter women.

In a similar way, a man who senses that his exchange partner is unable to produce gifts of yams of equal quantity and size to his own, will strive to make even more lavish prestations to underscore the disparity. While people take covert pride in these displays, they also realize that such behavior is unwise and can cause all sorts of problems. The established precedent, in fact, states that all exchanges of yams between exchange partners should be scrupulously equal. Informants say that people generally try to match rather than outdo their rivals in yam exchanges in order to prevent the exchanges from escalating.

There is thus a social tension underlying all contexts of competitive exchange. The socially sanctioned impulse to defeat an adversary conflicts with the strict parity mandated by the need to preserve social harmony. In this way, a young man's bikhet seduction of a woman contributes to broadly based points of tension in Bumbita society.

The vandalism by the young avengers also plays on some of these tensions. Sketched in the broadest terms, all Bumbita social action produces a moral dilemma—the extremely high degree of mutual interest that typifies small kin-based societies means that each act of allegiance implies the betrayal of someone else, and each assertion of individual interests implies a betrayal of the community.[1] Bumbita individuals face this dilemma daily. When the Bumbita adolescents flagrantly ignored the community's efforts to discourage Bumbita youths from seeking out Buter women, the Buter adolescents felt that their own village's honor needed defending, and in that spirit they vandalized what they thought were Bumbita gardens. Their actions were regarded as bikhet because they jeopardized larger social harmony in favor of more parochial interests (that is, Buter's honor and the boys' own reputations). The fact that they destroyed property was of lesser import. Everyone understood that the vandalism was not gratuitous.

The Buter adolescents had asserted themselves in defense of their village; they had decided to "play rough." In so doing, they were contributing to a social dialogue between two villages. Some in their own village may have applauded their assertion of masculine strength, but at the same time some knew that this breach in harmonious relations between the villages could cause future trouble. In short, people are almost always ambivalent about bikhet behavior.

Another characteristic of bikhet behavior is verbal intimidation. People disapprove of verbal insults or threats for the obvious reason that such acts inflame hostility and invite conflict. The consensus was that the Bumbita man, in berating the Buter pair as they walked past the clearing, had done little to help matters. In addition to being potentially dangerous, verbal intimidation is regarded as blatantly opportunistic. People told me that this man aspired to be a village leader, and he wanted everyone to think that he had masculine courage and initiative. In this case, most people saw right through it. The man in question did not hold the stature and influence to make his threats effective. However, had he been an esteemed leader, the public appraisal of his behavior may have been quite different. People have considerable respect for a leader who jeopardizes his own well-being (those with harsh words always run the risk of falling victim to wrathful sorcery) by standing up in defense of the group.

THE BIKHET MYSTIQUE AND IMAGES OF LEADERS

The question of public posturing and verbal intimidation has relevance for adolescents and others who are thinking about the kinds of persons they want to be and about the positions they aspire to hold in the community of adults. For those who aspire to positions of leadership, the options are troublesome because the Bumbita ideology of leadership contains contradictory messages. In fact, the tensions over social action become most evident on the issue of leadership. As in many areas of Melanesia, there are basically two types of Bumbita political leaders—the bikhet and the consensus builder. Leaders of both types build their reputations by first establishing their masculine spiritual credentials through demonstrated superiority in the spiritually supervised activities of yam production, pig hunting, polygyny, and commitment to the men's cult. However, once a certain stature is attained, the bikhet leader adds to his reputation through intimidation and coercion. He corresponds to what Read (1959), in describing leadership among the Gahuku-Gama, has called the "strong man." He is "an individual who is not likely to defer to others, a person who tends to act precipitately" (433). He stands in contrast to the "autonomous man," a leader who demonstrates strength but also solicits opinions of others and acts only when backed by consensus. The two stereotypes of leaders help explain not only why adolescents might find it appealing to cultivate the bikhet image, but also why senior men of the village might be interested in accusing young men of bikhet tendencies. A look at a pair of Bumbita leaders helps to clarify the relationship between bikhet behavior and Bumbita leadership.

In the Bumbita village, one leader in particular, Botena, was legendary for having cultivated the bikhet—or "strong man"—style. Botena was the first village councilor following independence, had two wives, and supervised the last series of Tambaran initiations. People in Bumbita attributed their belated interest in Christianity to his earlier intimidation of missionaries and others who had come to proselytize. It was only after Botena died, they said, that anyone in Bumbita converted. Before that, he would not allow it. Stories circulated about how Botena used to spit in people's faces when he was angry with them. He once forced two men to stand still in front of his house in the hot sun simply because they had opposed him over some controversy. Botena was able to wield his power in this way, people said, because he was an uncompromising bikhet.

By contrast, Arehin, a leader who was still alive when I was in Bumbita, espoused a completely different philosophy of leadership. In contrast to most men, he said, a leader had to subordinate completely his own interests to those of his fellow villagers. He indicated that as a leader he could not exhort or even encourage others to change:

> SL: You have seen everything change and no one is interested in planting. Are you bothered a little by that or are you agreeable?
> A: Me, I have been put into too many leadership positions, in government [as *komiti* to the councilor], as the boss of our coffee business, [as one for] looking after the court and taking people to court, and now the youth group has asked me to advise them. How can I contradict [*senisim*] them? True, if I were just an average person [*pipol nating*], then yes, [but as a leader] I can't change their minds and tell them what to do. You see, I'm a leader, right? I can't contradict them. Whatever it is that they want to do, I can't disagree, I must sit there and listen and say, "All right, you all go and try it. Whatever bears fruit, you follow that." I can't go against them.

Arehin here expresses an opinion on leadership that stands in opposition to the style of leadership that Botena exemplified. Arehin's comments are so pointed that it is easy to infer a deliberate attempt to impugn Botena's character. Botena was, after all, a rival. Nevertheless, by framing the essentials of leadership in terms of subordinating one's interests and following the consensus of the people, Arehin suggests that one's sense of identity as a leader comes from the tension between the bikhet style and the consensus style.

It is also not insignificant that Arehin himself, when describing himself as a young man, says with some pride that he too was a bikhet. He wants to capitalize on the bikhet reputation without sacrificing the cultivated image of being a wise and consensus-building leader. This kind of image, though difficult to maintain, is the one to which most Bumbita leaders aspire. The bikhet or "strong man" type of leader, while effective in building a powerful reputation, faces serious dangers (compare Brison 1991). Karen Brison (1996) describes leadership among the Kwanga, a group closely related to the Bumbita:

> People admire forceful leaders, but believe that the very strength which enables these men to keep order in the village . . . can also be used to ride roughshod over fellow community members. In fact, it seems to be virtually inevitable that anyone "strong" will also be seen as a "bad man" who pursues selfish goals at the expense of others. (12)

Bikhet leaders run the risk of inviting resentment and malicious gossip or of being ensorcelled outright. For most of them, then, it is advantageous to cultivate the reputation of standing up to opponents and presiding over village affairs without having to take responsibility for specific disruptive acts. Thus, in the case of the conflict with Buter, Arehin and other leaders tacitly supported the young men's efforts to acquire Buter women (they offered advice on techniques of seduction during gatherings at my house), but publicly took the lead in pronouncing the adolescents' behavior as "bikhet" after the violence had erupted. The Bumbita leaders would benefit from Bumbita's reputation as a bikhet village, but would risk damaging reprisal (from even their own constituents) if they became associated too closely with such behavior. The young men, with no grand consensus-building reputation to defend, were simply interested in cultivating a bikhet reputation.

THE BIKHET AS DEFENDER OF TRADITION

One final dimension of the definition of bikhet behavior involves the commitment to tradition and the opposition to Christian conversion. In Bumbita discourse, the traditionalists, those who oppose Christianity and wish to retain what is left of the customs, are considered bikhet, both by themselves and by others. We have already seen how Bumbita gained the reputation for being a bikhet village by opposing Christianity under the guidance of Botena, the bikhet leader. In addition, local Christian ideology portrays the Christian life as a modern alternative to a bikhet tradition. Local Christian ideology states that the arrival of Christ in the Second Coming ultimately depends upon there being, on the ground, a state of *"wan bel,"* translated roughly as "collective harmony with a unified purpose" (Leavitt 1995b; 1995c). In fact, the Bumbita believe that it is their demonstrated failure to be able to get along with one another that is an essential difference between themselves and the Europeans. In the Bumbita view, Europeans possess an almost miraculous ability to coordinate their actions, and they have demonstrated a capacity to subjugate petty personal aspirations in favor of collective goals. Some Bumbita also see an explicit practical association between collective harmony and material wealth. They feel their collective enterprises are failing because of bikhet behavior which is manifested in petty disputes, theft, and personal ambition. Through the course of the revival, "wan bel" became a rallying cry for Christians. Whenever lured into arguments, Christians would call out to their adversaries with "Wan bel! Wan bel!" rather than continue the conflict. It was their equivalent to turning the other cheek. In addition, "wan bel" replaced "good morning" or "good day" as the standard salutation when greeting someone or shaking hands. Those who opposed the Christian movement were bikhet in a double sense. First, they retained allegiance to a system of competitive exchange that the Christians—and missionaries—saw as inimical to cooperative and harmonious communities like those of the Europeans. Exchange was bad, Christians said, because it encouraged "competition." In addition, traditionalists were bikhet because their opposition to Christianity constituted defiance against a wave of popular sentiment that looked to the future. The traditionalists were being stubborn and self-interested. As Christians saw it, converting implied the ultimate sacrifice of personal interests in favor of a vision of a new community, one that would flourish without strife after the arrival of the New Age.

Thus, for the Bumbita, the concept of bikhet involves a cluster of characteristics related to some of the fundamental tensions in sociality. Being bikhet includes active assertion of will, defiance against opposition, stubborn resolve, and a certain reckless disregard for dangerous consequences. While people disapprove of bikhet behavior for its tendency to interfere with social harmony, they also admire those who assert themselves against the burdensome demands of others. For the individual who is able to pull it off, being a bikhet can add significantly to one's reputation. Such an individual is admired for accomplishing what others dare contemplate only in fantasy.

An adolescent male participates in this elaborate constellation of meanings when he decides to engage in bikhet behavior. For the Bumbita adolescent male, the choice to aspire to be a bikhet, in contrast to the non-bikhet alternative, becomes more pressing when we look at Bumbita definitions of what it is to be a man.

ADOLESCENCE AND MANHOOD

While the concept of the bikhet applies to several different domains, including acts by adults and children, men and women, adolescent males have a particular reputation for engaging in bikhet behavior. This tendency is related in several ways to the position of marginality held by adolescent males in the

Bumbita conceptualization of development. The term for *adolescent males* in Bumbita Arapesh is *ounohi*.[2] It applies to the period of time from the development of secondary sexual characteristics to the time when a young man marries, usually in his early twenties. While the term itself no longer applies after marriage, people feel that a man is not fully mature until he has children. Thus, for the Bumbita male, adolescence begins as a category of physical development and ends with a change in social status. The adolescent male is marginal in the sense that his immature status is prolonged ideologically by Bumbita culture. Long after they are physically mature, Bumbita men are regarded as sociologically adolescent. To a certain extent, the denunciation of adolescent males for their bikhet behavior derives from the fact that they are still considered immature. Had a group of initiated older men vandalized the gardens, for example, the community's reaction would have been quite different. While still regarded as bikhet behavior, it may have been interpreted as a strategic maneuver of some significance rather than as a case of some kids getting out of hand in their desire for vengeance.

But Bumbita adolescents themselves are also particularly concerned with bikhet behavior, regardless of the community's reaction to it. A search for all instances of the use of the term *bikhet* in a series of some sixty personal interviews revealed that single men used the term about ten times more frequently than did women and other men. The adolescent male's concern with bikhet behavior derives from another dimension of marginality that applies specifically to him: as an unmarried male, his spiritual development is radically incomplete. The Bumbita hold, with many Melanesian societies, that there are significant differences in the physical development of males and females. While females achieve womanhood naturally, as an inherent part of their development, boys must be turned into men. The central contrast in the Bumbita understanding of male and female identity lies not so much in their physical development as with their spiritual development as men and women. Thus, for example, the Bumbita do not hold that a boy's physical development will be hampered if he is not initiated into the Tambaran; rather, the primary effect will be on his ability to produce a thriving and abundant crop of yams, an ability intimately connected with spiritual, and masculine, power. A man must actively create his being so that he is not merely male in body but also masculine in spirit. As the Bumbita see it, a woman's inherent femininity makes her naturally desirable to a man, while men must actively seduce women, using magic and other ploys, as it is likely that women would not otherwise desire them. Similarly, a woman's natural functions, her menstruation, her vaginal secretions, her immanent sexuality, are dangerous to men and can make them ill. Dangers of men to women, by contrast, come almost entirely from the powers created in them traditionally through their Tambaran initiations or through their involvement with the magical arts of curing or sorcery. Uninitiated men are not dangerous to women.

These beliefs have significant implications for the experiences of adolescent males as they strive to become men. In the ritual domain, the cultivation of masculine energy fell traditionally under the province of the Tambaran. The first stage of initiation in childhood was oriented around ridding the boy of feminine and maternal substances; the second (in late adolescence and early adulthood) concentrated on generating purely male spiritual energy. Through these first two stages of initiation, the young man's spiritual essence was nurtured through carefully controlled ritual procedures. Without such procedures, the theory goes, a young man's spiritual power remained stunted. In the domestic sphere, the young man is expected to take control of his own development, avoiding certain foods and associations with women to optimize his development and demonstrating his masculine prowess through assertive action. Especially now that initiations are no longer being practiced, being a bikhet provides a young man with evidence that he is indeed cultivating his masculinity in the proper manner.

In this emotional environment, the celebration of masculine spiritual power becomes synonymous with assertive action. The significance of male action can be seen by examining the symbolic association of female menstruation with male penile bloodletting. Throughout the Sepik, men periodically let blood from their penises as a hygienic measure by jabbing the glans with a razor after inducing an erection (cf. Tuzin 1980:73–78). The Bumbita see menstruation and penis bleeding as equivalents; a woman rids herself of "bad blood" through her period, and a man does the same by cutting his penis. However, the purification process is different in men and women because of the initiative involved with penis bleeding. While menstruation is a natural event over which women have no control, men can carefully monitor their bloodletting so as to maintain optimum masculine spiritual energy. Bumbita men assert that, unlike women, men gain spiritual renewal through something done by "we ourselves." Masculine assertive control over spiritual energy constitutes an essential difference between men and women (Leavitt 1991).

While this ideology allows men to celebrate their freedom to control their own spiritual destinies, it also presents a potential problem for adolescents, for those young men who have yet to demonstrate any substantial masculine energy. They cannot rely on natural processes to lead them into adulthood; they must cultivate their masculine identity through action. The initiative involved in the penis bleeding procedure is merely an icon for a larger sense of initiative that they must generate throughout this period of development. Adolescent males develop a preoccupation with demonstrating competence, not only to indicate maturity, as in our society, but also to indicate (to themselves and others) that they are actually developing properly in the spiritual domain. Bikhet behavior, with its emphasis on assertive action and its opportunity for identification with established and successful senior males, offers a means for reassurance.

These strivings are often demonstrated through the use of magic. As the Bumbita conceptualize it, an important component of masculine spiritual energy lies in the power to transform the world and influence other people—compelling all external elements to respond to the masculine will. A primary tool that men use is magic—to enhance the growth of their crops, to lure pigs into their nets, to practice sorcery, to attract women, and more recently, to insure success in gambling games with playing cards. Performing magic lies almost exclusively within the domain of men, and it is intimately associated with the Bumbita conception of what men are. The ability to perform magic is an indication of men's belief that they create themselves through action.

For adolescents, the most significant magic is love magic for the courting of women, and in the domain of soliciting love relationships adolescents are often accused of being bikhet. Spiritual power in the case of love magic comes from objects noted for their peculiarities. The most common are a red soil of mysterious origin and marked by distinctive color, ginger root which when bitten has a "hot" taste that is otherwise unknown to the Bumbita palate, and bottled cologne. One Bumbita man describes how he first used magic on a woman:

> Before, I had really worked it on her here! It was something else, what I did to her. I cooked her with ginger . . . I burned her when we were doing the dances. . . . When I arrived at the dance, I got ready by putting it into my mouth. . . . When she walked past me, I spit and I got her. That's all, there wasn't anything else. This is ginger for getting women. . . . When we go to a dance or a party or whatever, when we spit and the breath gets her, then just like that she must come and take you! So I did it to her like that.

What is significant about this description is the rhetoric of control and manipulation. He emphasizes the transformative power of his masculine essence working in conjunction with the magic. His power was such that he needed only the smallest procedure ("that's all, there wasn't anything else") to manipulate the woman's will ("just like that").

When Bumbita adults complain about adolescents, they see love magic as only one element in a larger pattern of objectionable coercion and harassment. Adolescents may resort to intimidation or even violence, for magic does not usually work as well as this speaker implies. But whether subtle or blunt, soliciting or abusive, the bikhet behavior of adolescent males toward young women involves a fundamental assertion of power in the service of cultivating a masculine identity.

BIKHET BEHAVIOR IN THE RITUAL DOMAIN

When Tambaran initiations were still practiced, the period of adolescence for males was bracketed ritually by two stages of initiation—Rehin and Maolomu', respectively. From the completion of the first stage to the completion of the second, ritual activities concentrated on two aims: the cultivation of a pure spiritual masculine essence and the demonstration of masculine transformative powers. The latter aim included a pattern of sanctioned behaviors consistent with the bikhet ethos, thus underscoring the intimate association between masculine development and bikhet behavior, as the Bumbita see it.

Completion of the Rehin stage of initiation established for young adolescent boys the prerogative to don the *songohowa* (sg. *songomu'*), referred to in the Sepik literature by the Tok Pisin term *tumbuan*. The *tumbuan* is a costume used by men to represent materialized spirits and has ritual importance throughout the Sepik region. In the Bumbita area, these costumes are used to terrify women and children during harvesting seasons and when Tambaran activities are occurring. The costume is comprised of a woven fiber mask covered with clay and painted red, yellow, and black; a wide collar of coiled fibers adorned with rings of orange fruits; and a long skirt of thatch made from sago fibers.[3] Adolescents who had passed through the Rehin initiation would occasionally don the costume during the harvest season and prance around the village demanding food. All Bumbita, including men, report feelings of fear when confronted by a *songomu'*, for it is said that the *songomu'* sometimes commits homicide without warning. Initiated men know that these are not in fact spirits, that only young men are inside, but they also say that even they are afraid, for they do not know *who* is inside.

The *songomu'*'s antics reflect prototypical bikhet behavior. They use their anonymity and ghoulish appearance to coerce people into giving them food with no regard for the established precedents governing food transactions. Young men report that when they put on the mask the spiritual power of the mask itself causes a transformation in their thinking so that they no longer have any regard for social conventions. Some young men assured me that, under the mask, they would have no qualms whatsoever in stabbing their mothers or sisters with a spear. The *songomu'* appears to convey a symbolic recognition of the special charge assigned to adolescent males—that under ritual guidance, they are to assert their wills in flagrant disregard for usual social conventions.

During the Maolomu' Tambaran stage that marked the end of the ritual period analogous to adolescence, the emphasis on disregard for convention persisted, but under the overarching theme of demonstrating to the community the transformative powers of males and their spiritual energy (cf. Tuzin 1980:74–115). Women and children were told that the initiates had been transformed into flying foxes *(maolomu'),* animals whose prominent male genitals associate them strongly with sexual prowess (Tuzin 1980:91). Women were told that during their seclusion in the forest, initiates were engaging in promiscuous sexual encounters with women from all over the area. The most profound secret of the initiation was feasting on pork, which enabled the men, upon their return after a period of weeks, to actually appear fatter—literally transformed. Just before the end of the initiation sequence, the villages were cleared of all people, and the initiates, along with initiators and other participants, stormed through the village. They attached long ropes to the tops of coconut trees and pulled on them until the trees snapped near their base. When the women and children returned to the village, they saw fallen trees scattered about, some of them crushing houses. They were told that flying foxes are capable of tremendous force when alarmed.

The pronouncements to women and children were thinly veiled demonstrations of the potential of masculine power when cultivated correctly and set free from the bonds of conventional social decency. For adolescents, the Maolomu' Tambaran marked the culmination of a life period devoted to establishing one's credentials as a mature man. Even with the initiations gone, the bikhet behavior for which they are so often maligned is an essential part of a process of maturation.

BEING A BIKHET: CREATING AN IDENTITY

The ritual initiation system, with its ideology of masculine development, provided an image of "natural" masculine identity as radically incomplete, as something that needed to be supplemented by ritual acts and procedures. For young Bumbita men who are interested in establishing themselves in the adult world today, the issue of masculine identity can also become a preoccupation on a very personal level. When young men talk explicitly about their own behavior in relation to the bikhet phenomenon, they reveal themselves to be quite conscious of the identity that they seek to construct through their behavior, and often they actively seek out a bikhet image, which has significant effects on their personal experiences.

One young man of about twenty years, Aminguh, spoke with me extensively about his bikhet reputation, and his attitudes emerged most clearly in the context of our discussions about his fleeting association with the Christian movement.[4] As he describes it, as a Christian he was not able to be the kind of person that he wanted to be, that he *had* been before his conversion:

> SL: I want you to go back to your true thinking about becoming a believer again, what you really think.

A: What I really think. I can't go back and be a believer with them. If I became a believer, I wouldn't be able to do the bikhet things that my father before used to do, no. I'd just sit and be good. I wouldn't get up and yell [at people], like now... If I were to believe, I wouldn't be able to talk. If I were to talk, I'd then have to be afraid of God. . . . I'd just stay at my house, I wouldn't be able to go around, go around in the middle of the night. I wouldn't be able to go to parties or do the customs. . . I would go and hear them say, "Ah, Jesus is coming very soon." I would wait and I wouldn't see this thing happen. I'd just go and get old and then die. . . . What sorts of things would I have done? Nothing. And later when they would talk about me to the children, say what kind of man I was, like say, "Oh, this man before, he was a real bikhet," like this or that. They wouldn't be able to say that. I would just follow the straight way and die. . . . All of the time my thoughts go to the side of being a heathen. I must be a bikhet, so then later all of my children and my grandchildren must tell stories about me and my name must stay on.

As Aminguh presents it, being unable to engage in bikhet behavior interferes with his sense of who he wants to be and prevents his acquiring a reputation like that of his father. If he were not a bikhet he would not be remembered by future generations; he sees being vocal in public as an essential component to a man's reputation. What is noteworthy about his statements is the explicit contemplation of alternative ways of being. If he were Christian, he would have another identity, one that is not bikhet. He wouldn't participate in disputes, travel around at night with his friends, or be a part of the customs. It would be a bleak existence. His rhetoric creates a dichotomy between the bikhet man and man who does nothing in life. Thus, Aminguh's identification with the image of his father as a bikhet and his self-conscious reflection on what it would mean to him to live as a Christian indicate that the bikhet mystique lies at the heart of a cultivated identity.

The life of a Christian man might at this point be a somewhat abstract alternative for Aminguh, one that he could easily avoid. But there looms another alternative to the bikhet life that is much less easily avoided, one that seriously threatens his sense of masculinity and generates considerable anxiety: marriage. Young Bumbita men are in fact notorious for their reluctance to enter into marriage. They put it off as long as possible, even after all the proper arrangements have been made. Bumbita lore tells of young couples being forcibly locked and guarded in their house until the marriage was consummated (Leavitt 1991). For young men marriage not only interferes with an easy style of life and companionship with other young men, it also threatens to undo a precarious sense of masculine identity, one often based on a bikhet model. When I talked with Aminguh about his upcoming marriage, the topic was clearly one he had concerns about. At one point, I asked him if he was going to marry soon, and he responded:

> Sorry my friend, marriage, marriage I think about. It is not good for me to marry because then I would sit down and be good. Plenty of men tell me to marry, but I myself don't think of being married. If I were married, I wouldn't be a bikhet now. If I wanted to be a bikhet, then I would think, "Ah, I would leave my wife to go to jail and who would look after her now?" I would sit quietly and do my work, but I still want to have sex around. I myself don't want to get married. . . .
>
> I told [my fiancée], "Later, when you're old and I'm old we can get married and it's finished. Now look, you're still young and I'm still young. Why should I marry?" . . . I told her, saying, "You shouldn't yearn too much to be married." I told her, "Marriage is not a good thing! Marriage will make us old in a hurry. We will have many children and we will go to nothing, we will become no good. You stay young and I stay young, that's the good way."

As Aminguh frames it, after getting married he would no longer be a bikhet. He would be a different kind of person. It is not so much that he would no longer be able to do the things that he can do as a single man; it is rather that he would no longer be *inclined* to do them. He would become a different person, one that thinks about his responsibilities, one that checks his desire to act in a disruptive way. As he describes it, the man who thinks twice before acting up, who thinks of his wife's well-being ("who will look after her?" etc.) is Aminguh himself, as a married man, an image of himself that he (as yet) wants to avoid.

When he talks with his fiancée about marriage, he suppresses the bikhet theme and frames his objection in another way, restricting himself to talking about physiological, not spiritual, deterioration. Marriage, he says, hastens the aging process. There is a time for marriage, and his time has not yet come. But throughout his entire discussion of marriage there is an implied dichotomy between the married man and the bikhet man, much like with his earlier contrast between the Christian and the bikhet. By getting married and assuming responsibilities, his bikhet tendencies will become domesticated. In fact, for many adult men, the "domesticated bikhet" image is the one that they regularly choose as a description of themselves. Recall, for example, that Arehin, the local Bumbita leader who refers to himself as having bikhet past, has a bikhet core to his identity in spite of his current emphasis on consensus and wisdom. In Aminguh's mind, though, the domestication that comes with marriage is something that he is not yet willing to accept.

Underlying all of this is a subtle notion about identity that is instructive: Life experiences and life events can have a transformative influence on one's identity. Thus, for example, when Aminguh says that marriage would prevent

him from being bikhet, he is not referring simply to new constraints and obligations; he is saying, rather, that marriage would *make him a different person.*
Bumbita ideas about events transforming people in fact appear across a broad
spectrum of issues. They believe, for example, that children, in eating the food
that parents have grown and given them, literally sap the parents of their
strength. When Aminguh talks of aging fast after having children, he is speaking
in literal terms. Children cause aging. Similarly, initiation ideology states that
performing certain ritual acts transforms a man into a different kind of spiritual being. By participating in the initiations, young men were creating themselves in a literal sense. Aminguh and other young men apply a similar model to
the bikhet pattern. When they act in a disruptive or disobedient way, it is not
simply that they seek to broadcast a bikhet image of themselves to the community; rather, they are also actively creating a bikhet identity for themselves, an
identity intimately associated with who they are as men. The Bumbita bikhet
mystique must be appreciated in this light.

In Aminguh's case, the Bumbita view of the transformative power of events
had the effect of heightening his anxiety about the future. The bikhet identity
was one that he felt he had to hold on to, one that he associated with his father.
The alternatives that the future might bring were as yet too disturbing. He made
one revealing comment to me on the eve of my departure. I asked him what he
thought was in store for him—would he become Christian, would he marry?
He took the occasion to say that he would have to remain as he was, unmarried,
a "heathen," adding,

> that way I'd be able to write a letter to you and tell you what sorts of things I
> had been doing. If I were a bikhet then later I'd write a letter, saying "I have
> been a bikhet like this or like that." I think about this.

He suggests here that if in the future he did not continue on his course as a
bikhet, any letters he may write me would not fit with the image of himself that
he had recorded on my machine. Only by remaining a bikhet could he send appropriate addenda to his interviews. For Aminguh, at least, being a bikhet had
become central to his sense of who he was.

CONCLUSION: THE EFFECT OF SOCIAL CHANGE?

I began this chapter with the Bumbita observation that in recent years the
bikhet behavior of adolescents has gotten more pronounced and disruptive. The
short duration of my stay made it impossible to make definitive statements
about the extent of—and motivations for—the putative local rise in bikhet behavior. However, it appears that the rise of Christianity and the subsequent demise of the traditional male initiation cult have had two relevant effects on the

experience of Bumbita adolescent males. Increased Christian consciousness in Bumbita communities has shifted the moral debate to the ultimate "virtue" or "sin" of various acts and away from the appropriate social context for various kinds of threatening, retaliatory, or predatory behavior brought on by the bikhet pattern. Young men like Aminguh feel they have to take an active "bikhet" stand against the Christian cause which would, as he sees it, leave him no context whatsoever in which to generate a reputation that would enable him to leave his name to subsequent generations. Second, the extinction of traditional practices of competitive exchange and Tambaran initiations have left young men with the need to demonstrate their active cultivation of a masculine identity without any controlled context in which to do it. Bumbita elders lament that young Bumbita men, without the ritually induced spiritual power, are no longer able to produce large crops of yams, but for young men, their very identity seems to be at stake. They may be compensating by developing bikhet reputations outside of traditional ritual domains.

Harris (1987) has argued that the delinquent behavior that has beset Port Moresby in recent years should not be conceptualized necessarily as a lapse into immoral behavior or even the formation of a "delinquent" subculture. He suggests that the rise in crime reflects concerted efforts to redress perceived wrongs and cultivate social organizations to adapt to the unfamiliar elements of the urban setting. The Bumbita case, while bearing little relationship to the problems Harris addresses, nevertheless demonstrates how a particular notion of masculine identity, in conjunction with general social tensions over what is appropriate behavior, can contribute to a pattern of behavior that has usually been glossed as "delinquency."

Notes
Bibliography
Index

NOTES

2. "Adolescence in the Pacific," by Carol M. Worthman

Thanks to all contributors to this volume who supplied initial drafts of their chapters, and particularly to those who responded to my questionnaire of February 1990 on the social construction of adolescence as it relates to physical development. Respondents were Aletta Biersack (Pajela), Paula Brown (Chimbu), Vicky Burbank (Aboriginals of Mangrove), Eileen Cantrell (Gebusi females), Bruce Knauft (Gebusi males), and Steve Leavitt (Bumbita). I thank them all for generously providing the information that supported and stimulated much of this paper; however, responsibility for any misinterpretations, misrepresentations, and misunderstandings must be fully my own. Information supplied in the surveys that is cited in the text of this paper is referenced by the name of the investigator and the designation of "survey." Finally, recognition should be given the many stimulating discussions with Gil Herdt that doubtless, in numerous ways, find resonance in this paper.

This paper was written with the support of a Faculty Scholarship from the William T. Grant Foundation.

Methodological note: Citations denoted as "survey" in the text are drawn from responses that provide ethnographic material unavailable elsewhere. An earlier version of this chapter originally drew on the societies discussed at a symposium on adolescence at the 1990 meeting of the Association for Social Anthropology in Oceania. Some of the studies presented at that symposium appear as chapters in this volume.

1. Gilbert Herdt, personal communication, September 1991, has observed gynaecomastia among Sambia.

2. Fredrik Barth (pers. comm., 10/90) suggests that gynaecomastia may fit hermaphroditic themes found in some societies of highland New Guinea. In these societies, hermaphrodites possess high symbolic potency because they combine features of both producers and consumers of energy.

3. Researchers in Papua New Guinea regularly remark that the only plump highlanders they see are adolescent girls.

4. Instances include the Etoro (Kelly 1976) and Bimin Kukusmin (Poole 1982).

5. For a prescient discussion on the relationship of culture and biology in terms of caregiving and socialization practices in relation to physical maturation, see Mead and Macgregor (1951):24–35.

6. More precisely, the Gainj figure is based on median age at onset of luteal function.

7. Physiologic-phenomenologic bases of cultural constructions of mind-body distinction are insightfully explored by Leder (1990).

8. Schieffelin (1985) describes a similar instrumental role for expressions of anger among Kaluli men.

9. Psychologists who are most concerned with intracultural variation have suggested that persons "make" their own environments through their perceptions, actions, and interactions with others (Scarr and McCartney 1983), and that "goodness of fit" between child and context influences the person-environment interaction (Lerner and Busch-Rossnagel 1981; Lerner 1987).

10. For an extended examination of the social production of difference, as well as processes of its social valuation and hence of the social construction of meaningful differences, see Kelly 1993.

3. "Adolescent Pregnancy and Parenthood in an Australian Aboriginal Community," by Victoria K. Burbank and James S. Chisholm

We wish to acknowledge the support of the Australian Institute of Aboriginal and Torres Strait Islander Studies, the Fulbright Foundation, the Menzies School of Health Research, and the Northern Territory Department of Health. We also wish to thank the men and women of Mangrove, Neil Pelkey, and Dr. Ernesto Pollitt for their help with this work.

1. While there is no ethnographic data from the presettlement period, statements of Aboriginal people about a premenarcheal marriage age are corroborated by ethnographic reports on nearby groups little disturbed by Western culture (see, e.g., Warner 1937; Rose 1960).

2. Statements made by Aboriginal people during formal interviews were recorded by hand, more or less verbatim. When comments were made in casual conversation, we tried to remember and record them word for word, but they can only be regarded as approximations. Many of the statements presented here have also been translated and edited.

3. With reference to Mangrove, Burbank (1996) has suggested that actions of young men are most productively interpreted as attempts to solve problems arising from a history of inadequate education, disappointing employment prospects, racism, and political domination.

4. At Mangrove it is said that a man gives his children his face and his feet. Like faces, feet mark the individuality of people. An individual's footprints, for example, are distinguished from those left by other people.

5. Mangrove seems to provide an example that does not support the idea that male control of women's reproductive capacities is essential for reproduction of the social formation (see Meillassoux [1973] discussed in Harris and Young [1981]). That is, at

Mangrove, women's product, children, are socially appropriated, but women's reproductive powers are left largely uncontrolled. For a further discussion of this topic, see Burbank 1996; Bern 1979; Hiatt 1985.

6. Burbank asked several women if today's single mothers would have difficulties if they wished to marry later on. None of the answers indicate these women think that they would, if they chose "straight" partners. In the answers there is no indication of a stigma being attached to having borne a child out of wedlock.

4. "Horticulture and Hierarchy," by Aletta Biersack

My original fieldwork in Paiela was conducted under a National Science Foundation dissertation grant (1974–1978). Work was begun on this paper while I held a fellowship for university teachers from the National Endowment for the Humanities. My research on these practices has continued in the 1990s through a grant in aid from the Wenner-Gren Foundation at the end of 1993 and the beginning of 1995 and as a Fulbright Research Scholar during the second half of 1995. I thank all of these institutions and agencies for their support and encouragement.

I acknowledge with gratitude my continuing debt to my Paiela and Porgera hosts and hostesses. The research on which this chapter is based involved both males and females. In Paiela, those I talked to about these matters included, among the women, Mata, Kongolome, Limbame, Matia (mother of Kolo), Siata, and Wandiokoleme, and, among the men, Nikolas, Luke, Kau, and Simion. At Porgera Station, I talked, among the men, to Kualata, Koipanda, and, among the women, to Lombome. The chapter is dedicated to my now-deceased Paiela mother, Mata, who first told me about a girl's magical plants and their wondrous effects, who shared with me her store of knowledge, including magic, and who brought me my daily allotment of sweet potatoes while I conducted my doctoral research.

My thanks also to Gil Herdt and Cliff Sather for their readings of an earlier draft, and to Steve Leavitt for his patience. Frances Ingemann has been wonderfully informative in linguistic matters, though I accept all responsibility for matters of translation and interpretation here.

1. Kongolome also said a spell to postpone menstruation so that the breasts would be allowed their period of growth before menarche. When the young woman menstruates, she will be ready to do "menstrual blood work" *(tatama peape);* she will be ready to conceive and reproduce. The maturation of the breasts is to courtship as menses is to marriage, therefore. Kongolome said this very same spell when she was nursing her children to preclude conceiving before she was ready to wean her child. Again, the breasts and their functions are serially related to menstruation and its functions. The reader should note that while Paiela women might say spells to grow their breasts, breast milk was thought to "come nothing," without intervention, and the same is true of menstrual blood, the flow of which might be curbed but not initiated by an agent.

2. In my first reporting on the *omatisia* ritual (Biersack 1982), I claimed that *omatisia* was ginger. I now believe that, while "ginger" *(palena)* may be a metaphorical term for the plant, the plant is not gingerroot, but something else. A generic term of magical

plants used in the ways that I have described here is *kandolopa*. Another generic term that is used is *pole*, which Ingemann translates as "sweet-flag (Araceae, Acorus)" (1997:60). According to Ingemann, *pole* is synonymous with *sialangai* and may be synonymous with *omatisia* (ibid., 60). Unfortunately, through a series of mishaps and misadventures, I am not yet able to supply the scientific term for the various magical plants I discuss in this chapter. I do have a botanical assessment of the cordyline *pitu*, and I supply the scientific terms when and if Ingemann supplies them.

3. Elsewhere (Biersack 1996a), I have provided a detailed account of the *omatisia* ritual of the Yokone clan, which is based at Kolombi, on the eastern side of the Paiela Valley. The account was given to me by one of the most knowledgeable traditional leaders in the Paiela Valley—Luke, son of Botane.

4. Ingemann glosses *aiya* as handsome (1997:2). *Aiya* is the male equivalent of *maya,* or "beautiful," and, according to Mata, the origin of *sialangai* is *maya* house *(maya anda),* presumably the female equivalent of the young men's *aiya anda,* the upper forest where the female spirit hides in the bamboo tube.

5. *Kinambuli* also refers to females who are old enough to have married and borne children, but who have not.

6. Birds are associated with the sky, for obvious reasons, and they, together with the most important inhabitant of the sky, the sun, are symbols of omniscience and all that omniscience represents (see Biersack 1990, 1991, and 1996c).

7. In explaining the various leaves used to form the duct, Kualata emphasized the need to cleanse the eyes of any menstrual blood–related filth. Women staunch their menstrual flow and collect their menstrual blood in preparation for discarding it by plugging their vagina with tampax-like moss pads, and Kualata used this same moss *(kamalumbi)* to draw water toward his eyes when he washed them. The cordyline leaf that is used, *pitu* (Cordylina fructicosa) is associated with ancestral figures and perhaps represents their staying power. The entire *omatisia* area is enclosed in a ring of *pitu* cordyline plants.

8. I have discovered several differences between Paiela and Porgera practices. According to the information on the *omatisia* rituals of the Maipangi and Anga clans, participants planted two cultigens rather than the one cultigen, *omatisia,* which alone was planted by Paiela clans such as Takali and Yokone. The solid dark green plant, or *omatisia,* represents the boy's hair, and the striped green and yellow plant, or *sialangai,* represents the boy's skin, according to Koipanda. Both plants were planted near a lake or swamp. The third plant, a plant called *sandalu,* is white, and it, too, symbolizes the boy's body. Also, in the Paiela Valley, the boys spent the first and last night at a halfway house called the *palipai* or *palipali anda,* which marked the entranceway to the forest retreat. Neither the Maipangi nor the Anga clans of the Porgera Valley appear to have had such a house.

9. No Paiela has ever mentioned the loss of the bamboo tube element to me. In the Enga version of the ritual, there are no bamboo tubes (Meggitt 1964).

10. This procedure is similar to the procedure that men follow if they have intercourse with a menstruating woman.

11. According to Ingemann, *yange* is "a long-tailed bird of paradise, variously

identified as Taeniaparadiseae mayeri, Epimachus meyeri, Paradisornis rudolphi, and Trichoparadisea guilielmi; also a racket-tail (Tanysiptera carolinae and Tanysipteri galatea)" (1997:82–83). She tells me, in discussing the *yange* metaphor, that the back panel of a woman's traditional skirt, longer than the front panel, was "compared to the tail of a bird of paradise" (e-mail message, January 14, 1998).

12. The *wambia* bird of paradise is "variously identified as Paradisornis rudolphi, Drepanornis albertisii, Trichoparadisea guilielmi and Paradisaea minor" (Ingemann 1997:78).

13. Like the *omatisia* woman, the Melpa female goddess of which Strathern writes is a virginal bride, "but this marriage is not, like a human marriage, consummated by sexual intercourse. Instead, she brings the power of granting fertility to others, acting like a third operator on the human female-male pair" (A. Strathern 1994:232).

14. A woman's decline is tied particularly to childbearing and nursing. Pendulous breasts are a product of these activities, and the difference between a young and desirable woman, on the one hand, an old and less desirable woman, on the other, lies, quite simply, in the length of the breast. If a woman can take a break from childbearing and nursing, she can recover some of her allure, but not otherwise. Men's decline follows from their sexual activity, but, as long as a male does not engage in adultery, intercourse will be merely intermittent. A male should not have intercourse while his wife is menstruating, pregnant, or nursing, which means that he effectively is chaste for long periods. During these stretches, if he has the wealth, he will court in the hope of marrying again; and courting males that are looking for a second or third wife are considered "beautiful" as long as they are still relatively young.

15. It may seem contradictory to emphasize, on the one hand, courtship and beautification in preparation for it and, on the other, the social, organizational work of marriage. Spouse seekers are always positioned within a broad and complex field of potential mates and matchmakers. This field will always offer multiple opportunities for marrying strategically, giving any one person choices and stiff competition.

16. The spirit woman is also thought to be the source of her boy-husband's wealth and, in that, is wifely. A wife feeds and fattens the pigs she owns jointly with her husband, increasing their value. In the Yokone clan magic I collected, when a participant in the *omatisia* ritual purchased his bamboo tubes with cowrie shells, the spirit woman was told to "go to her husband" along with the bamboo tube and to bring pearl shells with her. The spirit woman is a "wealthy" woman, Luke, the Yokone spellmaster, told me, and when the bamboo tubes and the bark that would ring them were cut, they were first etched with a valuable pearl shell as the spellman said a spell referring to the participants as "wealthy men one and all."

17. Like Errington and Gewertz (1996), we must be cautious in making predictions and pronouncements and must be aware that, far from being uniform, present-day trends may conflict and contradict each other. Susanne Bonnell conducted a survey among households that the Porgera Joint Venture had resettled to clear the way for gold mining in the later 1980s, and she discovered that polygyny was on the rise rather than on the decline (Bonnell 1994:table 16), suggesting that traditional marriage—with its gender politics of exchange—is proving resilient if not resurgent, however much

countervailing foreign ideologies might tend to undermine it (see Biersack 1998b).

18. Informants in Paiela tended to say that the *omatisia* plant represented the boy's hair while the bamboo tubes represented the boy's skin. However, there is no question that in Paiela versions of the *omatisia* ritual, a boy-girl, ritual husband/ritual wife relationship is the core relationship of the ritual.

5. "Woman the Sexual, a Question of When," by Eileen M. Cantrell

I wish to thank Gilbert Herdt, Raymond Kelly, Bruce Knauft, Stephen Leavitt, and Harriet Whitehead for their thoughtful comments on earlier drafts of this paper.

1. On exchange, see, for instance, Lederman 1986, 1989; on economic development, see, for instance, Sexton 1986; Rosi and Zimmer-Tamakoshi 1993; on oral narrative, see, for instance, Kyakas and Wiessner 1992; Keesing 1985; cf. Polier n.d.; on women's overall status, see, for instance, Lepowsky 1993; on male domination and/or female resistance, see, for instance, Godelier 1986; Josephides 1985.

2. Field work was initially conducted between 1980 and 1982. Additional information on the Gebusi can be found in Cantrell 1989; n.d. See also Knauft 1985; 1986; 1989; 1991.

3. Two small mission stores existed in neighboring tribal territories. However, due to longstanding intergroup hostilities, the Gebusi were reluctant to travel through these territories to reach the stores.

4. For a detailed statistical discussion of the decrease in Gebusi homicide rates from pre- to post-contact periods, see Knauft 1985, chapter 5, especially pp. 116–18. My comments concerning violence are restricted to acts of physical violence observable by ordinary persons. Gebusi believe the risk of violence caused by the covert acts of sorcerers have continued unabated since pacification. Enactments of sorcery can be seen only by spirit people *(todi os)*, who then orally communicate their observations to humans at séances.

5. I use "adult women" to refer to all persons of the female sex who have attained the age status of "true womanhood" *(oifor deb)*, that is, women over the age of approximately sixteen. Gebusi do not employ a gender-free term comparable to the English term "adult"; all adult age categories in the Gebusi lexicon are simultaneously gender categories.

6. These terms refer to age/gender categories as well as the age/gender status of individuals. This means that a term such as *oifor elem* may be translated as "emerging woman" as well as "emerging womanhood."

7. See Sørum 1982 and n.d. for discussion of male initiation among the Bedamini, a language group located to northwest of the Gebusi. See also R. D. Shaw 1990 concerning initiation among the Samo who live to the northwest of Gebusi lands.

True young women play important roles at numerous points throughout the male initiation. However, participation is optional for any given woman. Furthermore, neither men nor women think of women's participation as constituting a female initiation (for contrast, see R. D. Shaw 1990). Even though young Gebusi women dress in ritual costume similar to that of the initiates and stand beside them during several ceremonial enactments, female participation is meant to highlight the initiates' assumption to manhood, particularly those aspects of manhood that entail heterosexual relations.

8. In regard to boys between the ages of approximately seven and seventeen, it was said that hearing women's conversations about female maturation was detrimental to male maturational processes. It was also said that overhearing such conversations would result in decreased growth, coughing, or shortness of breath among boys who were "still growing." Although this belief also applies to uninitiated males in late adolescence, approximately eighteen to twenty-three years old, regard for their health was not the main reason for women's secrecy. Although it is forbidden for uninitiated young men to engage in heterosexual intercourse, adult women believe that they have an ever-increasing desire to do so, making young men's commitment to preinitiation heterosexual celibacy tenuous. Concerned more with the "pragmatics" of protecting pubescent females than loss of lung power among uninitiated males, adult women did not want any male whom they considered predisposed toward a sexualized view of young women to be reminded that certain females were beginning to mature sexually.

9. There is a strong similarity in the way the Gebusi use the terms *suskay/suskay de* (muscle/bold) and the way Americans use the terms "gut" and "gutsy."

10. Occasionally, exceptions are made to the all-male composition of the séances. Of the 101 séances known to have occurred between June 1980 and February 1982, participants in four séances included both men and women. Women were allowed to participate when the minimum number of men considered requisite to conduct the séance could not be met. For further information on spirit women, Gebusi women, and séances, see Cantrell n.d. For more information on the Gebusi séances in general, see Knauft 1985; 1989.

11. This life cycle metaphor is fairly widespread among Strickland-Bosavi groups. See Kelly 1976; also Sørum n.d.

12. For further discussion on this topic, see Cantrell n.d.; cf. also Knauft 1985:chaps. 10–12; 1986; 1989.

13. This is the Gebusi appropriation of the cognate Tok Pisin term for power.

14. *Wa gisay* literally means "child grown up (matured)." Although a young man is not a "child grown up true" *(wa gisay dep)* until he is initiated, the term *wa gisay* is nonetheless used with increasing frequency as the time for his initiation nears. Men are typically initiated sometime between the ages of eighteen and twenty-three years. Referring to uninitiated men as "children grown" is, I believe, an implicit acknowledgment that visual assessments of adult body attainment precede and are temporarily out of synchrony with cultural practices that affirm adult status. Young men in their late teens and early twenties who are still being inseminated and who have not yet been initiated are *wa kawisum* "children continuing to grow." This term of reference notwithstanding, women trust their own visual assessments of young men's maturational status over cultural terminology, particularly when sexual assessments enter into judgments regarding appropriate female behavior in the presence of these young men.

15. All names cited in this chapter are pseudonyms.

16. The ashes of the *kafis* plant are added to a kava mixture, which Gebusi men drink at feasts. It is said that the ashes reduce kava's bitter taste.

17. The term used by Yob, *buala,* has number of interrelated meanings and is difficult

to translate into English. *Buala* is, first, "to physically struggle against another person(s)." This meaning is used in a number of contexts: in reference to the armed physical aggression between groups of men ("to fight") and in reference to the behavior of men and women during sexual intercourse. The second meaning of *buala* is "to sit." Depending on conversational cues, *buala* may refer to either fighting or sitting as these pertain to the way marriage negotiations are conducted in which fighting signifies rejection of a proposed marriage and sitting communicates acceptance. In conversations on marriage, either of these meanings may stand for the whole, and indeed, *buala* also means "to marry." In conversations on sexual intercourse, *buala* may refer to the way men and women relate to each other physically prior to sexual climax, as in "to struggle physically against one another," or it may be used to indicate one's willingness to engage in sex, as in, "Come sit with me." In conversations on heterosexual intercourse, *buala* may also serve as a metonymic reference and glossed simply as "to have sex" or "to engage in sexual intercourse."

In the context of her narrative, it is clear that Yob did not want to do any of the following: to fight, struggle, sit down with, have sex with, or marry Baya. Although Baya may have had marriage to Yob as an ultimate goal, his behavior in this situation is not consistent with the way ritualized bride capture is used to make formal marriage claims on women. Yob's refusal to *buala* is only a distant reference to her wish "not to marry" Baya. The immediate reference of her refusal is sexual. Yob's use of the term *buala* is contextualized by her understanding that Baya wanted to have sex with her in that situation. She did not want to "fight or struggle" with him either as part of sexual intercourse or as part of refusing sexual relations with him—hence the somewhat awkward translation of *buala golem mwi da* as "do not want to fight/struggle/have sex."

18. Auled is actually Baya's father's brother's wife. After Baya's true father and mother died, Auled became his adoptive mother. Auled is Mebay's true mother, making Baya and Mebay classificatory brother and sister.

19. Boys enter into homosexual relations with young initiated men about the age of twelve or thirteen. Gebusi believe that, without oral insemination, boys will not achieve manhood. Gebusi men undergo initiation only once, typically between the ages of eighteen and twenty-three. Until manhood is recognized and celebrated at their initiation, uninitiated male youth may receive but are, in principle, not supposed to give semen. This would preclude, of course, both heterosexual and homosexual transfers of semen. Upon initiation, these injunctions are lifted, giving men the right to assume the role of semen donor to both adolescent males and women (cf. Knauft 1986, 1987; Herdt 1981; 1987).

20. By age seven, young boys sleep in the men's section of the longhouse on a regular basis. Although their participation in séances increases with age, especially during adolescence, no effort is made to prevent boys in early childhood from hearing séances. Knauft reports (pers. comm.) a boy as young as four or five years old may fall asleep in his father's lap while listening to the refrains of the séance songs and his father's repartee with the spirit women. If, on the average, men attend séances even once a month (one is given on the average of every eleven days [Knauft 1985:296]), they would attend twelve séances a year. Between the ages of seven and twenty years, a young man

would have heard 156 séances. This estimate is low, and it is safe to say that most Gebusi men, by age twenty, have heard all or part of well over one hundred séances.

21. The spirit people, *todi os,* are thought of as invisible, sentient beings who share with humans many physical, intellectual, and emotional attributes. A Gebusi man becomes a spirit medium only by marrying a spirit woman and producing a spirit child. The medium's soul is said to leave his body during the séance, during which time his spirit wife and spirit son may enter and speak to the men attending the séance. Other spirit women, not married to the medium, may do the same. The spirit women, regardless of whether their individual identities are known (many are not), are of a generic stock. Almost all spirit women are portrayed as "true young women" (that is, over the age of sixteen, but not yet the mother of two children). Spirit women are said to be exceedingly beautiful, with slim waists, large breasts, and unblemished skin. Their legendary and highly admired sexual desire and boldness cause spirit women to pursue men, spirit and human, for sexual gratification. Marriage, in the spirit world, far from acting as a deterrent to serial adultery, acts as a catalyst for it. The nearly constant absence of the spirit woman's husband is said to leave her "sad and longing," causing her to seek sexual liaisons with other men. Spirit women who are not married are *ipso facto* thought to be alone and longing for sex with men. In séance narratives, spirit women do not suffer violent retribution from men for their sexual promiscuity, nor does their behavior inspire jealousy or competitive violence among men. Spirit women, sexually desirable and ever-longing for sex, are said to be abundant in number. Over 80 percent of the songs sung over the course of the eight- to nine-hour séance in question depicted some aspect of the erotic life of the spirit women. The spirit woman persona is, in symbolic terms, "woman the sexual," a highly eroticized and widely praised representation of womanhood. This construct of female sexuality is also the product of the collective male imagination. The impact of this image of womanhood on the lives of Gebusi women over the life cycle is the subject of my dissertation (Cantrell n.d.). For a broader description of Gebusi spirit séances as well as their role in sorcery accusations, see Knauft 1985, ch. 11, and Knauft 1989.

22. There were, in a sense, two Manwis. One Manwi was the thirteen-year-old adolescent female who lived in our settlement. The other was the persona of Manwi as represented by the men attending the séance. For clarity as well as brevity's sake, I shall use the name Manwi to refer to the séance persona while I shall refer to the living person as "the real Manwi."

23. Manwi's mother's brothers were true mother's brothers and were thus precluded, through incest prohibition, from marriage with her.

24. For discussions of similar beliefs among other Strickland-Bosavi tribes, see Sørum 1982; 1984; Kelly 1976; 1977; Schieffelin 1976; 1982.

25. Because women, including female anthropologists, are decidedly unwelcome visitors at both séance performances and subsequent translation sessions, I am grateful to Knauft for his generosity in giving me access to the séance material presented in this chapter.

26. A morphemic translation of *fayi wasi fala* is "sickness spinning hit" and refers to a mental state in which a person's mind has been "hit" and is "spinning around" with

sexual desire. As sex is believed to rob a person of strength (here, good judgment), such a state is also associated with illness.

27. See note 13 for the meanings of *buala*. In this séance song, the (male) representation of Manwi is that of a thirteen-year-old girl who is enticing a spirit man into having sexual relations *(buala)* with her. This contrasts dramatically with Yob's account of resisting male sexual advances during her own adolescence.

28. It is logically possible that the reference here is to fellatio. Herdt and Stoller (1990) report that this practice is preferred among Sambia men with their wives, especially in the early years of marriage. Since homosexual fellatio is practiced among the Gebusi, I asked three Gebusi women if this was also a heterosexual practice. All three women were in their mid-twenties to early thirties, two of whom were currently married and one of whom was widowed. All three said no. One woman spontaneously said that the practice would make her throw up, whereupon she dramatically imitated the act of vomiting. Each woman was questioned in complete privacy. Each of these women had agreed to be interviewed for five to six sessions, each session lasting one to two hours. I worked from a broad set of questions designed to elicit understandings governing young womanhood, sex, marriage, motherhood, widowhood, and old age. The question concerning heterosexual fellatio came in the context of these sessions.

29. A code letter for a clan name is used to further the anonymity of individual séance participants.

30. Gebusi women are not reluctant to comment on the sexual attributes and assertiveness of spirit women in the presence of men. In fact they do so enthusiastically with a mixture of earthy humor and admiration. The existence of spirit women per se is not taboo knowledge for women. In addition, the morning after an all-night séance, women may comment, in a good-natured fashion, on the raucous behavior of the men during the previous night. Such references are typically oblique comments about how sleepy they or the men are going to be during the upcoming day. Beneath the chiding remarks, women's knowing smiles indicate approval. This positive reaction underscores, by contrast, the disapproval with which Manwi's kinswomen responded to the erotic portrayal of "their child" in the séance.

31. This is not to imply that adult men do not also have protective responsibilities toward adolescent males. Adult men do instruct and caution against the dangers of a predatory, sexual greed in adult women. But whereas men's obligations are both generative and protective, women's obligations entail protection only. Whereas the celebratory aspects of ritual highlight men's power to reproduce men, the uncelebrated pride of women notes the "natural" transition of females to womanhood. My representation of women's duty as "protection" is meant to convey a restricted same-sex relation, not a gender-exclusive attribute. However, the representation of men's duty as the generation of manhood in social others is understood as a gender-exclusive ability. Women are (understood to be) unable to bring forth womanhood in social others.

32. In four of the ten cases of child/adolescent betrothal, the designated bride was residentially separated from her premarital coresident kin. This is the same rate of postmarital bride/kin separation that occurs in a survey of 35 first unions. The larger sample includes marriages that were publicly negotiated when the bride was an *oifor*

deb (between sixteen and twenty years old) as well as marriages that were publicly negotiated when the bride was younger. Twenty-one first marriages (60 percent) involved the immediate co-residence of the bride's kin and the groom's kin.

33. For further discussion on the relationship between the understanding of marriage as "reciprocal sexual longing" and the understanding of marriage as "the reciprocal exchange of women between men from different clans" see Cantrell (1989).

34. In other Strickland-Bosavi tribes betrothal, daughter-familial co-residence, and bride transfer are configured differently. Kelly (1977) reports that, in the late 1960s, Etoro girls were typically betrothed by the age of five. However, it was customary for a betrothed girl to remain a member of her parental household until she communicated emotional maturity and personal acceptance of the groom and her role as wife. It was common, though not mandatory, for the designated groom to co-reside with her family during the betrothal period or for the bride's family to live with the kin of the designated groom. Kelly writes that the "transition to the status of wife is gradual in every respect" (1977:214).

Sørum (pers. comm.) reports just the opposite situation among the Bedamini, the largest tribe in the Strickland-Bosavi area, neighboring the Etoro to the west and the Gebusi to the northeast. Sørum reports that Bedamini girls are typically betrothed between the ages of five and eight. An initial meat prestation is formally given by the prospective groom to the girl's mother as an acknowledgment of the strong mother-daughter bond and the grief anticipated by the termination of the mother-daughter co-residence. The bride resides with her family until she enters puberty, when marital transfer is effected through a symbolic form of bride capture in which the groom's agnatic kin stage a ritualized bow-and-arrow attack upon her family's house and successfully "capture" the bride despite the "attempt" of her own kin to protect her. In a day or two, when the bride's kin visit the groom's settlement for a marriage feast, the young adolescent Bedamini girl is given license to swear angrily, publicly, and lewdly at her kin for deserting her. She is allowed to belittle her affines as well. Co-residence between the wife's kin and groom's kin is not common during or after betrothal. Among the Bedamini, betrothal does not appear to prepare the designated bride for her abrupt residential transfer or for the adjustment to living without close kin, among whom maternal ties are acknowledged as preeminent.

My data indicate that, in cases of child/adolescent betrothal, Gebusi bride transfer encompasses two forms. The first is similar to that practiced by the Etoro in regard to daughter-familial co-residence during the betrothal period and a gradual transition to married life. The other is similar to that practiced by the Bedamini in the abrupt nature of the bride-family separation and the emotional significance accorded the mother-daughter bond. Unlike either the Etoro or the Bedamini, 71 percent of all first unions among the Gebusi are publicly negotiated or revealed when the bride is between the ages of sixteen and twenty. This not only means that the majority of women reside with their family until "true womanhood"; it also means a young woman is able to exercise a significant influence in the selection of her first husband regardless of her betrothed status or sister exchange commitments. This pattern is consistent with the prominence of the spirit women in Gebusi séances, a sexualized construction of womanhood in which women initiate their own heterosexual partnerships (see note 10). In Etoro and Bedamini séances, the promiscuous voices of spirit women are not heard to the same extent they are heard in Gebusi séances, a pattern consistent with their tighter social control over women (girls) in contracting marriage (cf. Sørum 1982; Kelly pers. comm.).

6. Coming of Age on Vanatinai, by Maria Lepowsky

Portions of this chapter were presented in the "Symposium on Adolescence in Pacific Island Societies: Change and Continuity," held at the Association for Social Anthropology in Oceania Annual Meetings on Kauai, Hawai'i in March 1990. I thank Gilbert Herdt and the other symposium participants for their comments. Thanks to Victoria Burbank, Fitz Poole, Stephen Leavitt, and an anonymous reviewer for their helpful comments on various written drafts.

1. Male initiations are not found anywhere in the Massim culture area. They are characteristic of Melanesian societies with strong ideologies of male dominance (Allen 1967; Herdt 1982; Poole 1981; Godelier 1986). Female puberty ceremonies are far less frequent in Melanesia, and when they occur they are less elaborate than their male counterparts (see, e.g., Powdermaker 1971; Godelier 1986). Their significance as reflections and reinforcements of gender ideologies, and as practices that create and signify the gendered person, is more variable and open to debate. See Lutkehaus and Roscoe (1995) and the introduction by Lutkehaus (1995) for excellent overviews and ethnographic accounts.

2. Vanatinai people attribute this phenomenon, and the island's overall low birthrate, to the practices of a variety of contraceptive techniques, magical and herbal. They also tell me that sleeping with more than one man sequentially will keep a girl or woman from becoming pregnant, recommending this as a contraceptive technique and as a good reason why a girl should not settle down too early with one boy. This is why married women are much more likely to conceive, they say. Menarche on Vanatinai is about fifteen, and ovulation is unlikely to be regular for another couple of years. Biologists have long noted this phenomenon of adolescent subfecundity. I have also learned about first trimester spontaneous abortions in late adolescent girls. These are common in industrialized countries as well. Gonorrhea is prevalent and is probably a major reason for the sterility of about one out of eight long-married couples I observed in the southwestern portion of the island. In addition, adolescent girls on Vanatinai are unlikely to have regular sex lives: on an island of small hamlets of closely related people, sexual contacts are often almost literally a matter of "feast or famine," with bursts of sexual activity at feasts, or when exchange visitors arrive, and tedious periods of chastity in between for many, though not all, young people (Lepowsky 1993).

3. See, for example, Condon (1995) on Canadian Inuit youth; Davis and Davis (1989), and Davis (1995) on adolescence in a Moroccan town; Hollos and Leis (1986, 1989) on Nigeria; Abu-Lughod (1990) on Egyptian Bedouin adolescent girls; Lebra (1995) on Japanese aristocratic women; Liechty (1995) on young urbanites in Kathmandu, Nepal; and Jourdan (1995) on the urban migrant Kwaio youths of the Solomon Islands.

7. Youth in Rotuma, Then and Now, by Alan Howard

1. See Howard and Howard 1964; Howard 1970. Major sections of this chapter are adapted from these publications. I want to point out that much of the "knowledge" obtained was based on gossip and talk among adolescent males. Since much of this talk is self-serving, intended to impress listeners concerning the speakers' bravado and exploits, it needs to be tempered with caution, especially where courtship is involved. Margaret Mead was not the first, nor the last, anthropologist to be duped by adolescent discourse.

2. My first field trip was for two years, from August 1959 to August 1961. One year was spent on Rotuma and one year researching Rotuman enclaves in Fiji. I spent almost all of 1960 on Rotuma (December 1959 to December 1960), so refer to the time period of concern by that year. My return to the island in 1987 was brief, but I spent three months there in 1988, six months in 1989, two months in 1990, a week in 1991 and two weeks in 1994, on each occasion with my wife, Jan Rensel, who is also an anthropologist who has studied Rotuma. The account of changes is based on these latter excursions.

3. See Howard 1991 and Rensel 1991 for descriptions of changes over the past thirty years.

4. I use the latter term in reference to physical age, corresponding roughly to the period from the onset of puberty to physical maturity, or to the teenage years.

5. Rotuma is divided into seven districts, each headed by a paramount chief. Districts are divided into villages and hamlets headed by subchiefs.

6. According to my 1960 records nearly 100 percent of the twelve and thirteen year olds were in school, compared with only about 50 percent of the fourteen year olds, and 32 percent of the fifteen and sixteen year olds. These figures were arrived at by comparing school rolls with demographic data from a census I conducted of the whole island.

7. For information concerning the political significance of this division, see Howard 1985; 1986.

8. A game of *tika* begins with members of the visiting team throwing first, followed by the host team. Points are scored each time a throw by the host team exceeds the longest throw by the visiting athletes. A number of the visitors' longer throws are left on the course while the remainder are picked up. If none of the host team's throws are farther than the longest of the visitors', the latter gain a point for each of their efforts exceeding the longest throw of their opponents. After all the players have thrown from one end of the course, they go to the other end and throw in the opposite direction, the order in which the teams throw being reversed. They go back and forth until one team reaches a score of twelve, ending the game. The first team to win two games wins the match. A challenge is ordinarily reciprocated by the other side, after which interest in the sport wanes.

9. Rotuma was missionized by English Methodists and French Catholics in the latter part of the nineteenth century. In 1960 approximately two-thirds of the population were Methodist and one- third were Catholic.

10. According to Hereniko (1977), a group of Rarotongans visited Rotuma in the late 1940s and greatly impressed the people with their dancing. The Rotumans eagerly adopted Rarotongan style dancing, which involves vigorous knee and hip movements.

11. There was some evidence of homosexual play among children and episodic encounters among adolescents, but no one was cast into a homosexual role and all adult males appeared to be actively heterosexual.

12. I was told of marriages never consummated because the girl went through with a marriage so as not to defy her parents, then ran off with her true lover afterwards.

13. This underestimates the proportion of Rotuman children who go on to high school since it does not include individuals in these age groups who left the island for further education or employment. My data indicate that nearly 90 percent of the latter group have some high school education, and a significant portion of those have had some tertiary education.

14. During the one-hundred and fiftieth anniversary celebration of the coming of Christianity to Rotuma, which took place in November and December 1989, a *tika* match was held between the island residents and their visiting kinsmen from Fiji. Almost all the participants were middle-aged men.

15. The Rotuman term *hanisi*, like the Samoan term *alofa* and its cognates, is difficult to translate into English. Churchward defines it as "to feel pity, sorrow, sympathy, or solicitude; to take pity on, be kind to; to be kindly disposed to, to love" (1940:216). However, the emphasis is more on *behaving* in a loving or kindly manner than on *feeling* an emotion.

8. The Bikhet Mystique, by Stephen C. Leavitt

This essay was written under a Rockefeller Humanities fellowship at the Center for Pacific Island Studies, University of Hawaii. My thanks to Gilbert Herdt for comments on an earlier draft.

1. The conflict between following one's own interests and adhering to the demands of kin finds expression in many dimensions of Bumbita culture. For example, in the spiritual realm, ancestral spirits are invoked by the living to perform both good and bad acts. At the same time, these same ancestral spirits have autonomous wills, and they pursue their actions following their own interests. This double nature of ancestral spirits leads to the situation in which spirits may protest against their own essences being invoked in the service of causes that they themselves disavow. It is safe to say that in many contexts, Bumbita feel similarly "invoked" by the demands of their kin. For an eloquent discussion of this fundamental social tension and its relation to the spiritual realm, see Bercovitch 1989.

2. It is possible that the term *ounohi* drives from *ounump*, the Bumbita term for "penis." The possibility is strengthened by the fact that the term for "adolescent female" is *ounuweri'uri*, where -*weri* is a negative term (meaning "no" or "not") and -*'uri* is a singular female possessive suffix. The term for "adolescent female" could thus be glossed as meaning "she without penis."

3. Tuzin (1980) provides a detailed description of the *tumbuan* in Ilahita and outlines its ritual significance in connection with Tambaran initiations (40–42, 47–54).

4. For a more detailed account of Aminguh's narrative and its relation to the loss of his father, see Leavitt 1995c.

BIBLIOGRAPHY

Abu-Lughod, L.
1990   The Romance of Resistance. *In* Beyond the Second Sex: New Perspectives on the Anthropology of Gender. P. Sanday and R. Goodenough, eds., pp. 311–37. Philadelphia: University of Pennsylvania Press.

Allardyce, W. L.
1885–86   Rotooma and the Rotoomans. Proceedings of the Queensland Branch of the Geographical Society of Australasia. 1st sets:130–44.

Allen, M. G.
1967   Male Cults and Secret Initiations in Melanesia. Melbourne: Melbourne University Press.

Amit-Talai, V., and H. Wulff, eds.
1995   Youth Cultures: A Cross-Cultural Perspective. London: Routledge.

Anderson, W. W., and D. D. Anderson
1986   The Muslim Adolescents' Self, Sexuality, and Antinomy. Ethos 14: 368–94.

Angold, A., and C. M. Worthman
1993   Puberty Onset of Gender Differences in Rates of Depression: A Developmental, Epidemiologic and Neuroendocrine Perspective. Journal of Affective Disorders 29:145–58.

Apter, D.
1980   Serum Steroids and Pituitary Hormones in Female Puberty: A Partly Longitudinal Study. Clinical Endocrinology 12:107–20.

Ariès, P.
1962   Centuries of Childhood: A Social History of Family Life. New York: Random House.

Armstrong, W. E.
1928   Rossel Island: An Ethnological Study. Cambridge: Cambridge University Press.

Bane, M. J., and D. Ellwood
1989   One Fifth of the Nation's Children: Why Are They Poor? Science 245:1047–53.

Bateson, G.
1936   Naven. Cambridge: Cambridge University Press.

Beck, E.
1985   The Enigma of Aboriginal Health. Canberra: Australian Institute of Aboriginal Studies.

Bennett, G.
1831   A Recent Visit to Several of the Polynesian Islands. United Service Journal 33:198–202, 473–482.

Bercovitch, E.
1989   Mortal Insights: Victim and Witch in Nalumin Imagination. In The Religious Imagination in New Guinea. G. H. Herdt and M. Stephen, eds., pp. 122–159. New Brunswick, N.J.: Rutgers University Press.

Berger, P. L., and T. Luckmann
1966   The Social Construction of Reality. New York: Doubleday.

Bern, J.
1979   Ideology and Domination: Toward a Reconstruction of Australian Aboriginal Social Formation. Oceania 50:118–32.

Bielicki, T.
1986   Physical Growth as a Measure of the Economic Well-being of Populations: The Twentieth Century. In Human Growth, 2nd ed. F. Falkner and J. M. Tanner, eds., vol. 2, pp. 283–305. New York: Plenum Press.

Biersack, A.
1982   Ginger Gardens for the Ginger Woman: Rites and Passages in a Melanesian Society. Man 17:239–58.
1987   Moonlight: Negative Images of Transcendence in Paiela Pollution. Oceania 57:178–94.
1990   Histories in the Making: Paiela and Historical Anthropology. History and Anthropology 5:63–85.
1991   Prisoners of Time: Millenarian Praxis in a Melanesian Valley. In Clio in Oceania: Toward a Historical Anthropology. A. Biersack, ed., pp. 231–96. Washington, D.C.: Smithsonian Institution Press.
1995   Heterosexual Meanings: Society, the Body, and the Economy Among Ipilis. In Papuan Borderlands: Huli, Duna, and Ipili Perspectives on the Papua New Guinea Highlands. A. Biersack, ed., pp. 231–68. Ann Arbor: The University of Michigan Press.
1996a   Reproducing Patriarchy: The Gender Politics of Male Cults in the Papua New Guinea Highlands and Amazonia. Paper given at the Wenner-Gren conference, "Amazonia and Melanesia: Gender and Anthropological Comparison," Mijas, Spain, September 7–15, 1996.
1996b   "Making Kinship": Marriage, Warfare, and Networks Among Paielas. In Work in Progress: Essays in New Guinea Highlands Ethnography in Honour of Paula Brown Glick. H. LeVine and A. Ploeg, eds., pp. 19–42. Frankfurt: Peter Lang.
1996c   Word Made Flesh: Religion, the Economy, and the Body in the Papua New Guinea Highlands. History of Religions 36:85–111.
1998a   Sacrifice and Regeneration Among Ipilis: The View from Tipinini. In Fluid Ontologies: Myth, Ritual, and Philosophy in the Highlands of Papua New Guinea. L. Goldman and C. Ballard, eds. Westport, Conn.: Greenwood Press.
1998b   Notes from an Anthropologist. Afterword to Dilemmas of Development: The Social and Economic Impact of the Porgera Mine, 1989–1994. C. Filer, ed. Port Moresby, Papua New Guinea: National Research Institute, and Canberra: National Centre for Development Studies (Pacific Policy Paper series), Australian National University.

Biggs, B.
1965   Direct and Indirect Inheritance in Rotuman. Lingua 14:383–415.

Bindon, J. R., and S. Zansky
1986   Growth and Body Composition. *In* The Changing Samoans: Behavior and
            Health in Transition. P. T. Baker, J. M. Hanna, and T. S. Baker, eds., pp. 222–53.
            Oxford: Oxford University Press.

Blos, P.
1967   The Second Individuation Process of Adolescence. Psychoanalytic Study of
            the Child 22:162–86.

Bogin, B.
1988   Patterns of Human Growth. Cambridge: Cambridge University Press.

Bonnell, S.
1994   Dilemmas of Development: Social Change in Porgera, 1989–1993. Porgera
            Social Monitoring Programme, report no. 2. A report to Porgera Joint
            Venture, August 1994.

Boxer, A. M., H. P. Gerschenson, and D. Offer
1984   Historical Time and Social Change in Adolescent Experience. *In* Patterns of
            Adolescent Self-Image. D. Offer et al., eds., pp. 83–95. San Francisco: Jossey-
            Bass.

Brindis, C., and R. Jeremy
1988   Pregnancy and Parenting in California: A Strategic Plan for Action. San
            Francisco: Sutter.

Brison, K.
1991   Just Talk: Gossip, Meetings and Power in a Papua New Guinea Village.
            Berkeley: University of California Press.
1996   Becoming Savage: Western Representations and Cultural Identity in a Sepik
            Society. Anthropology and Humanism 21:5–18.

Brooks-Gunn, J., A. C. Petersen, and D. Eichorn, eds.
1985   Time of Maturation and Psychosocial Functioning in Adolescence. Journal of
            Youth and Adolescence, parts I and II, vol. 14, nos. 3–4.

Brooks-Gunn, J., and M. P. Warren
1988   Mother-Daughter Differences in Menarcheal Age in Adolescent Girls
            Attending National Dance Company Schools and Non-Dancers. Annals of
            Human Biology 15:35–44.

Brown, J. K.
1981   Cross-cultural Perspectives on the Female Life Cycle. *In* Handbook of Cross-
            Cultural Human Development. R. H. Munroe et al., eds., pp. 581–609. New
            York: Garland Pub.

Brown, P.
1978   Highland Peoples of New Guinea. Cambridge: Cambridge University Press.
1988   Gender and Social Change: New Forms of Independence for Simbu Women.
            Oceania 59:123–42.

Brown, P., and G. Buchbinder, eds.
1976   Man and Woman in the New Guinea Highlands. Washington, D.C.: American
            Anthropological Association Special Publication Number 8.

Brudevoll, J. E., K. Liestøl, and L. Walløe
1979   Menarcheal Age in Oslo During the Last 140 Years. Annals of Human Biology
            6:407–16.

Brundtland, G. H., K. Liestøl, and L. Walløe
1980   Height, Weight, and Menarcheal Age of Oslo Schoolchildren During the Last
        60 Years. Annals of Human Biology 7:307–22.

Brunstein, G. D.
1996   Gynecomastia. Endocrine News 21:5.

Buchbinder, G., and R. A. Rappaport
1976   Fertility and Death Among the Maring. In Man and Woman in the New
        Guinea Highlands. P. Brown and G. Buchbinder, eds., Special Publications no.
        8, pp. 3–35. Washington, D.C.: American Anthropological Association.

Bullough, V. L.
1981   Age at Menarche: A Misunderstanding. Science 213:365–66.

Burbank, V. K.
1987   Premarital Sex Norms: Cultural Interpretations in an Australian Aboriginal
        Community. Ethos 15:226–33.
1988   Aboriginal Adolescence: Maidenhood in an Australian Community. New
        Brunswick, N.J.: Rutgers University Press.
1994   Fighting Women. Berkeley: University of California Press.
1995   Gender Hierarchy and Adolescent Sexuality: The Control of Female Repro-
        duction in an Australian Aboriginal Community. Ethos 23:33–46.
1996   A Critical Psychological Anthropology of Teenage Pregnancy in Aboriginal
        Australia. In Aboriginal Health: Social and Cultural Transitions. G. Robinson,
        ed., pp. 101–04. Darwin: Northern Territory University Press.

Burbank, V., and J. Chisholm
1990   Old and New Inequalities in a Southeast Arnhem Land Community:
        Polygyny, Marriage Age, and Birth Spacing. In Emergent Social and Economic
        Inequalities Among Contemporary Hunters and Gatherers. F. Merlan and J.
        Altman, eds., pp. 85–93. Sydney: Oceania Monographs.
1992   Gender Differences in the Perception of Ideal Family Size in an Australian
        Aboriginal Community. In The Father's Role: Cultural and Evolutionary
        Perspectives. B. Hewlett, ed., pp. 177–90. New York: Aldine de Gruyter.

Burrows, E. G., and M. Spiro
1953   An Atoll Culture. New Haven: Human Relations.

Burton, L.
1990   Teenage Childbearing as an Alternative Life-Course Strategy in
        Multigeneration Black Families. Human Nature 1:123–43.

Busse, M.
1990   Continuities and Discontinuities in the Transition from Adolescence to
        Marriage Among the Marind-anim and Boazi of Southern New Guinea.
        Paper presented at the Association for Social Anthropology in Oceania
        annual meeting, Hawaii, March 20–26.

Cantrell, E. M.
1989   When Sisters Become Brides: Choosing a Spouse in a Sister Exchange Society:
        Pre-marital Experience Among Gebusi Women). Paper presented at the
        annual meeting of the American Anthropological Association, Washington,
        D.C., Nov. 15–19.
n.d.   Gebusi Gender Relations. Ph.D. dissertation (in progress). Department of
        Anthropology. The University of Michigan, Ann Arbor.

Carrier, J. G., and A. H. Carrier
1989   Wage, Trade, and Exchange in Melanesia: A Manus Society in the Modern

State. Berkeley: University of California Press.

Cavan, R. S.
1961   The Concepts of Tolerance and Contraculture as Applied to Delinquency. Sociological Quarterly 2:243–58.

Chowning, A.
1973   Childrearing and Socialization. *In* Anthropology in Papua New Guinea: Readings for the Encyclopedia of Papua and New Guinea. Ian Hogbin, ed., pp. 61–79. Carlton, Australia: Melbourne University Press.
1990   Adolescence in Four Papua New Guinea Societies. Paper presented at the biannual meeting of the Association for Social Anthropology in Oceania, Kauai. March 21–25.

Churchward, C. M.
1940   Rotuman Grammar and Dictionary. Sydney: Australasian Medical Publishing Co.

Clifford, W., L. Morauta, B. Stuart
1984   Law and Order in Papua New Guinea, vol. 1: Report and Recommendations. Papua New Guinea: Institute of National Affairs.

Cloward, R. A., and L. E. Ohlin
1960   Delinquency and Opportunity. New York: Free Press.

Cohen, A. K.
1955   Delinquent Boys: The Culture of the Gang. Glencoe, Ill.: The Free Press.

Cole, M., J. Glick, and D. Sharp
1971   The Cultural Context of Learning and Thinking. New York: Basic Books.

Coleman, J.
1961   The Adolescent Society: The Social Life of the Teenager and Its Impact on Education. New York: Free Press.

Collier, J. F., and M. Z. Rosaldo
1981   Politics and Gender in Simple Societies. *In* Sexual Meanings: The Cultural Construction of Gender and Sexuality. S. B. Ortner and H. Whitehead, eds., pp. 273–329. Cambridge: Cambridge University Press.

Condon, R. G.
1987   Inuit Youth: Growth and Change in the Canadian Arctic. New Brunswick, N.J.: Rutgers University Press.
1995   The Rise of the Leisure Class: Adolescence and Recreational Acculturation in the Canadian Arctic. Ethos 23:47–68.

Cowlishaw, G.
1979   Women's Realm: A Study of Socialization, Sexuality and Reproduction Among Australian Aborigines. Ph.D. dissertation. Department of Anthropology, University of Sydney.

Cramer, J.
1989   Patterns of Poverty and Financial Assistance Among Premature Mothers. Paper presented at the Population Association of America Meetings, Chicago. Mar. 31–Apr. 1.

Crittenden, R., and J. Baines
1985   Assessment of the Nutritional Status of Children on the Nembi Plateau in 1978 and 1980. Ecology and Food Nutrition 17:131–47.

Crockenberg, S., and B. Soby
1989   Self-Esteem and Teenage Pregnancy. *In* The Social Importance of Self-Esteem.

A. Mecca, N. Smelser, and J. Vasconcellos, eds., pp. 125–64. Berkeley: University of California Press.

Davis, D.
1995   Modernizing the Sexes: Changing Gender Relations in a Moroccan Town. Ethos 23:69–78.

Davis, S., and D. Davis
1989   Adolescence in a Moroccan Town: Making Social Sense. New Brunswick, N.J.: Rutgers University Press.

Davis, A., and J. Dollard
1940   Children of Bondage: The Personality Development of Negro Youth in the Urban South. Washington, D.C.: American Council on Education.

D'Emilio, J., and E. B. Freedman
1988   Intimate Matters: A History of Sexuality in America. New York: Harper and Row.

Dennett, G., and J. Connell
1988   Acculturation and Health in the Highlands of Papua New Guinea: Dissent on Diversity, Diets, and Development. Current Anthropology 29:273–99.

Dettwyler, K. A., and C. Fishman
1992   Infant Feeding Practices and Growth. Annual Review of Anthropology 21:171–204.

Douglas, B.
1979   Rank, Power, Authority: A Reassessment of Traditional Leadership in South Pacific Societies. Journal of Pacific History 14:2–27.

Ducharme, J. R., M. G. Forest, E. de Peretti, M. Sempé, R. Collu, and J. Bertrand
1976   Plasma Adrenal and Gonadal Sex Steroids in Human Pubertal Development. Journal of Clinical Endocrinology and Metabolism 42:468–76.

Elder, G. H., Jr.
1975   Age Differentiation and the Life Course. In Annual Review of Sociology, vol. 1, A. Inkeles, ed., pp. 165–90. Palo Alto, Calif.: Annual Reviews.
1980   Adolescence in Historical Perspective. In Handbook of Adolescent Psychology. J. Adelson, ed., pp. 1–46. New York: Wiley & Son.

Ellison, P.
1981   Morbidity, Mortality, and Menarche. Human Biology 53:635–43.

Elwin, V.
1947   The Muria and Their Ghotul. Bombay: Oxford University Press.
1968   The Kingdom of the Young. Bombay: Oxford University Press.

Erikson, E.
1968   Identity: Youth and Crisis. New York: W. W. Norton.

Errington, F., and D. Gewertz
1996   The Individuation of Tradition in a Papua New Guinean Modernity. American Anthropologist 998:114–26.

Eveleth, P. B., and J. M. Tanner
1976   Worldwide Variation in Human Growth. Cambridge: Cambridge University Press.

Eyre, S. L.
1988   Revival Christianity Among the Urat of Papua New Guinea—Some Possible

Motivational and Perceptual Antecedents. Ph.D. dissertation. University of California, San Diego.

Feil, D.
1987   The Evolution of Highland Papua New Guinea Societies. Cambridge: Cambridge University Press.

Field, T., S. Widmayer, S. Stoller, and M. de Cubas
1986   School-aged Parenthood in Different Ethnic Groups and Family Constellations: Effects on Infant Development. *In* School-Aged Pregnancy and Parenthood. J. Lancaster and B. Hamburg, eds., pp. 263–72. New York: Aldine de Gruyter.

Fine, M.
1988   Sexuality, Schooling, and Adolescent Females: The Missing Discourse of Desire. Harvard Education Review 58:29–53.

Forbes, G. B.
1986   Body Composition in Adolescence. *In* Human Growth: A Comprehensive Treatise, vol. 2. F. Falkner and J. M. Tanner, eds., pp. 119–45. New York: Plenum Press.

Forbes, L.
1875   Two Years in Fiji. London: Longmans, Green, and Co.

Fortune, R.
1932   Sorcerers of Dobu: The Social Anthropology of the Dobu Islanders of the Western Pacific. New York: E. P. Dutton.

Freeman, D.
1983   Margaret Mead and Samoa: The Making and Unmaking of an Anthropological Myth. Cambridge Mass.: Harvard University Press.

Freud, A.
1958   Adolescence. Psychoanalytic Study 13: 255–78.
1966   The Ego and the Mechanisms of Defense. New York: International University Press.

Furstenberg, F.
1976   Unplanned Parenthood: The Social Consequences of Teenage Childbearing. New York: Macmillan.

Galler, J. R., F. C. Ramsey, P. Salt, and E. Archer
1987   Long-term Effects of Early Kwashiorkor Compared with Marasmus. I. Physical Growth and Sexual Maturation. Journal of Pediatric Gastroenterology and Nutrition 6:841–46.

Galler, J. R., F. Ramsey, and G. Solimano
1985   A Follow-up Study of the Effects of Early Malnutrition on Subsequent Development. Vol. I. Physical Growth and Sexual Maturation During Adolescence. Pediatric Research 19:518–23.

Geertz, C.
1963   The Integrative Revolution: Primordial Sentiments and Civil Politics in the New States. *In* Old Societies and New States. C. Geertz, ed., pp. 105–57. New York: Macmillan.
1973   Thick Description: Toward an Interpretive Theory of Culture. *In* The Interpretation of Cultures: Selected Essays by C. Geertz, pp. 3–30. New York: Basic Books.

Gellner, E.
1992   Postmodernism, Reason, and Religion. New York: Routledge.

Geronimus, A.
1987   On Teenage Childbearing and Neonatal Mortality in the United States.
            Population and Development Review 13:245–79.
1996   What Teen Mothers Know. Human Nature 7(4):323–52.

Gewertz, D.
1982   The Father Who Bore Me: The Role of *Tsambunwuro* During Chambri
            Initiation Ceremonies. *In* Rituals of Manhood: Male Initiation in Papua New
            Guinea. G. H. Herdt, ed., pp. 286–330. Berkeley: University of California Press.
1983   Sepik River Societies. New Haven: Yale University Press.

Gladwin, T., and S. Sarason
1953   Truk: Man in Paradise. Viking Fund Publications in Anthropology, no. 20.
            New York: Wenner-Gren Foundation for Anthropological Research.

Godelier, M.
1986   The Making of Great Men: Male Domination and Power Among the New
            Guinea Baruya. Cambridge: Cambridge University Press.

Godelier, M., and M. Strathern, eds.
1991   Big Men and Great Men: Personifications of Power in Melanesia. Cambridge:
            Cambridge University Press.

Goffman, E.
1961   Asylums. New York: Doubleday.

Goldman, L.
1993   The Culture of Coincidence. Oxford: Oxford University Press.

Good, T. L., and R. S. Weinstein
1986   Schools Make a Difference: Evidence, Criticisms, and New Directions.
            American Psychologist 41:1090–97.

Goodale, J.
1971   Tiwi Wives. Seattle: University of Washington Press.

Grace, G.
1959   The Position of the Polynesian Languages Within the Austronesian (Malayo-
            Polynesian) Language Family. Bloomington: Memoir 16 of the International
            Journal of American Linguistics.

Greenfield, P. M., and J. S. Brown
1966   Culture and Cognitive Growth. International Journal of Psychology 1:89–107.

Grumbach, M. M., P .C. Sizonenko, and M. L. Aubert, eds.
1990   Control of the Onset of Puberty. Baltimore: Williams and Wilkins.

Hamburg, B.
1986   Subsets of Adolescent Mothers: Developmental, Biomedical, and Psychosocial
            Issues. *In* School-Age Pregnancy and Parenthood. J. Lancaster and B.
            Hamburg, eds., pp. 115–45. New York: Aldine de Gruyter.

Hamilton, A.
1982   Child Health and Child Care in a Desert Community, 1970–1971. *In* Body,
            Land, and Spirit: Health and Healing in Aboriginal Society. J. Reid, ed., pp.
            49–71. St. Lucia: University of Queensland Press.

Harkness, S., and C. M. Super, eds.
1996   Parents' Cultural Belief Systems: Their Origins, Expression, and Consequences.
            New York: Guildford Press.

Harris, B. M.
1987   The Rise of Rascalism: Action and Reaction in the Evolution of Rascal Gangs. Papua New Guinea: Institute of Applied Social and Economic Research.

Harris, O., and K. Young
1981   Engendered Structures: Some Problems in the Analysis of Reproduction. *In* The Anthropology of Pre-Capitalist Societies. J. Kahn and J. Llohera, eds., pp. 109–47. London: MacMillan Press.

Hart, C. W. M., A. R. Pilling, and J. C. Goodale
1988   The Tiwi of North Australia. New York: Holt, Rinehart, and Winston.

Hartup, W. W.
1979   The Social Worlds of Childhood. American Psychologist 34:944–50.

Hayes, C., ed.
1987   Risking the Future, vol. 1. Washington, D. C.: National Academy Press.

Heath, S. B.
1989   Oral and Literate Traditions Among Black Americans Living in Poverty. American Psychologist 44:367–73.

Hebdige, D.
1979   Subculture: The Meaning of Style. London: Methuen.

Herdt, G.
1981   Guardians of the Flutes: Idioms of Masculinity. New York: McGraw-Hill.
1982   Fetish and Fantasy in Sambia Initiation. *In* Rituals of Manhood: Male Initiation in Papua New Guinea. G. Herdt, ed., pp. 44–98. Berkeley: University of California Press.
1984   Ritualized Homosexual Behavior in the Male Cults of Melanesia, 1862–1983: An Introduction. *In* Ritualized Homosexuality in Melanesia. G. Herdt, ed., pp. 1–81. Berkeley: University of California Press.
1987   The Sambia: Ritual and Gender in New Guinea. New York: Holt, Rinehart and Winston.
1989a   Introduction: Gay and Lesbian Youth, Emergent Identities, and Cultural Scenes at Home and Abroad. Journal of Homosexuality 17:1–42
1989b   Spirit Familiars in the Religious Imagination of Sambia Shamans. *In* The Religious Imagination in New Guinea. G. Herdt and M. Stephen, eds., pp. 91–121. New Brunswick, N.J.: Rutgers University Press.
1989c   Father Presence and Ritual Homosexuality: Paternal Deprivation and Masculine Development in Melanesia Reconsidered. Ethos 17:326–70.
1990a   Sambia Nosebleeding Rites and Male Proximity to Women. *In* Cultural Psychology: Essays on Comparative Human Development. J. Stigler, R. A. Schweder, and G. Herdt, eds., pp. 366–400. Cambridge: Cambridge University Press.
1990b   Developmental Discontinuities and Sexual Orientation Across Cultures. *In* Homosexuality/Heterosexuality: Concepts of Sexual Orientation. D. P. McWhirter, S. A. Sanders, and J. M. Reinisch, eds., pp. 208–36. New York: Oxford University Press.

Herdt, G., ed.
1982   Rituals of Manhood: Male Initiation in Papua New Guinea. Berkeley: University of California Press.
1984   Ritualized Homosexuality in Melanesia. Berkeley: University of California Press.

Herdt, G., and F. J. P. Poole
1982   "Sexual Antagonism": The Intellectual History of a Concept in New Guinea Anthropology. Social Analysis 12:3–28.

Herdt, G., and M. Stephen
1989   Introduction. *In* The Religious Imagination in New Guinea. G. Herdt and M. Stephen, eds., pp. 1–11. Rutgers University Press.

Herdt, G., and R. J. Stoller
1990   Intimate Communications: Erotics and the Study of Culture. New York: Columbia University Press.

Hereniko, V. T.
1977   Dance as a Reflection of Rotuman Culture. *In* Rotuma: Hanua Pumue (Precious Land). A. Fatiaki et al., eds., pp. 120–42. Suva: Institute for Pacific Studies, University of the South Pacific.

Hiatt, L.
1985   Maidens, Males, and Marx: Some Contrasts in the Work of Frederick Rose and Claude Meillassoux. Oceania 56:34–46.

Hill, J. P., et al.
1985   Menarcheal Status and Parent-Child Relations in Families of Seventh-Grade Girls. Journal of Youth and Adolescence 14:301–16.

Hogbin, I.
1970   The Island of Menstruating Men. Scranton, Pa.: Chandler.

Hollingshead, A. B.
1949   Elmtown's Youth: The Impact of Social Classes on Adolescents. New York: John Wiley and Sons.

Hollos, M., and P. E. Leis
1986   Descent and Permissive Adolescent Sexuality in Two Ijo Communities. Ethos 14: 395–408.
1989   Becoming Nigerian in Ijo Society. New Brunswick, N.J.: Rutgers University Press.

Howard, A.
1970   Learning to be Rotuman. Enculturation in the South Pacific. New York: Columbia Teachers College Press.
1985   History, Myth and Polynesian Chieftainship: The Case of Rotuman Kings. *In* Transformations of Polynesian Culture. A. Hooper and J. Huntsman, eds., pp. 39–77. Auckland: Polynesian Society.
1986   Cannibal Chiefs and the Charter for Rebellion in Rotuman Myth. Pacific Studies 10:1–27.
1989   The Resurgence of Rivalry: Politics in Post-Colonial Rotuma. Dialectical Anthropology 14:145–58.
1991   Reflections on Change in Rotuma, 1959–1988. *In* Rotuma: Hanua Pumue (Precious Land). A. Fatiaki et al., eds., pp. 227–64. Suva: Institute for Pacific Studies, University of the South Pacific.
1995   Rotuman Seafaring in Historical Perspective. *In* Seafaring in the Contemporary Pacific Islands. R. Feinberg, ed., pp. 114–43. DeKalb: Northern Illinois University Press.

Howard, A., and I. Howard
1964   Pre-marital Sex and Social Control Among the Rotumans. American Anthropologist 66:266–83.

Hrdy, S. B.
1990   Sex Bias in Nature and in History: A Late 1980s Reexamination of the "Biological Origins" Argument. Yearbook of Physical Anthropology 33:25–37.

Hutchins, E.
1987   Myth and Experience in the Trobriand Islands. *In* Cultural Models in Language and Thought. D. Holland and N. Quinn, eds., pp. 269–89. Cambridge: Cambridge University Press.

Ingemann, F.
1997   Ipili Dictionary. Working draft. Typescript in author's files.

Inkeles, A.
1966   Social Structure and the Socialization of Competence. Harvard Education Review 36:265–83.

Jenkins, C.
1994   National Study of Sexual and Reproductive Knowledge and Behavior in Papua New Guinea. Papua New Guinea Institute of Medical Research Monograph, no. 10. Goroka, Papua New Guinea.

Johnson, P. L.
1981   When Dying Is Better Than Living: Female Suicide Among the Gainj of Papua New Guinea. Ethnology 20:325–34.

Jolly, M., and M. Macintyre
1989   Family and Gender in the Pacific: Domestic Contradictions and the Colonial Impact. Cambridge: Cambridge University Press.

Josephides, L.
1985   The Production of Inequality: Gender and Exchange Among the Kewa. New York: Tavistock.

Jourdan, C.
1995   Masta Liu. *In* Youth Cultures: A Cross-Cultural Perspective. V. Amit-Talai and H. Wulff, eds., pp. 202–22. London: Routledge.

Keesing, R. M.
1982   Introduction. *In* Rituals of Manhood: Male Initiation in Papua New Guinea. G. Herdt, ed., pp. 2–43. Berkeley: University of California Press.
1985   Kwaio Women Speak: The Micropolitics of Autobiography in a Solomon Island Society. American Anthropologist 87:27–39.

Keesing, R. M., and R. Tonkinson, eds.
1982   Reinventing Traditional Culture: The Politics of Kastom in Island Melanesia. Mankind 13(4).

Kelly, R. C.
1976   Witchcraft and Sexual Relations: An Exploration in the Social and Semantic Implications of the Structure of Belief. *In* Man and Woman in the New Guinea Highlands. P. Brown and G. Buchbinder, eds., pp. 36–53. Special publication no. 8. Washington, D.C.: American Anthropological Association.
1977   Etoro Social Structure: A Study in Structural Contradiction. Ann Arbor: University of Michigan Press.
1993   Constructing Inequality: The Fabrication of a Hierarchy of Virtue Among the Etoro. Ann Arbor: University of Michigan Press.

Khan, A. W., K. G. Schroeder, R. Martorell, and J. A. Rivera
1995   Age at Menarche and Nutritional Supplementation. Nutrition 125:1090S–96S.

Kiki, A. M.
1968   Ten Thousand Years in a Lifetime. Melbourne: Melbourne University Press.

Kirkpatrick, J.
1983   The Marquesan Notion of the Person. Studies in Cultural Anthropology, no.
            3. Ames, Iowa: Iowa State University Press.
1987   Taure'are'a: A Liminal Category and Passage to Marquesan Adulthood. Ethos
            15:382–405.

Knauft, B. M.
1985   Good Company and Violence: Sorcery and Social Action in a Lowland New
            Guinea Society. Berkeley: University of California Press.
1986   Text and Social Practice: Narrative "Longing" and Bisexuality Among the
            Gebusi of New Guinea. Ethos 14:252–81.
1987   Homosexuality in Melanesia. The Journal of Psychoanalytic Anthropology
            10:155–91.
1989   Imagery, Pronouncement, and the Aesthetics of Reception in Gebusi Spirit
            Mediumship. In The Religious Imagination in New Guinea. G. H. Herdt and
            M. Stephen, eds., pp. 67–98. New Brunswick, N.J.: Rutgers University Press.
1991   Gebusi: A Cultural Summary. Encyclopedia of World Cultures: Oceania
            Volume. New Haven: Human Relations Area Files Press.
1993   South Coast New Guinea Cultures: History, Comparison, Dialectic. Cam-
            bridge: Cambridge University Press.

Kulick, D.
1993   Heroes from Hell: Representations of "Rascals" in a Papua New Guinea
            Village. Anthropology Today 9:9–14.

Kulin, H., M. A. Frontera, L. M. Demers, M. J. Bartholomew, and T. A. Lloyd
1989   The Onset of Sperm Production in Pubertal Boys. American Journal of
            Diseases of Children 143:190–93.

Kyakas, A., and P. Wiessner
1992   From Inside the Women's House: Enga Women's Lives and Traditions.
            Buranda, Queensland: Robert Brown.

Lancaster, J., and B. Hamburg, eds.
1986   School-Age Pregnancy and Parenthood. New York: Aldine de Gruyter.

Landauer, T. K., and J. W. M. Whiting
1981   Correlates and Consequences of Stress in Infancy. In Handbook of Cross-
            Cultural Human Development. R. H. Munroe, R. L. Munroe, and B. B.
            Whiting, eds., pp. 355–75. New York: Garland Press.

Langness, L. L.
1967   Sexual Antagonism in the New Guinea Highlands: A Benabena Example.
            Oceania 37:161–77.

Laron, Z., J. Arad, R. Gurewitz, M. Grunebaum, and Z. Dickerman
1980   Age at First Conscious Ejaculation: A Milestone in Male Puberty. Helvetica
            Paediatrica Acta 35:13–20.

Latukefu, S.
1980   The Definition of Authentic Oceanic Cultures with Particular Reference to
            Tongan Culture. Pacific Studies 4: 60–81.

Lawrence, P.
1964   Road Belong Cargo. Manchester: Manchester University Press.

Leavitt, S. C.
1991   Sexual Ideology and Experience in a Papua New Guinea Society. Social
            Science and Medicine 33(8):897–907.
1995a   Suppressed Meanings in Narratives About Suffering: A Case from Papua New

Guinea. Anthropology and Humanism 20(2):1–20.

1995b　　Political Domination and the Absent Oppressor: Images of Europeans in Bumbita Arapesh Narratives. Ethnology 34:177–89.

1995c　　Seeking Gifts from the Dead: Long-Term Mourning in a Bumbita Arapesh Cargo Narrative. Ethos 23:453–73.

1997　　Cargo Beliefs and Religious Experience. *In* Conformity and Conflict, 9th ed. J. P. Spradley and D. W. McCordy, eds., pp. 337–46. New York: Harper-Collins.

Lebra, T.

1995　　Skipped and Postponed Adolescence of Aristocratic Women in Japan: Resurrecting the Culture/Nature Issue. Ethos 23:79–102.

Leder, D.

1990　　The Absent Body. Chicago: Chicago University Press.

Lederman, R.

1986　　What Gifts Engender: Social Relations and Politics in Mendi, Highland Papua New Guinea. Cambridge: Cambridge University Press.

1989　　Contested Order: Gender and Society in the Southern New Guinea Highlands. American Ethnologist 16:230–47.

Lee, P. A.

1980　　Normal Ages of Pubertal Events Among American Males and Females. Journal of Adolescent Health Care 1:26–29.

Lee, P. A., and C. J. Migeon

1975　　Puberty in Boys: Correlation of Plasma Levels of Gonadotropins (LH, FSH), Androgens (Testosterone, Androstenedione, Dehydroepiandrosterone and Its Sulfate), Estrogens (Estrone and Estradiol) and Progestins (Progesterone and 17-hydroxyprogesterone). Journal of Clinical Endocrinology and Metabolism 41:556–62.

Lee, P. A., T. Xenakis, J. Winer, and S. Matsenbaugh

1976　　Puberty in Girls: Correlation of Serum Levels of Gonadotropins, Prolactin, Androgens, Estrogens, and Progestins with Physical Changes. Journal of Clinical Endocrinology and Metabolism 43:775–84.

Leenhardt, M.

1979　　Do Kamo. B. M. Gulati, trans. Chicago: University of Chicago Press.

Lepowsky, M.

1983　　Sudest Island and the Louisiade Archipelago in Massim Exchange. *In* The Kula: New Perspectives on Massim Exchange. J. Leach and E. Leach, eds., pp. 467–501. Cambridge: Cambridge University Press.

1989a　　Death and Exchange: Mortuary Ritual on Vanatinai (Sudest Island). *In* Death Rituals and Life in the Societies of the Kula Ring. F. H. Damon and R. Wagner, eds., pp. 199–229. De Kalb: Northern Illinois University Press.

1989b　　Soldiers and Spirits: The Impact of World War II on a Coral Sea Island. *In* The Pacific Theater: Island Representations of World War II. G. White and L. Lindstrom, eds., pp. 205–30. Pacific Monograph Series, no. 8. Honolulu: University of Hawaii Press.

1990a　　Gender in an Egalitarian Society: Lessons from a Coral Sea Island. *In* Beyond the Second Sex: New Perspectives on the Anthropology of Gender. P. Sanday and R. Goodenough, eds., pp. 171–223. Philadelphia: University of Pennsylvania Press.

1990b　　Big Men, Big Women, and Cultural Autonomy. Ethnology, 29:35–50.

1993　　Fruit of the Motherland: Gender in an Egalitarian Society. New York: Columbia University Press.

Lerner, R. M.
1985   Adolescent Maturational Changes and Psychosocial Development: A Dynamic Interactional Perspective. Journal of Youth and Adolescence 14:355–72.
1987   A Life-Span Perspective for Early Adolescence. *In* Biological-Psychosocial Interactions in Early Adolescence. R. M. Lerner and T. T. Foch, eds. Hillsdale, N.J.: Lawrence Erlbaum Associates.
1989   Organismic and Contextual Bases of Development in Adolescence: A Developmental Contextual View. *In* Biology of Adolescent Behavior and Development. G. R. Adams, R. Montemayor, and T. P. Gullotta, eds., pp. 11–37. Newbury Park, Calif.: Sage Publications.

Lerner, R. M., and N. A. Busch-Rossnagel, eds.
1981   Individuals as Producers of Their Development: A Life Span Perspective. New York: Academic Press.

Lerner, R. M., and T. T. Foch, eds.
1987   Biological-Psychosocial Interactions in Early Adolescence. Hillsdale, N.J.: Lawrence Erlbaum Associates.

LeVine, R. A.
1982   Culture, Behavior and Personality: An Introduction to the Comparative Study of Psychosocial Adaptation, 2nd ed. New York: Aldine Publishing Company.
1990   Enculturation: A Biosocial Perspective on the Development of Self. *In* The Development of the Self. D. Cicchetti, ed. Chicago: University of Chicago Press.

LeVine, R., and M. White.
1987   Parenthood in Social Transformation. *In* Parenting Across the Life Span. J. Lancaster, J. Altmann, A. Rossi, and L. Sherrod, eds., pp. 271–93. New York: Aldine de Gruyter.

Levy, R. I.
1973   Tahitians: Mind and Experience in the Society Islands. Chicago: University of Chicago Press.

Liestøl, K.
1982   Social Conditions and Menarcheal Age. Annals of Human Biology 9:227–33.

Liechty, M.
1995   Media, Markets, and Modernization: Youth Identities and the Experience of Modernity in Kathmandu, Nepal. *In* Youth Cultures: A Cross-Cultural Perspective. V. Amit-Talai and H. Wulff, eds., pp. 166–201. London: Routledge.

Lincoln, B.
1991   Afterword. *In* Emerging from the Chrysalis, 2nd ed. B. Lincoln, ed., pp. 110–19. Oxford: Oxford University Press.

Lindenbaum, S.
1984   Sociosexual Forms in Transition in Melanesia. *In* Ritualized Homosexuality in Melanesia. G. Herdt, ed., pp. 337–61. Berkeley: University of California Press.
1987   The Mystification of Female Labors. *In* Gender and Kinship: Essays Toward a Unified Analysis. J. F. Collier and S. Yanagisako, eds., pp. 221–43. Stanford: Stanford University Press.

Linnekin, J.
1990   Sacred Queens and Women of Consequence: Rank, Gender, and Colonialism in the Hawaiian Islands. Ann Arbor: University of Michigan Press.

Linney, J. A., and E. Seidman
1989   The Future of Schooling. American Psychologist 44(2):336–40.

Linton, R.
1940   A Neglected Aspect of Social Organization. American Journal of Sociology
          45:870–86.
1942   Age and Sex Categories. American Sociological Review 7(5):589–603.

Lowie, R.
1920   Primitive Society. New York: Harper and Row.

Lowrey, G. H.
1978   Growth and Development of Children, 7th ed. Chicago: Year Book Medical.

Luker, K.
1991   Dubious Conceptions: The Controversy Over Teen Pregnancy. The American
          Prospect 5:73–83.

Lutkehaus, N.
1995   Feminist Anthropology and Female Initiation in Melanesia. In Gender
          Rituals: Female Initiation in Melanesia. N. Lutkehaus and P. Roscoe, eds., pp.
          3–29. New York: Routledge.

Lutkehaus, N., and P. Roscoe, eds.
1995   Gender Rituals: Female Initiation in Melanesia. New York: Routledge.

Lutz, C.
1985   Ethnopsychology Compared to What? Explaining Behavior and Conscious-
          ness Among the Ifaluk. In Person, Self, and Experience. G. White and J.
          Kirkpatrick, eds., pp. 35–79. Berkeley: University of California Press.

Lynd, R. S., and H. M. Lynd
1929   Middletown. New York: Harcourt Brace and Co.

Maccoby, E. E.
1980   Social Development. New York: Harcourt Brace Jovanovitch.

Maddock, K.
1974   The Australian Aborigines: A Portrait of Their Society. Ringwood, Victoria,
          Australia: Penguin.

Malcolm, L. A.
1970   Growth and Development in New Guinea: A Study of the Bundi People of the
          Madang District. Institute of Human Biology Monograph Series, no. 1.
          Madang, Papua New Guinea: Institute of Human Biology.
1976   Growth and Development Patterns and Human Differentiation in Papua New
          Guinean Communities. In Youth in a Changing World: Cross-Cultural
          Perspectives on Adolescence. E. Fuchs, ed., pp. 65–77. The Hague: Mouton
          Publishers.

Malina, R. M.
1986   Growth of Muscle Tissue and Muscle Mass. In Human Growth: A Compre-
          hensive Treatise, vol. 2. F. Falkner and J. M. Tanner, eds., pp. 77–99. New York:
          Plenum Press.

Malinowski, B.
1922   Argonauts of the Western Pacific. New York: E. P. Dutton.
1927a   Sex and Repression in Savage Society. New York: Harcourt, Brace.
1927b   The Father in Primitive Psychology. New York: W. W. Norton and Company,
          Inc.
1929   The Sexual Life of Savages in Northwestern Melanesia. New York: Liveright.

1935   Coral Gardens and Their Magic. New York: American Book Co.

Malo, T.
1973   Rotuman Marriage. Suva, Fiji: The South Pacific Social Sciences Association.

Marshall, M.
1979   Weekend Warriors: Alcohol in a Micronesian Culture. Palo Alto, Calif.:
            Mayfield Publishing Co.

Marshall, W. A., and J. M. Tanner
1969   Variations in Pattern of Pubertal Changes in Girls. Archives of Disease in
            Childhood 44:291–303.
1970   Variations in the Patterns of Pubertal Changes in Boys. Archives of Disease in
            Childhood 45:13–23.
1986   Puberty. In Human Growth: A Comprehensive Treatise, vol. 2. F. Falkner and
            J. M. Tanner, eds., pp. 171–209. New York: Plenum Press.

Mead, M.
1928   Coming of Age in Samoa. New York: William Morrow.
1930   Growing Up in New Guinea. New York: William Morrow. Reprinted 1975.
1935   Sex and Temperament in Three Primitive Societies. New York: William
            Morrow.
1970 [1938]
            The Mountain Arapesh, Volume II: Arts and Supernaturalism. Garden City,
            N.J.: The Natural History Press.
1949   Male and Female: A Study of the Sexes in a Changing World. New York:
            William Morrow.
1956   New Lives for Old: Cultural Transformation—Manus, 1928–1953. New York:
            Dell.
1961   Cultural Determinants of Sexual Behavior. In Sex and Internal Secretions.
            W. C. Young, ed., pp. 1433–79. Baltimore: Williams and Wilkins.
1963   Socialization and Enculturation. Current Anthropology 4:184–88.

Mead, M., and F. C. Macgregor
1951   Growth and Culture: A Photographic Study of Balinese Childhood. New
            York: G. P. Putnam's Sons.

Meggitt, M. J.
1964   Male-Female Relationships in the Highlands of Australian New Guinea.
            American Anthropologist 66(4): 204–24.

Merton, R. K.
1938   Social Structure and Anomie. American Sociological Review 3:672–82.

Metcoff, J.
1986   Association of Fetal Growth and Maternal Nutrition. In Human Growth: A
            Comprehensive Treatise, vol. 2. F. Falkner and J. M. Tanner, eds., pp. 333–88.
            New York: Plenum Press.

Meyer-Bahlberg, H. F. L.
1985   Idiopathic Precocious Puberty in Girls: Psychosexual Development. Journal
            of Youth and Adolescence 14: 339–53.

Myers, F.
1986   Pintupi Country, Pintupi Self: Sentiment, Place, and Politics Among Western
            Desert Aborigines. Washington, D.C.: Smithsonian Institution Press.

Narokobi, B.
1980   The Melanesian Way. Henry Olela, ed., Boroko, Papua New Guinea: Institute
            of Papua New Guinea Studies.

Neugarten, B. L., and N. Datan
1973   Sociological Perspectives on the Life Cycle. *In* Life-Span Developmental Psychology: Personality and Socialization. P. B. Baltes and K. W. Schaie, eds., pp. 53–69. New York: Academic Press.

Niswander, K., and M. Gordon
1972   The Collaborative Perinatal Study of the National Institute of Neurological Diseases and Stroke: Women and Their Pregnancies. Philadelphia: Sanders.

Nottelmann, E .D., E. J. Susman, L. D. Dorn, G. Inoff-Germain, D. L. Loriaux, G. B. Cutler, and G. P. Chrousos
1987   Developmental Process in Early Adolescence. Journal of Adolescent Health Care 8:246–60.

Offer, D., E. Ostrov, K. I. Howard, and R. Atkinson
1988   The Teenage World: Adolescents' Self-Image in Ten Countries. New York: Plenum Medical Book Company.

Ortner, S. B.
1990   Gender Hegemonies. Cultural Critique 14:35–80.

Ortner, S. B., and H. Whitehead
1981   Introduction. *In* Sexual Meanings: The Cultural Construction of Gender and Sexuality. S. Ortner and H. Whitehead, eds., pp. 1–27. Cambridge: Cambridge University Press.

Parsons, T.
1942   Age and Sex in the Social Structure of the United States. American Sociological Review 7:604–16.

Pawley, A.
1979   New Evidence on the Position of Rotuman. Department of Anthropology, University of Auckland. NTIS, Working Paper No. 56.

Petersen A. C.
1988   Adolescent Development. Annual Review of Psychology 39: 583–607.

Petersen A. C., and L. Crockett
1985   Pubertal Timing and Grade Effects on Adjustment. Journal of Youth and Adolescence 14:191–206.

Phoenix, A.
1988   Narrow Definitions of Culture: The Case of Early Motherhood. *In* Enterprising Women: Ethnicity, Economy, and Gender Relations. S. Westwood and P. Bhachu, eds., pp. 153–76. New York: Routledge.
1993   The Social Construction of Teenage Motherhood: A Black and White Issue? *In* The Politics of Pregnancy: Adolescent Sexuality and Public Policy. A. Lawson and D. Rhode, eds., pp. 74–97. New Haven: Yale University Press.

Polakow, V.
1993   Lives on the Edge: Single Mothers and Their Children in the Other America. Chicago: University of Chicago Press.

Polier, N.
n.d.   Stella's Stori: Colonialism, Christianity, and Conflict in the Life of a Papua New Guinea Migrant Woman. Unpublished manuscript, author's files.

Poole, F. J. P.
1981   Transforming "Natural" Woman: Female Ritual Leaders and Gender Ideology Among Bimin-Kuskusmin. *In* Sexual Meanings. S. Ortner and H. Whitehead, eds., pp. 116–65. Cambridge: Cambridge University Press.

1982 The Ritual Forging of Identity: Aspects of Person and Self in Bimin-Kuskusmin Folk Psychology. *In* Rituals of Manhood. G. Herdt, ed., pp. 99–154. Berkeley: University of California Press.

1985 Among the Boughs of the Hanging Tree: Male Suicide Among the Bimin-Kuskusmin of Papua New Guinea. *In* Culture, Youth and Suicide in the Pacific Guinea: Papers from an East-West Center Conference. F. X. Hezel, D. H. Rubinstein, and G. M. White, eds., pp. 152–79. Honolulu: Institute of Culture and Communication, East-West Center.

1990 The Cultural Shape, Psychological Force, and Social Form of "Adolescence": Betwixt and Between *Rites de Passage:* The Interplay of Ritual and Non-Ritual Dimensions of Bimin-Kuskusmin "Adolescence." Paper presented at the Association for Social Anthropology in Oceania annual meeting, Hawaii, March 20–25.

Powdermaker, H.
1971 Life in Lesu: The Study of a Melanesian Society in New Ireland. New York: W. W. Norton. Originally published 1933.

Read, K.
1952 Nama Cult of the Central Highlands, New Guinea. Oceania. 23:1–25.

1955 Morality and the Concept of the Person Among the Gahuku-Gama. Oceania 25:233–82.

1959 Leadership and Consensus in a New Guinea Society. American Anthropologist 61:425–36.

Rensel, J.
1991 Housing and Social Relationships on Rotuma. *In* Rotuma: Hanua Pumue (Precious Land). A. Fatiaki et al., eds., pp. 185–203. Suva: Institute for Pacific Studies, University of the South Pacific.

Rogoff, B., and G. Morelli
1989 Perspectives on Children's Development from Cultural Psychology. American Psychologist 44: 343–48.

Roscoe, P.
1995 "Initiation" in Cross-Cultural Perspective. *In* Gender Rituals: Female Initiation in Melanesia. N. Lutkehaus and P. Roscoe, eds., pp. 219–38. New York: Routledge.

Rose, F.
1960 Classification of Kin, Age Structure, and Marriage Amongst the Groote Eylandt Aborigines. Berlin: Akademie-Verlag.

Rosi, P., and L. Zimmer-Tamakoshi
1993 Love and Marriage Among the Educated Elite in Port Moresby. *In* The Business of Marriage: Transformations in Oceanic Matrimony. R. A. Marksbury, ed., pp. 175–204. Association for Social Anthropology in Oceania Monograph. Pittsburgh: University of Pittsburgh Press.

Rosow, I.
1978 What Is a Cohort and Why? Human Development 21:65–75

Ross, J.
1965 The Puberty Ceremony of the Chimbu girl in the Eastern Highlands of New Guinea. Anthropos 60:423–32.

Rossi, A. S.
1980 Life-Span Theories and Women's Lives. Signs 6:4–32.

1987   Parenthood in Transition: From Lineage to Child to Self-Orientation. *In* Parenting Across the Life Span. J. Lancaster, J. Altmann, A. Rossi, and L. Sherrod, eds., pp. 31–81. New York: Aldine de Gruyter.

Rubinstein, D. H.
1983   Epidemic Suicide Among Micronesian Adolescents. Social Science and Medicine 17:657–65.
1992   Suicide in Micronesia and Samoa: A Critique of Explanations. Pacific Studies 15:51–75.
1995   Love and Suffering: Adolescent Socialization and Suicide in Micronesia. The Contemporary Pacific 7(1):21–53.

Ruel, M. T., J. Rivera, J .P. Habicht, and R. Martorell
1995   Differential Response to Early Nutrition Supplementation: Long-Term Effects on Height at Adolescence. International Journal of Epidemiology 24:404–12.

Sahlins, M.
1963   Poor Man, Rich Man, Big Man, Chief: Political Types in Melanesia and Polynesia. Comparative Studies in Society and History 5:285–303.
1976   Culture and Practical Reason. Chicago: University of Chicago Press.

Samuel, G.
1990   Mind, Body and Culture. Cambridge: Cambridge University Press.

Scarr, S., and K. McCartney
1983   How People Make Their Own Environments: A Theory of Genotype and Environment Effects. Child Development 54:424–35.

Schepher-Hughes, N., and H. Stein.
1987   Child Abuse and the Unconscious in American Popular Culture. *In* Child Survival. N. Schepher-Hughes, ed., pp. 339–58. Boston: Reidel.

Schieffelin, E. L.
1976   The Sorrow of the Lonely and the Burning of the Dancers. New York: St. Martin's.
1982   The *Bau a* Ceremonial Hunting Lodge: An Alternative to Initiation. *In* Rituals of Manhood: Male Initiation in Papua New Guinea. G. Herdt, ed., pp. 155–200. Berkeley: University of California Press.
1985   Anger, Grief and Shame: Towards a Kaluli Ethno-Psychology. *In* Person, Self and Experience: Exploring Pacific Ethnopsychologies. G. White and J. Kirkpatrick, eds., pp. 168–82. Los Angeles: University of California Press.

Schieffelin, E. L., and R. Crittendon
1991   Like People You See in a Dream: First Contact in Six Papuan Societies. Stanford: Stanford University Press.

Schlegel, A.
1995a   Introduction. Ethos 23:3–14. Special issue on adolescence.
1995b   A Cross-Cultural Approach to Adolescence. Ethos 23:15–32.

Schlegel, A., and H. Barry
1991   Adolescence: An Anthropological Inquiry. New York: Free Press.

Schneider, D.
1953   Abortion and Depopulation on a Pacific Island. *In* Health, Culture, and Community. B. D. Paul, ed., pp. 211–35. New York: Russell Sage.

Schreiber, G., and B. Baron
1984   Differences Between Somatic Growth Curves of Males and Females Are a

Secondary Sex Characteristic. Medical Hypotheses 14:227–32.

Schwartz, T.
1976   Relations Among Generations in Time-Limited Cultures. *In* Socialization as Cultural Communication. T. Schwartz, ed., pp. 217–30. Berkeley: University of California Press.

Scott, K., T. Field, and E. Rubertson
1981   Teenage Parents and Their Offspring. New York: Grune and Stratton.

Seligman, C.
1910   The Melanesians of British New Guinea. Cambridge: Cambridge University Press.

Sexton, L.
1982   Wok Meri: A Woman's Savings and Exchange System in Highland Papua New Guinea. Oceania 52:167–98.
1986   Mothers of Money, Daughters of Coffee: The Wok Meri Movement. Ann Arbor, Mich.: University Microfilms International Research Press.

Shaw, B.
1986   The Children of the Kyaka Enga: Culture, Diet, Environment, and Health in a Papua New Guinea Highlands Society, 1950–1960. *In* Shared Wealth and Symbol: Food, Culture, and Society in Oceania and Southeast Asia. L. Manderson, ed., pp. 191–217. Cambridge: Cambridge University Press.

Shaw, R. D.
1990   Kandila: Samo Ceremonial and Interpersonal Relationships. Ann Arbor: University of Michigan Press.

Shore, B.
1988   Interpretation Under Fire. Anthropology Quarterly 61:161–76.
1996   Culture in Mind: Cognition, Culture, and the Problem of Meaning. Oxford: Oxford University Press.

Shweder, R.
1991   Thinking Through Cultures: Expeditions in Cultural Psychology. Cambridge: Harvard University Press.

Simmons, R. G., and D. A. Blyth
1985   Moving Into Adolescence. The Impact of Pubertal Change and School Context. New York: A. de Gruyter.

Smith, D.
1989   Book review of Aboriginal Adolescence: Maidenhood in an Australian Community. Australian Aboriginal Studies 1:80–83.

Somare, M.
1975   Sana. Port Moresby, Papua New Guinea: Niugini Press.

Sørum, A.
1980   In Search of the Lost Soul: Bedamini Spirit Séances and Curing Rites. Oceania 50:273–96.
1982   Seeds of Power: Patterns in Bedamini Male Initiation. Social Analysis 10:42–62.
1984   Growth and Decay: Bedamini Notions of Sexuality. *In* Ritualized Homosexuality in Melanesia. G. Herdt, ed., pp. 318–37. Berkeley: University of California Press.
n.d.   The Forked Branch: A Study of Meaning in Bedamini Ceremonial. University of Trondheim, Norway.

Spindler, G.
1974 The Transmission of Culture. *In* Education and Cultural Process: Toward an Anthropology of Education. G. Spindler, ed., pp. 279–336. New York: Holt, Rinehart and Winston, Inc.

Spiro, M. E.
1986 Culture Relativism and the Future of Anthropology. Current Anthropology 1:259–86.

Stattin, H., and Magnusson, D.
1990 Pubertal Maturation in Female Development. Hillsdale, N.J.: Lawrence Erlbaum Associates.

Steinberg, L. D.
1987 Adolescence. New York: Knopf.

Steinberg, L. D., and J. P. Hill
1978 Patterns of Family Interaction as a Function of Age, the Onset of Puberty, and Formal Thinking. Developmental Psychology 14:683–84.

Stigler, J. W., R. A. Shweder, and G. Herdt, eds.
1990 Cultural Psychology: Essays on Comparative Human Development. Cambridge: Cambridge University Press.

Stinson, S.
1985 Sex Differences in Environmental Sensitivity During Growth and Development. Yearbook of Physical Anthropology 28:123–47.

Strathern, A.
1970 The Female and Male Spirit Cults in Mount Hagen. Man n.s. 5:571–85.
1979 Men's House, Women's House: The Efficacy of Opposition, Reversal and Pairing in the Melpa Amb Kor Cult. Journal of the Polynesian Society 88:37–54.
1994 Lines of Power. *In* Migration and Transformations: Regional Perspectives on New Guinea. A. Strathern and G. Stürzenhofecker, eds., pp. 231–55. Association for Social Anthropology in Oceania Monograph. Pittsburgh: University of Pittsburgh Press.

Strathern, M.
1972 Women in Between: Female Roles in a Male World, Mount Hagen, New Guinea. London: Seminar (Academic) Press.
1981 Self-Interest and the Social Good: Some Implications of Hagen Gender Imagery. *In* Sexual Meanings. S. B. Ortner and H. Whitehead, eds., pp. 166–91. Cambridge: Cambridge University Press.
1987 Introduction. *In* Dealing with Inequality. M. Strathern, ed., pp. 1–32. Cambridge: Cambridge University Press.
1988 The Gender of the Gift: Problems with Women and Problems with Society in Melanesia. Berkeley: University of California Press.

Styne, D. M.
1991 Puberty and Its Disorders in Boys. Endocrinology and Metabolism Clinics of North America 20:43–69.

Super, C.
1986 A Developmental Perspective on School-Aged Parenthood. *In* School-Aged Pregnancy and Parenthood. J. Lancaster and B. Hamburg, eds., pp. 379–86. New York: Aldine de Gruyter.

Sutherland, E. H., and D. R. Cressey
1974   Criminology, 9th ed. Philadelphia: Lippincott.

Suvulo, N.
1988   Social Indicators of Papua New Guinea, 1980–1985. Papua New Guinea: National Statistical Office.

Tanner, J. M.
1978   Fetus Into Man. Cambridge: Harvard University Press.
1981   A History of the Study of Human Growth. New York: Cambridge University Press.

Tharp, R. G.
1989   Psychocultural Variables and Constants: Effects on Teaching and Learning in Schools. American Psychologist 44(2):349–59.

Thomas, N.
1989   The Force of Ethnology: Origins and Significance of the Melanesia/Polynesia Division. Current Anthropology 30:27–34.

Tobias, P. V.
1985   The Negative Secular Trend. Journal of Human Evolution 14:347–56.

Townsend, P. K.
1985   The Situation of Children in Papua New Guinea. Boroko, Papua New Guinea: Institute of Applied Social and Economic Research.

Triandis, H. C.
1988   Commentary. In The Teenage World. D. Offer et al., eds., pp. 127–28. New York: Plenum Publishing Corp.

Tuzin D. F.
1976   The Ilahita Arapesh: Dimensions of Unity. Berkeley: University of California Press.
1980   The Voice of the Tambaran: Truth and Illusion in Ilahita Arapesh Religion. Berkeley: University of California Press.
1989   The Rise of Christian Consciousness. In The Varieties of Religious Imagination in New Guinea. M. Stephen and G. Herdt, eds. New Brunswick, N.J.: Rutgers University Press.
1995   Art and Procreative Illusion in the Sepik: Comparing the Abelam and the Arapesh. Oceania 65:289–303.
1997   The Cassowary's Revenge: The Life and Death of Masculinity in a New Guinea Society. Chicago: University of Chicago Press.

Van Baal, J.
1984   The Dialectics of Sex in Marind-anim Culture. In Ritualized Homosexuality in Melanesia. G. Herdt, ed., pp. 128–66. Berkeley: University of California Press.

Van Gennep, A.
1960   The Rites of Passage. M. K. Vizedom and G. L. Caffee, trans. Chicago: University of Chicago Press.

Ward, M. C.
1994   Marriage Belong Bisnis. In The Business of Marriage: Transformations in Oceanic Matrimony. R. A. Marksbury, ed. Association for Social Anthropology in Oceania Monograph. Pittsburgh: University of Pittsburgh Press.

Warner, W.
1937   A Black Civilization, rev. ed. Gloucester, Mass.: Peter Smith.

Warren, M. P.
1980   The Effects of Exercise on Pubertal Progression and Reproductive Function in Girls. Journal of Clinical Endocrinology and Metabolism 51:1150–57.

Warry, W.
1986   Kafaina: Female-Wealth and Power in Chuave, Papua New Guinea. Oceania 57:4–21.

Weber, M.
1946   The "Rationalization" of Education and Training. In From Max Weber: Essays in Sociology. H. H. Gerth and C. W. Mills, eds., pp. 240–44. New York: Oxford University Press.

Weiner, A. B.
1976   Women of Value, Men of Renown: New Perspectives in Trobriand Exchange. Austin: University of Texas Press.
1992   Inalienable Possessions: The Paradox of Keeping-While-Giving. Berkeley: University of California Press.

White, G., and J. Kirkpatrick
1985   Exploring Ethnopsychologies. In Person, Self, and Experience. G. White and J. Kirkpatrick, eds., pp. 3–34. Berkeley: University of California Press.

Whiteman, J.
1965   Girls' Puberty Ceremony Amongst the Chimbu. Anthropos 60:410–22.

Whiting, B. B., and C. P. Edwards
1988   Children of Different Worlds: The Formation of Social Behavior. Cambridge, Mass.: Harvard University Press.

Whiting, B. B., and J. W. M. Whiting
1987   Foreword to Adolescents in a Changing World series. In Inuit Youth: Growth and Change in the Canadian Arctic. R. G. Condon, pp. xiii–xx. New Brunswick, N.J.: Rutgers University Press.

Whiting, J. W. M.
1941   Becoming a Kwoma. New Haven: Yale University Press.
1965   Menarchal Age and Infant Stress in Humans. In Sex and Behavior. F. A. Beach, ed., pp. 221–34. New York: Wiley.

Whiting, J. W. M., V. K. Burbank, and M. Ratner
1986   The Duration of Maidenhood Across Cultures. In School-Age Pregnancy and Parenthood: Biosocial Dimensions. J. Lancaster and B. Hamburg, eds., pp. 273–302. New York: Aldine.

Whiting, J. W. M., and E. H. Chasdi
1994   Culture and Human Development: The Selected Papers of John Whiting. Cambridge: Cambridge University Press.

Wilcox, K.
1982   Ethnography as a Methodology and Its Application to the Study of Schooling: A Review. In Doing the Ethnography of Schooling: Educational Anthropology in Action. G. Spindler, ed., pp. 456–88. New York: Holt, Rinehart and Winston.

Wood, J. W., P. L. Johnson, and K. L. Campbell
1985   Demographic and Endocrinological Aspects of Low Natural Fertility in Highland New Guinea. Journal of Biosocial Science 17:57–79.

World Health Organization (W.H.O.)
1983   Measuring Change in Nutritional Status. Geneva: W.H.O.

Worthman, C. M.
1986   Development Dyssynchrony as Normative Experience: Kikuyu Adolescents. *In* School-Age Pregnancy and Parenthood: Biosocial Dimensions. J. Lancaster and B. Hamburg, eds., pp. 95–112. New York: Aldine.
1987   Interactions of Physical Maturation and Cultural Practice in Ontogeny: Kikuyu Adolescents. Cultural Anthropology 2:29–38.
1992   Cupid and Psyche: Investigative Syncretism in Biological and Psychological Anthropology. *In* Self and Society. T. Schwartz, G. White, and C. Lutz, eds., pp. 150–78. Cambridge: Cambridge University Press.
1993   Bio-cultural Interactions in Human Development. *In* Juvenile Primates: Life History, Development and Behavior. M. Pereira and L. Fairbanks, eds., pp. 339–58. Oxford: Oxford University Press.
1995   Ethnopediatrics: A Beginning Outline. Items 49:6–10.
1996   Survivorship, Selection, and Socialization: Biosocial Determinants of Sex Ratios. *In* Long Term Consequences of Early Environments. S. J. Ulijaszek and C. J .K. Henry, eds., pp. 45–68. Cambridge: Cambridge University Press.

Wulff, H.
1995   Introduction: Introducing Youth Culture in Its Own Right: The State of the Art and New Possibilities. *In* Youth Cultures: A Cross-Cultural Perspective. V. Amit-Talai and H. Wulff, eds., 1–18. London: Routledge.

Young, M.
1971   Fighting with Food: Leadership, Values and Social Control in a Massim Society. Cambridge: Cambridge University Press.

Zemel, B., and C. Jenkins
1989   Dietary Change and Adolescent Growth Among the Bundi (Gende-speaking) People of Papua New Guinea. American Journal of Human Biology 1:709–18.

Zemel, B., C. M. Worthman, and C. Jenkins
1993   Differences in Endocrine Status Associated with Urban-Rural Patterns of Growth and Maturation in Bundi (Gende-speaking) Adolescents of Papua New Guinea. *In* Urban Health and Ecology in the Third World. L. M. Schell, M. T. Smith, and A. Bilsborough, eds., pp. 38–60. Cambridge: Cambridge University Press.

INDEX